More Advance Praise for
What Doesn't Kill Us

"In this fascinating book, Stephen Joseph maps out the rarely explored positive consequences of trauma, reminding us that growth is possible even in the most adverse circumstances. Although essential reading for clinicians working with traumatized patients, *What Doesn't Kill Us* is so accessibly written that it should appeal to anyone interested in the human condition."

—**Richard Bentall, Professor of
Clinical Psychology, University of Liverpool**

"Beautifully written, drawing on leading-edge scientific research to reveal one of humankind's noblest qualities: the capacity to find meaning and growth in the face of near-unbearable suffering."

—**Mick Cooper, Professor of Counseling,
University of Strathclyde**

"Convincingly challenging, highly enlightening, and compulsively readable, *What Doesn't Kill Us* is thoroughly recommended for both those who have and have not experienced trauma. A transformational new perspective."

—**Elaine Iljon Foreman, author of**
Fly Away Fear: Overcoming Your Fear of Flying

WHAT
DOESN'T
KILL US

WHAT DOESN'T KILL US

The New Psychology of Posttraumatic Growth

STEPHEN JOSEPH, PhD

BASIC BOOKS
A Member of the Perseus Books Group
New York

Published by Basic Books,
A Member of the Perseus Books Group

Books published by Basic Books are available at special discounts for bulk purchases in
the United States by corporations, institutions, and other organizations. For more
information, please contact the Special Markets Department at the Perseus Books
Group, 2300 Chestnut Street, Suite 200, Philadelphia, PA 19103, or call (800) 255-
1514, or e-mail special.markets@perseusbooks.com.

Designed by Brent Wilcox

Library of Congress Cataloging-in-Publication Data
Joseph, Stephen.
    What doesn't kill us: the new psychology of posttraumatic growth / Stephen Joseph.
      p.   cm.
    Includes bibliographical references and index.
    ISBN 978-0-465-01941-0 (hardcover : alk. paper) — ISBN 978-0-465-02792-7
(e-book)   1. Post-traumatic stress disorder.   I. Title.
    RC552.P67J673 2011
    616.85'21—dc22
                                                                    2011012343

10 9 8 7 6 5 4 3 2 1

To Vanessa

CONTENTS

NIETZSCHE'S DICTUM

What doesn't kill me makes me stronger.

—NIETZSCHE

As a child of the 1960s and 1970s I loved American comic books. Hard as they were to get in Belfast, they were dear to me because of the superheroes they depicted: Daredevil, Batman, and the Fantastic Four. But Spiderman was my favorite of all. Physically transformed after a bite from a radioactive spider, he finds himself gifted with strange superpowers. But that is not what made him my favorite. It isn't until after his Uncle Ben dies at the hands of a criminal that Peter Parker realizes his calling in life, turning his newfound powers to fighting crime.

Peter Parker's life as Spiderman is not easy. J. Jonah Jameson, editor of the *Daily Bugle*, seeks to make headlines by exposing him as a criminal. His romance with Mary Jane is tortured by the stress of his secret identity.

What Spiderman had in common with the other comic book characters was that, through no fault of their own, something happened to each of them that challenged them to set a new, exciting, though difficult course in life.

As a young boy growing up in Belfast at the height of the political violence in Northern Ireland, I discovered in these stories a different world, of skyscrapers, of romance, where people with the courage to stand up for what they believe in can make a difference. I loved that tragedy could be the springboard for transformation. If only real life were like that!

As I have gotten older I realize that it is.

Stories about superheroes are metaphors for the challenges we face in life. Heroes encounter a life-changing traumatic event. They could crumple in the face of the tragedy, but instead it awakens them to new strength and wisdom. Life is forever changed: Their tragedy redefines who they are, and what they must do with their lives.

What I have learned is that these metaphors have real-life counterparts. Ordinary people have the power to live lives just as dramatic and driven as those of superheroes, overcoming traumas no less daunting. Their stories are all the more impressive for being real.

Leon Greenman was one of those people. Born into a Dutch-Jewish family in 1910 in East London, he trained as a boxer and worked as a barber, eventually specializing in the trade of antiquarian books. With his Dutch wife, Esther, Greenman was living in Rotterdam in 1938 as tensions rose across Europe. Set to return to London, he heard British Prime Minister Neville Chamberlain on the radio declaring "peace for our time." He put his plans on hold, thinking there was no rush to move back to London.

The following year, war broke out; then, in 1940, Germany invaded Holland. Greenman gave his passport and life savings to a friend for safe-keeping. Later, he heard that British citizens were being allowed to go home in exchange for German prisoners. So he asked his friend for the passport back. But to Greenman's horror, his friend had burnt the passport in fear of reprisals for helping Jews.

Unable to elude the Nazis, in 1942 Greenman, Esther, and their two-year-old son, Barney, were sent to Westerbork and then deported to Birkenau, otherwise known as the death camp of Auschwitz. On arrival he was separated from his wife and child. Esther held his child up for him to see and blew him a kiss. He never saw them again. As a fit young man, Greenman could work as a barber; his arm was tattooed with the number 98288 and he was sent to work in the camps.

On April 11, 1945, now at the Buchenwald camp after a sixty-mile death march, he woke up to find the camp deserted of guards. The camp had been liberated by General Patton's 3rd Army. After two more days at the hospital barracks, now free to move around the camp, he visited the ovens where so many lives had been destroyed. There were heaps of ashes and bones. He took some of the bones as tokens of remembrance and as evidence to show the world.

Unlike millions of others, Greenman had escaped the gas chambers. He returned to London and worked as a market vendor and a professional singer under the name of Leon Maure. People did not want to hear about the experiences of the camps and he did not think to tell them. Everything changed when in 1962 he witnessed a rally for the National Front, a white nationalist party that denied that the Holocaust had ever happened. It was then that he realized that it could all happen again.

For the next forty-six years, Greenman protested the rise of the Far Right and devoted himself to giving talks about what had happened. As a result he received hate mail and death threats and had to install mesh shutters on his windows at home to prevent bricks being thrown in. Despite this, he continued to give talks, take people on tours at Auschwitz, and speak out against fascism. Many schoolchildren got to hear him talk and through him learned about the horrors of the war. About his new mission, he said: "My purpose now—my duty—is to tell people what happened." In 1998 the Queen of England awarded him with the Order of the British Empire for his services against fascism.[1] He continued his mission up until his death in 2008 at the age of ninety-seven.

Greenman's story encapsulates what this book is all about: how trauma can transform the course of one's life. Our way of seeing the world can be so completely and radically dismantled and then rebuilt that, in a sense, we step into a new world.

The idea of transformation through trauma goes against the grain of all that is written about the devastating and destructive effects of trauma. Psychological studies have shown that adverse life-events are often the trigger for depression, anxiety, or posttraumatic stress. Psychiatrists, too, recognize that life-events such as serious illness, accident or injury, bereavement, and relationship breakdown can be threatening to mental health.[2]

What, then, are we to make of the stories of people who have encountered a life-threatening illness, a harrowing natural disaster, even a man-made horror, and then go on to tell of how it was a transformational turning point in their lives? Such stories seem to point to the truth of Nietzsche's dictum: "What doesn't kill me makes me stronger."[3] But are these merely the articulations of the lucky few? Or can psychological trauma really have a silver lining for all of us? Surprisingly, the answer to this second question seems to be yes.

Adversity, like the grit that creates the oyster, is often what propels people to become more true to themselves, take on new challenges, and view life from a wider perspective. Think, for example, of the great American cyclist Lance Armstrong. He managed to overcome the adversity of his struggle with testicular cancer and went on to win the Tour de France. And not just once did he win, but seven times in a row. In his autobiography, he wrote of how cancer changed his life:

> There are two Lance Armstrongs, pre-cancer, and post. Everybody's favorite question is "How did cancer change you?" The real question is how didn't it change me? I left my house on October 2, 1996, as one person and came back home another. . . . The truth is that cancer was the best thing that ever happened to me. I don't know why I got the illness, but it did wonders for me, and I wouldn't want to walk away from it. Why would I want to change, even for a day, the most important and shaping event of my life?[4]

For all the inspiration and hope they offer, real-life stories like this one do not tell us how transformation comes about. In recent years, however, psychologists have begun to sit up and take notice of the benefits of adversity, and to observe that it is not just the extraordinary few who find trauma transforming but people from all walks of life. This book will review the new research that is turning on its head what we thought we knew about how people cope with adversity.

This is not to suggest that people should wish for their trauma, tragedy, or misfortune to have happened, or that they should wish it on others. Rather, my point is simply that we must recognize adversity as a fact of life.

We all must face difficult events in our lives. What has happened cannot be undone. Our only choice is how to live with what has happened.

Consider the case of Harold Kushner, whose son died of a rare ageing disease. In his book *When Bad Things Happen to Good People*, he wrote:

> I am a more sensitive person, a more effective pastor, a more sympathetic counselor because of Aaron's life and death than I would have been without it. And I would give up all those gains in a second if I could have my son back. If I could choose, I would forego all the spiritual growth and depth which has come my way because of our experience, and be what I was fifteen years ago, an average rabbi, an indifferent counselor, helping some people and unable to help others, and the father of a bright, happy boy. But I cannot choose.[5]

Not until adversity strikes do many people begin to look deeply within themselves to reappraise what really matters. Adversity can awaken people to new and more meaningful lives.

This book is the culmination of over twenty years of study, research, and psychotherapy practice devoted to understanding the effects of adversity on our psychological systems. And, needless to say, I myself have had personal experiences of adversity during this time that have opened my eyes. As a therapist who has worked with people going through troubled times, and as a researcher who has read many personal accounts of people's experiences of adversity, I am convinced that people do often grow following adversity. In this book I want to share my experiences as a scientific researcher and therapist to answer this question of why it is that if two people encounter adversity, one may succumb but the other may thrive.

At the core of this book is the theory of the shattered vase. Imagine that a treasured vase sits in a place of prominence in your house. One day, you accidently knock it off its perch. It smashes. Sometimes when vases shatter, there is enough left intact to provide a base from which to start the process of reconstruction. In this case, however, only shards remain.

What do you do? Do you try to put the vase back together as it was, using glue and sticky tape? Do you collect the shards and drop them in the garbage, as the vase is a total loss? Or do you pick up the beautiful colored pieces and use them to make something new—such as a colorful mosaic?

When adversity strikes, people often feel that at least some part of them—their views of the world, their sense of themselves, their relationships—have been smashed. Those who try to put their lives back together exactly as they were remain fractured and vulnerable. But those who accept the breakage and build themselves anew become more resilient and open to new ways of living. The guiding principle that underscores this book is the belief, drawn from years of research and clinical practice, that focusing on, understanding, and deliberately taking control of what we do in our thoughts and actions can enable us to move forward in life following adversity.

There is no doubt that adversity can lead to great psychological suffering. We know that extremely frightening events can lead to very high levels of distress, which in turn can persist for many months, even years. Not everyone experiences full-blown posttraumatic stress disorder (PTSD), but most people will develop some of the emotional turmoil of posttraumatic stress following adversity. Research has documented what leads some people to be more vulnerable than others to the effects of trauma, and how best to help those people who are suffering from posttraumatic stress. Cognitive-behavioral treatments have been developed for the treatment of posttraumatic stress and are now recommended by the American Psychiatric Association. These seem to work. Many thousands upon thousands of people have benefited from these treatments. And thousands of mental health professionals are trained to deliver them.

An industry has grown up to help those who have gone through psychological trauma. For this army of counselors, psychotherapists, psychologists, psychiatrists, and social workers, business is booming. Surely this must be a good thing, right? At one time I would have agreed that it was. Yet as my own interests increasingly began to shift over the years away from the topic of PTSD and toward that of growth following adversity, I began to ask questions about the trauma industry and the extent to which it deals with this wider landscape. As our knowledge of PTSD has grown and the trauma industry has expanded, the idea of growth following adversity has become overshadowed. Our understanding of how people adapt following adversity has become lopsided, focusing only on the negative.

Trauma encompasses a landscape of human experience much wider than PTSD alone. It is a complex issue requiring that we take biology, culture, and politics into account to determine how to deal with adversity and make sense of our lives. This complexity has led me to three serious concerns about whether the trauma industry's success has had unintended consequences that have actually become part of the problem.[6]

First, the trauma industry has enthusiastically and single-mindedly adopted the language of medicine. As a diagnostic category, PTSD has been beneficial in providing recognition of the suffering experienced by many people—but the language of medicine puts therapists in a doctor-like position, which takes away from patients the responsibility for their own recovery. Indeed, the very word *patient* is problematic because it portrays the person as someone who is damaged, impaired, deficient, maladjusted, disordered. In short, it subtly shifts responsibility for the person's recovery into the hands of the therapist. *However, trauma is not an illness to be cured by a doctor.* Certainly, therapists can offer people guidance and be expert companions along the way, but ultimately people must be able to take responsibility for their own recovery and for the meaning that they give to their experiences.

Second, it has also created a culture of expectation in which there is a mistaken assumption that PTSD is both inevitable and inescapable. When disasters strike, often the message that follows is that people will be affected, that they will develop PTSD, and that they will need professional help for the foreseeable future. This may well be true of some people. But research over the past decade has shown us that trauma survivors are not necessarily destined for a life of unremitting despair and that the damaging effects of trauma have been overestimated. *If people are told that they are vulnerable and need help, these conditions become a self-fulfilling prophecy.* Indeed, what the research actually shows us is that the majority of those who face potentially traumatic events are relatively resilient, able to either resist stressors or recover quickly and then to maintain relatively high levels of functioning.[7] This is the message that needs to be conveyed—that the majority of people are resilient to the tragedies, misfortunes, and disasters that will befall them.

My third concern is one that I noted earlier: Our criterion for successful treatment has become confined to the alleviation of PTSD, which leads us to disregard the body of research showing not only that most people are resilient but also that many people find benefits in adversity that can provide a springboard to higher levels of functioning than before. Posttraumatic reactions are not one-sided phenomena but multifaceted, encompassing both distress and growth. *People are capable of finding pathways to reverse the destructiveness of trauma and turn it to their advantage.* Such observations have in the past been treated as exceptions to the rule—as little more than interesting anecdotes—rather than being seen as part of the very nature of trauma. Therapists who fail to recognize this possibility of growth in their clients do them a disservice.

In short, while the adoption of PTSD as a diagnostic category has been beneficial in terms of increasing access to psychological therapies for those who need them, it has been detrimental in these three ways: in taking responsibility away from people, in creating a culture of expectation, and ignoring the personal growth that often arises following trauma.

The aim of this book is to correct the imbalance—to show that trauma can have both negative and positive implications, and that the negative and the positive go hand in hand. I challenge the trauma industry by offering a new perspective: namely, that posttraumatic stress is a natural and normal process of adaption to adversity that marks the beginning of a transformative journey. Recovery from trauma consists of finding new meanings, creating new webs of understanding, and finding reparative methods centered on the sharing of memories. Viewed in this light, posttraumatic stress can be understood as a search for meaning in which the drive to revisit, remember, and think about the trauma is a normal urge to make sense of a shocking experience, to grasp new realities and incorporate them into one's own life story. At the heart of this book is the idea that posttraumatic stress is the engine of transformation— of a process known as posttraumatic growth.

Recognition of the journey of posttraumatic growth begins sooner for some than for others, but all are on the journey itself. A simple idea, but it stands in opposition to decades of psychiatric research that focused on suffering rather than on the transformation that can arise through suffering.

As human beings we are storytellers. Trauma triggers within us the need to tell stories to make sense of what has happened. These stories may take the form of conversations with family, friends, and colleagues. And our conversations are influenced by what we read in newspapers and see on television, and by the books, songs, and poetry that provide us with language that captures in words, music, and images what we are experiencing. Transformation arises through the stories we tell.

It is in the struggle to make sense of a traumatic event that growth can take hold.

For those curious about how to apply the new science of posttraumatic growth, I have included a postscript and set of appendices that provide specific details regarding the practical steps involved—including the Psychological Well-Being Post-Traumatic Changes Questionnaire (PWB-PTCQ)[8] and the THRIVE model of change, a six-stage process of exercises and reflections.

Drawing on the wisdom of the ancient philosophers, the insights of existential and evolutionary psychologists, and the optimism of modern positive psychology, I present the new psychology of adversity—a fresh, inspiring, and humanizing perspective on how to manage life and its inevitable challenges.

PART I

EVERYTHING CHANGES

I have returned
From a world beyond knowledge
And now must unlearn
For otherwise I clearly see
I can no longer live

CHARLOTTE DELBO,
Auschwitz and After

CHAPTER 1

The Flipside of Trauma

IN 1987, ON FRIDAY the 6th of March, a large passenger cruise ship called the *Herald of Free Enterprise* left the port of Zeebruggee in Belgium en route to England. Nearly five hundred passengers, eighty crew, and 1,100 tons of haulage were on board. Passengers were settling into their seats, queuing up at the restaurants, and ordering drinks at the bar. Below, water was flooding onto the car decks.

Unbeknownst to passengers and crew, one of the bow doors had not been secured. No one, neither crew nor passengers, noticed anything was wrong, until the ship attempted to turn. There was a lurch. Then, without warning, within forty-five seconds, the ship rolled over.

There was no time to sound alarms of any kind. Furniture, cars, trucks, and passengers alike were indiscriminately catapulted to port side. People collided with one another, crashed into walls, and slipped under the icy cold water as portholes imploded and water flooded the passenger areas. Electricity went out. The darkness reverberated with screams and shouts of pain and terror. As dead bodies floated in the icy water, many expected death, many lost loved ones, many witnessed unimaginable horrors.

One hundred and ninety-three people died in what was to become one of the most horrific maritime disasters of the twentieth century. It is hard to fathom what it must have been like to experience the *Herald* disaster. Imagine the room you are in right now lurching and then suddenly turning upside down, throwing its contents from one side to the other. The roof of the room becomes the floor, the lights go out, and water starts flooding in.

A few months after the disaster, lawyers acting on behalf of survivors and bereaved relatives contacted the psychology department at the Institute of Psychiatry in London to ask for help. Professor William Yule, who was then head of clinical services, quickly mobilized services to assist survivors and set up a research program. That is how I became involved. For the next three years my doctoral study was devoted to investigating the survivors and the roadblocks to recovery that they faced.

Immediately following the disaster, a number of survivors were asked to complete well-known psychological tests to measure posttraumatic stress disorder (PTSD). It was found that levels of psychological distress were high and that many met the criteria for PTSD in the first months following the disaster. Symptoms included recurrent and intrusive distressing recollections of what happened, upsetting dreams, detachment and emotional numbness, difficulty falling or staying asleep, difficulty concentrating, and a constant feeling of being on edge. These are all common experiences of people with PTSD.[1]

Not surprisingly, those who develop PTSD are also faced with considerable difficulties in their lives at home and at work. (See Appendix 1 for a list of problems often reported by survivors of trauma.) Many of the survivors surveyed at this first point in time found their work and relationships were affected, and many struggled to cope.[2] Of interest were the psychological processes that led to greatest difficulty. We found that psychological distress was most likely to be found in those who blamed themselves in some way.[3] As we listened to their stories, it was understandable that many would struggle to rebuild their lives. But little was known about the longer term effects and so a pressing research question was to find out how the lives of these survivors would unfold over the coming years.

Three years later, we carried out a follow-up survey with survivors. We asked similar questions as before about depression, anxiety, and PTSD. We found that the average level of psychological distress was now lower, although it remained a concern and many of the survivors were still struggling. To further explore the psychological processes that lead to difficulties, our survey also asked pointed questions about survivors' experiences during and after the disaster.[4]

We analyzed these responses to determine the extent to which the survivors' descriptions of their experiences were related to their current feelings. It turned out that those who were most distressed were the ones who reported feeling helpless during the accident, who prepared themselves for the worst, who thought they were going to die, and who felt paralyzed with fear. We also asked the survivors how they coped in the aftermath. Those who were most distressed were the ones who were least emotionally expressive, who lacked social support, and who had experienced other life-events in those preceding three years, such as serious illness, family bereavement, or loss of employment.[5]

In the time since we conducted this survey, many other studies have reported similar results. It is now commonly accepted that two major roadblocks to recovery are a lack of social support and a preponderance of other life-events to contend with in the aftermath of trauma.[6]

But people are not passive recipients of how their lives unfold. The feelings they have about what has happened distinctly influences their recovery. For example, feelings of guilt and shame can be another important roadblock to recovery. Our survey found that over half the survivors felt guilty that they had stayed alive when so many died, over two-thirds felt guilty about what they did not do in the accident, and one-third felt guilty about what they did do to survive. Those who reported such feelings tended to be the ones who were struggling the most psychologically.[7]

How people cope with their experiences is important. Some behaviors can help people feel better in the short term but lead to greater difficulties in the longer term. For example, our survey revealed that many of the survivors were using drink and drugs to help them cope—73 percent said that they were drinking more; 44 percent, that they were smoking more; 40 percent, that they were taking sleeping pills; 28 percent, that they were taking antidepressants; and 21 percent, that they were taking tranquilizers. In addition, we determined that those on either prescribed or nonprescribed medications were in poorer psychological health than those on no meds at all.[8]

In the process of identifying those factors that seem to be roadblocks to recovery, we were building a picture of how trauma can devastate people's lives. This very much accorded with accepted orthodoxy regarding the perils and processes of PTSD.

Yet during the research something unexpected happened. While our focus was on understanding the adverse affects of trauma, a new pattern began to emerge.

I had noticed during my interviews with the survivors that many also talked about positive changes in their lives. Strangely, it seemed that the trauma had left these people with a new outlook on life—one that contained a mix of negative and positive. To explore this, amidst the other questions on our survey three years after the tragedy, my colleagues and I included a brand new one: "Has your view of life changed since the disaster—and if so, has it changed in a positive way or a negative way?" It was only a brief question, one that had been squeezed into the survey at the last minute. Survivors were asked to tick a box indicating that their view of life had changed either for the worse, for the better, or neither.

The results were a shock. Although 46 percent said that their view of life had changed for the worse, 43 percent said that their view of life had changed for the better. I had expected some survivors to say "for the better"—but nearly half of the total? I checked the figures to be sure, but they were correct: A full 43 percent of the survivors of the *Herald of Free Enterprise* disaster reported some form of positive benefit. Intrigued by this initial observation, I wanted to find out whether the same was true of other such traumatic incidents. Was this finding unique to my survey participants, or did it reflect a more common occurrence among people who encounter adversity?

Fortunately, in the survey we had also asked survivors to tell us in their own words what sorts of changes they had experienced. Specifically, after the question asking survivors to tick the box saying if their view of life had changed, we had included a short follow-up question asking them how their view of life had changed. We left a space on the questionnaire for people to write their answers. Some wrote a few words, others a few sentences; still others took the opportunity to say much more, writing in the margins of the page.

I sat down and read through these results, carefully sorting what people said into two categories—descriptions of positive changes and descriptions of negative changes. I then sorted all the comments in terms of their similarity to one another until I had eleven piles of positive statements and fifteen piles of negative statements. I then picked the one statement in each pile that I thought best illustrated all the statements— so that in the end there were eleven positive statements and fifteen negative statements that seemed to capture in the survivors' own words the full range of what they had told us.

I could now ask other people how much they agreed or disagreed with these statements:

Please read each statement and rank it depending on how much you agree or disagree, where: 1 = strongly disagree, 2 = disagree, 3 = disagree a little, 4 = agree a little, 5 = agree, and 6 = strongly agree.

Negative changes in outlook:
- I don't look forward to the future anymore.____
- My life has no meaning anymore.____
- I no longer feel able to cope with things.___
- I fear death very much now.____
- I feel as if something bad is just waiting around the corner to happen.____
- I desperately wish I could turn the clock back to before it happened.____
- I sometimes think it's not worth being a good person.____
- I have very little trust in other people now.____
- I feel very much as if I'm in limbo.____
- I have very little trust in myself now.____
- I feel harder toward other people.____
- I am less tolerant of others now.____
- I am much less able to communicate with other people.____
- Nothing makes me happy anymore.____
- I feel as if I'm dead from the neck downward.____

Positive changes in outlook:
- I don't take life for granted anymore.____
- I value my relationships much more now.____
- I feel more experienced about life now.____
- I don't worry about death at all anymore.___
- I live every day to the fullest now.____
- I look upon each day as a bonus.____
- I'm a more understanding and tolerant person now.____
- I have greater faith in human nature now.____
- I no longer take people or things for granted.____
- I value other people more now.____
- I am more determined to succeed in life now.____

This survey yields two total scores—one that is the sum of all negative changes and one that is the sum of all positive changes. On the positive scale, the lowest a person can score is 11 and the highest is 66. On the negative scale, the lowest a person can score is 15 and the highest is 90. The higher the total scores, the more negative and positive changes, respectively.

Armed with this Changes in Outlook Questionnaire (CiOQ), as it came to be called, I was now ready to embark on a series of research studies to find out more about what leads to change. But before I could do anything, I had to determine whether survivors of other events were similar to the survivors of the *Herald* disaster in terms of what we had found out. Specifically, it was imperative to ask: Were positive changes unique to this particular group, or were they part of a larger pattern?

To find the answer to this question, I looked to the survivors of another cruise ship disaster. In the early evening of October 21, 1988, a school party of more than four hundred children and ninety teachers had set sail from Piraeus harbor in Greece on a ship called *The Jupiter*. They were taking an educational cruise of the eastern Mediterranean, and the excited children stood on deck as the ship embarked. Twenty minutes out of harbor, the unthinkable happened: An oil tanker collided amidships. *The Jupiter* was holed and rapidly took on water. As the ship began to list, the frightened passengers and crew dove into the oil- and debris-

TABLE 1.1 Percentage Agreeing with Positive Changes

I don't take life for granted anymore	94%
I value my relationships much more now	91%
I feel more experienced about life now	83%
I don't worry about death at all anymore	44%
I live every day to the fullest now	71%
I look upon each day as a bonus	77%
I'm a more understanding and tolerant person now	71%
I have greater faith in human nature now	54%
I no longer take people or things for granted	91%
I value other people more now	88%
I am more determined to succeed in life now	50%

Source: Adapted by author.

strewn water hoping to reach the safety of a rescue boat. Amidst the chaos, one schoolgirl, one teacher, and two seamen died.

I asked the adult survivors of the sinking of *The Jupiter* to complete the CiOQ. Would their answers match those of the survivors of the *Herald of Free Enterprise* disaster? As expected, some reported negative changes. The loss of life was not as great as in the *Herald* sinking, yet for all involved this was a tragic and traumatic event. However, what proved of interest was that so many reported positive changes. The percentage who agreed, at least a little, with each of the eleven positive statements is shown in Table 1.1.

Our initial results were not a fluke. They became the basis for one of the very first scientific studies ever published on the topic of positive changes following adversity.[9]

We now know, counterintuitively, that trauma can lead to positive developments in life. Even so, I was left with many questions. Why was it that some survivors reported positive changes when others did not? Can those other people be helped to find positive changes that they are apparently missing out on? Do those positive changes lead to an enriched life? And, most important, how can we reconcile these positive changes with the devastating impact of the trauma itself?

For the past twenty years I have devoted my career to answering these questions. Only now are we beginning to build the full picture of how people respond to adversity and to understand that trauma has both negative and positive sides. Crucially, we are beginning to understand that posttraumatic stress is an engine for transformation. Trauma forces people to confront a crossroads in their lives. The implications are profound. We must look at the most common diagnosis following trauma— posttraumatic stress disorder—and see it in a new light: as the process of personal transformation in action.

The idea that positive changes can arise out of trauma and adversity has long been present in the background,[10] but it never fully took hold in the imagination of mainstream psychology. Unstudied and undeveloped, this notion lay dormant for years, waiting to be rediscovered. Since the beginning of modern psychology in the late nineteenth century, studying positive change was unfashionable. Psychology was instead concerned with the various ways in which people become distressed and dysfunctional.

Indeed, although psychological trauma has been the subject of great fascination and inquiry for many decades, we still know relatively little about the experiences of those who fare well in the aftermath of traumatic events—and why it is that whereas one person struggles to cope, another flourishes and goes on to experience positive change.

The reason for this oversight is that psychologists are generally not interested in the positive effects of trauma. Nor is that much of a surprise. Psychologists and psychiatrists tend to see only distressed and dysfunctional people in their clinics. Their goal has been not to help these people live fulfilled and happy lives but, rather, to help them get back on their feet. In short, most psychologists and psychiatrists are satisfied if they can move their patients' outlook from just −5 to 0 rather than from −5 to +5. So it's not surprising that the vast bulk of research and analysis has been oriented toward psychological suffering.

This lopsided focus on suffering originated with Sigmund Freud. As a medical doctor himself, Freud brought to the new field of psychoanalysis a medical way of thinking. In turn, the early development of psychology was deeply influenced by psychoanalysis and the vocabulary of medicine—by words like *disorder, patient, cure,* and *treatment.* As psychology developed throughout the twentieth century, this early influence was hard to shake off. Psychology was well on its way toward becoming a profession that modeled itself on medicine and was interested only in the dark side of human experience.[11]

Yet along the way there were notable exceptions to this way of thinking. Although my colleagues and I were among the first to scientifically examine the idea of positive changes following adversity, a bit of digging into the history of psychology reveals that this concept had been theorized by scholars decades earlier. Among its most eloquent defenders was Viktor Frankl.

Frankl worked as a psychiatrist in Vienna during the 1930s. He treated suicidal patients until the Nazi regime banned Jewish doctors from practicing medicine. In 1942 he was sent to the Nazi concentration camp of Theresienstadt with his wife and parents. The family was divided when his wife was transported to Bergen-Belsen and he and his parents were sent to Auschwitz. By the time of liberation in 1945, Frankl had lost them all—alone among his family members, he had survived incredible trauma and distress.

After the war, Frankl became one of the most important psychologists of the twentieth century. He served as a professor of psychiatry at the University of Vienna and as a visiting professor at Harvard University. But he is most frequently remembered for his book *Man's Search for Meaning,* in which he wrote about his experiences in the Nazi death camps. The people best equipped for survival, he believed, were those most able to find meaning in life despite the horrors of the camps.

Frankl wrote:

The way in which a man accepts his fate and all the suffering it entails, the way in which he takes up his cross, gives him ample opportunity— even under the most difficult circumstances—to add a deeper meaning to his life. He may remain brave, dignified and unselfish. Or in the bitter fight for self-preservation he may forget his human dignity and become no more than an animal. Here lies the chance for a man either to make use of or to forgo the opportunities of attaining the moral values that a difficult situation may afford him.[12]

Later in his career, Frankl spoke of his patients' capacity to find meaning in the tragedies and misfortunes of life. He saw two sides of suffering, noting that while there might be nothing inherently good *in* misfortune, it might be possible to extract something good *out* of misfortune. To describe this outlook, he coined the phrase *tragic optimism*. Frankl maintained that man's confrontation with the "primordial facts" of existence offers the essential opportunity for finding meaning in life.

Another advocate of this outlook was the humanistic psychologist Abraham Maslow. His specialty was the study of self-actualized individuals—people who live their lives to the fullest of their potential. According to Maslow, the most important learning experiences in human life are tragedies, deaths, and other traumas that force people to take new perspectives on life.[13]

Likewise, the existential psychologist Irwin Yalom wrote about how meaning in life arises through the suffering caused by life-threatening illness. In Yalom's words: "A real confrontation with death usually causes one to question with real seriousness the goals and conduct of one's life up to then. . . . How many people have lamented: 'What a pity I had to wait till now, when my body is riddled with cancer, to know how to live!'"[14]

At the beginning of the twenty-first century, these exceptional ways of thinking began to be noticed. A new area of psychology was developing, and scientists started devoting themselves to understanding what leads to fulfillment, happiness, and a rewarding life. Sometimes an idea comes along that magnetically attracts the attention of scientists. *Positive psychology* was one such idea.

Before we go deeper into the topic of trauma and how it can be transformational, it is worth considering the ways in which positive psychology set a new agenda for psychological research. Prior to positive psychology, scientists' unspoken assumption was that psychological health was defined solely by the absence of suffering. Research was therefore single-mindedly fixated on understanding the various ways in which people suffer psychologically and how to end that suffering. But if well-being is more than simply the absence of suffering, then by definition all of this research has failed to tell us what actually makes people happy and makes life worth living. To remedy this, researchers began to turn their attention from pessimism to optimism, from depression to happiness—from topics focusing on what people cannot do to topics focusing on what they *can* do. New topics such as emotional intelligence, quality of life, and flow caught the imagination. Change was in the air.

Inevitably, psychology's topics reflect what's going on in the wider world. Thus it is interesting to note that the development of psychology took place in the context of two world wars and the Vietnam War, in contrast to the years leading up to the turn of the century, which were relatively peaceful and prosperous. Another factor related to the shift in topics is psychology's origin. As a science that had grown up in the shadow of medicine and psychiatry, psychology had modeled itself on psychiatry, using the same language of disorder. But by the mid-1990s psychology was a profession in its own right, its status no longer dependent on its association to psychiatry. There were many who were critical of psychology for being so close to psychiatry, and who called for it to stand on its own feet.

In 1999 Martin Seligman was elected president of the American Psychological Association. Picking up on the changing Zeitgeist, Seligman realized that psychology, in its enthusiasm for understanding life's problems, had largely neglected the study of what makes for a good life. Drawing upon his authority as the association's new president, he founded the positive psychology movement: the science of human strengths, virtues, happiness, and what makes life worth living.[15] The study of the positive was not wholly new, but Seligman succeeded in bringing scientists together, generating new interest, and creating a new movement. Since its emergence more than a decade ago, the idea of positive psychology has seeped into the profession of psychology—a profession that has been transformed by an outpouring of research on topics such as hope, gratitude, forgiveness, curiosity, humor, wisdom, joy, love, courage, and creativity. The ambition of the positive psychology move-ment was to change the face of mainstream psychology. Thanks to such efforts, we now know—based on hundreds of research studies—that pos-itivity is important to health and well-being.[16]

The goal of positive psychology was never to promote the idea that we should be concerned *only* with the positive side of human experience: That would be just as lopsided as the previous focus on the negative that the positive psychology movement railed against. In actuality, life consists of ups and downs, so we need to understand the interplay of negative and positive. The resulting picture is indeed more complicated—and, paradoxically, trauma has emerged as one of the key topics of positive psychology, because it shows us this fuller picture. Psychologists now re-alize that it is naive to seek to live a life in which there is no sadness, and no misfortune, and hence that the pursuit of happiness must include learning how to live with, and learn from, adversity.

Initially, the relevance of positive psychology to the scholarly study and clinical treatment of trauma was not fully acknowledged. Two decades ago, when I began talking to colleagues about my work on the positive side of trauma, I was met with blank looks. I remember wor-rying about whether my career was taking a turn that I would regret. Those who disagreed with me argued that there is nothing positive about trauma. Over and over again I explained that, indeed, there isn't—that it is in the struggle to deal with what has happened that pos-itive change can arise. But the notion that psychology ought to be con-cerned with the full spectrum of human functioning, from −5 to + 5, is no longer controversial. Indeed, this idea has penetrated the con-sciousness of psychologists at many universities and health-care clin-ics, and laboratories all over the world are generating research showing that positive changes are reported by people following all sorts of trauma and adversity.[17]

Various terms describe the positive changes that people can experi-ence, including *benefit-finding, growth following adversity, personal transformation, stress-related growth*, and *thriving*. But *posttraumatic growth*—coined in the mid-1990s by two clinical researchers, Professors Richard Tedeschi and Lawrence Calhoun—sparked the most interest of all and is now widely used to describe this new field of study and investigation into how trauma can sometimes be the springboard to greater well-being.[18]

Everything changed with the advent of positive psychology, which not only opened the door for psychologists to begin thinking about post-traumatic growth but also questioned what was meant by well-being in the first place.

Previously, psychologists had considered well-being simply the absence of negative states of mind. But positive psychologists questioned this notion, asserting that well-being was also the presence of positive states of mind. Having established the importance of studying the positive side of life, positive psychologists then went on to examine more carefully what well-being actually is.

This analysis led to the recognition that there are two distinct philosophical traditions to the study of well-being: eudaimonism and hedonism. *Eudaimonism* dates back to Aristotle, who held that the good life was defined as a life lived in accordance with one's virtues. *Hedonism*, in contrast, dates back to Aristippus, a Cyrenaic philosopher who emphasized the pursuit of pleasure as the goal of the good life. Eudaimonism, then, refers to a life dedicated to seeking meaning, engagement with the existential challenges of life, and the actualization of human potential, whereas hedonism refers to a life dedicated to seeking pleasure, happiness, and enjoyment. These two views of well-being reflect distinct perspectives on human nature that have held sway at varying times throughout the past millennia of intellectual history.[19]

Throughout the ages, philosophers have debated the question of what makes for a good life and have swung between views emphasizing the eudaimonic perspective and those emphasizing the hedonic perspective. But either taken to the extreme is not helpful; what we must seek is a balance between the two. The Roman philosopher Epicurus advocated a balanced life encompassing both virtue and pleasure.

The wisdom of this approach seems self-evident when we sit back and reflect on what the good life ought to look like, but the truth is that Western society in recent decades has lost its balance and swung toward hedonism at the expense of eudaimonism. When asked what is truly most important in life, most people respond by downplaying the importance of money and status, fully aware that these qualities do not guarantee a fulfilling life. In practice, however, many individuals lead lives that are inconsistent with what they clearly know to be true. They know, for example, that relationships are far more important than material success. Yet research indicates a general overemphasis on the value placed on wealth as well as increasing amounts of time spent at work and striving for status.

Perhaps this disconnect is less surprising if we take into account the constant bombardment of advertisements attempting to sell us the idea of happiness through materialism. The billions of dollars spent by marketers easily drown out the inner wisdom that tells us this is not the path to lasting happiness. As a result, wealth remains a common goal. Yet research has demonstrated not only that the correlation between wealth and happiness is quite small but also that overvaluing the attainment of materialistic goals is associated with a variety of negative outcomes, including mental illness, physical illness, alienation, and interpersonal problems.

Professor Tim Kasser and his colleagues have deeply explored this issue. In a study focusing on the content of people's values and goals and how these determine well-being, they described two types of goals and values. The first type they termed *extrinsic*; these are goals and values that predominate when people "buy into" the messages of consumer culture and organize their lives around the pursuit of money, possessions, image, and status. This pursuit is extrinsic in the sense that it is directed primarily toward the attainment of external rewards and praise. The second type they termed *intrinsic*; these are goals and values that involve personal growth, intimacy, and contributions to the community, all of which arise when people listen to their "inner voice." What Professor Kasser and his colleagues found is that personal well-being is diminished by the pursuit of extrinsic goals and heightened by the pursuit of intrinsic goals. Their message was clear: If you want to experience greater fulfillment in life, find meaning that is driven by intrinsic rather than extrinsic goals and values.[20]

Related studies conducted during the 1990s consistently showed that people who rated financial success as less important than relationships were happier than people whose priorities were reversed.[21] Faced with these reflections on consumerism and its relation to well-being, psychologists began to wake up to the fact that they, too, had been peddling visions of hedonism. A number of them started asking questions about what actually constitutes a good life, not simply a pleasurable life.

In modern psychology the eudaimonic and hedonic perspectives are referred to as psychological well-being (PWB) and subjective well-being (SWB), respectively. *Subjective well-being* refers to people's emotional states—the balance between their positive and negative feelings, and the extent to which they are satisfied with life. In everyday language, then, SWB is about happiness.

In contrast, *psychological well-being* refers to the more intrinsically motivated side of life—autonomy, a sense of mastery, personal growth, positive relations with others, self-acceptance, and purpose in life.[22]

Although the two types of well-being are moderately correlated (i.e., as levels of one increase, so do levels of the other), they should not be thought of as identical. Indeed, there are people who have much pleasure in life but whose lives are unfulfilled and lack meaning (high SWB, low PWB), just as there are people who are not perceived as "happy" but consider their lives deeply meaningful (low SWB, high PWB).[23] The good life, as Epicurus suggested, might be one that combines both pleasure and meaning (high SWB, high PWB).

While subjective well-being is necessarily a concern of therapists who are treating people in distress, the topic of posttraumatic growth offers a broader perspective whereby increases in psychological well-being are also of great interest.

With this distinction between hedonic and eudaimonic well-being clarified, psychologists were able to see that while trauma may not be a road to the pleasurable life, it can lead to a good life in other ways.

By focusing on eudaimonism, we are able to gain a more complete picture of how people struggle in the aftermath of trauma. As noted earlier,

the ideal life is characterized by high levels of both eudaimonic and hedonic well-being—but I would argue that, for too long, the helping pro-
fessions have directed their attention to hedonic well-being alone.
Certainly people strive to be happy, but the problem with seeking hedonic well-being as the road to happiness is that it does not automatically
lead to greater eudaimonic well-being. What we are beginning to realize, however, is that greater eudaimonic well-being *does* seem to lead to
greater hedonic well-being.[24]

Most people recognize that they could be happier in life. So what's
stopping them? Ironically it is the very pursuit of hedonic rather than
eudaimonic well-being that prevents them from leading a fulfilled life.
Whereas many books on happiness emphasize ways in which to attain
more pleasure in life, what research evidence points to is that pleasure is
fleeting in nature and, indeed, that more lasting fulfillment is actually
derived from having meaning in life.

According to one theory, known as the "hedonic treadmill," our emotional systems reset quickly to our usual level of hedonic well-being following a successful outcome. We all know the experience of looking
forward to something. Perhaps we have saved up for a new car, or jewelry,
or a new coat—and how excited we are on the day we get it. Our hedonic well-being is at a high level. But several days or weeks later, the eu-
phoria is gone and we have returned to our set point. Our hedonic
well-being has dropped down to its previous level!

On the other hand, there is no eudaimonic treadmill. Striving for eudaimonic well-being may not lead to immediate pleasure, but it is likely
that, in the longer term, satisfaction of the need for eudaimonic well-
being will lead to hedonic well-being as a by-product. Thus the pursuit
of happiness as a goal in itself is doomed to failure; happiness can be
achieved only as a by-product of other activities. By the same token, aiming for pleasure without thinking about meaning is less likely to lead to
fulfillment than aiming for meaning to begin with: Meaning does not
follow pleasure, whereas pleasure does follow meaning. Viktor Frankl recognized this phenomenon when he wrote: "Happiness cannot be pursued: it must ensue. One must have a reason to be happy. Once the
reason is found, however, one becomes happy automatically."[25]

The philosopher John Stuart Mill believed that the only people who are happy are those who "have their minds fixed on some object other than their own happiness; on the happiness of others, on the improvement of mankind, even on some art or pursuit, followed not as a means, but as itself an ideal end." This is a profound point; it challenges us to reflect on what our minds are fixed upon. Those who can honestly say they couldn't live more fully are few and far between. Most of us, if we are honest with ourselves, know that we don't live life as wisely, as responsibly, as compassionately, and as maturely as we could.

Trauma is like a wake-up call for us to reflect on what our minds are fixed upon.

Many survivors of trauma have experiences that haunt them for the rest of their lives, experiences they can never forget. They may struggle for many years with considerable psychological pain. The new psychology of posttraumatic growth does not deny this fact but, rather, simply recognizes that there is another side to the coin—that in the midst of great psychological pain there can also be new perspectives on life that are valuable to the survivor, including a new recognition of one's personal qualities and a deeper and more satisfying connection to others.

Three existential themes are at the core of posttraumatic growth. The first is the recognition that life is uncertain and that things change. This amounts to a tolerance of uncertainty that, in turn, reflects the ability to embrace it as a fundamental tenet of human existence. The second is psychological mindfulness, which reflects self-awareness and an understanding of how one's thoughts, emotions, and behaviors are related to each other as well as a flexible attitude toward personal change. The third is acknowledgment of personal agency, which entails a sense of responsibility for the choices one makes in life and an awareness that choices have consequences.

Trauma leads to an awareness of all three of these existential truths. In turn, this awareness seems to provoke changes in the way that people talk about themselves, the way they feel about life, and the way they go on to lead their lives. My point here is not that negative reactions to adversity should be avoided but, rather, that regrets, disappointments, and distress are inevitable in life—and it would be naive to think otherwise. Those who find growth in adversity accept this inevitability. They are realistic about themselves, objective in their outlook, able to experience deep and meaningful relationships, nonmaterialistic, and nondogmatic in their approach to life and they have common sense as well as a capacity for humor.

But their immediate concerns at the time of trauma are often the more pressing ones of survival—and then, just trying to cope with the devastating emotional aftermath. Thus treatment providers must focus on survivors' medical and emotional hurdles before beginning to deal with deeper issues of meaning and posttraumatic growth.

CHAPTER 2

The Emotional Toll
of Trauma

FOR MOST OF US, adversity is inevitable. Researchers have estimated that 75 percent of all people experience some form of trauma
in life—the loss or suffering of a loved one, the diagnosis of an illness, the
pain of divorce or separation, the shock of an accident, assault, or environmental disaster.[1] Around a fifth of all people are likely to experience
a potentially traumatic event within a given year.[2] By its very definition,
trauma is unexpected, unpredictable, and uncontrollable. Believing that
life can be lived without encountering adversity is a lost cause.

Horrible things happen every day. As I write this, a train travelling
between St. Petersburg and Moscow has been derailed by a bomb. At
least twenty-five people are known to have been killed; many others
are injured. In Southern Bangladesh, a ferry leaving Dhaka has cap-
sized. Fifty-eight people are confirmed dead, with many more thought
to have died. In America, four policemen have been shot dead in a coffee shop in Seattle. Wars, genocide, famines, political violence, and terrorism continue to rage into the second decade of the twenty-first century.
Disasters such as earthquakes, hurricanes, tornadoes, tsunamis, floods,
industrial accidents, and airplane crashes threaten the survival and well-
being of millions across the world. Many millions more are affected
every year by traffic collisions, accidents at home and at work, criminal
and sexual assaults, life-threatening illnesses, bereavement, divorce, separation, child abuse, and elder neglect. These kinds of adversity have

the power to shake us to the core of our being. When they do, we call them trauma.

The word *trauma*, which derives from the Greek word meaning "wound," was probably first used in the English language in seventeenth-century medicine to refer to piercing and wounding of the physical body. It is still used in this medical sense, but over time it has acquired the connotation of psychological wounding as well. In the twentieth century Freud used the term analogously to refer to how external events can rupture people's psychological boundaries.[3]

Psychologists still use *trauma* in the same way today—as a metaphor for life-events that tear at the psychological skin that protects us, leaving us emotionally wounded.

When we experience psychological trauma, our bodies go into shock and our minds are overwhelmed. Imagine a Christmas snow globe. Shake it and the snow flurries; over time, it settles. How long the snow remains unsettled depends on how vigorously the globe was shaken in the first place. So it is, with the trauma that shakes up our mental world.

Some victims of trauma emerge from their experiences severely psychologically distressed for a considerable period of time. These individuals are generally diagnosed with posttraumatic stress disorder (PTSD). I became familiar with PTSD back in the late 1980s, when I was investigating the reactions of survivors of the *Herald of Free Enterprise* disaster. PTSD was still a new diagnosis in those days, having been introduced into the psychiatric literature only a few years before.[4]

Back then, even the concept of PTSD was only just beginning to seep into public consciousness. Many of my colleagues in the clinical psychology department did not know what the acronym stood for, and the majority of the public were unaware of it altogether. Two decades later, the opposite is true. PTSD has become one of the most heavily researched of all the psychological conditions. In this day and age, it's hard to imagine *not* having heard of PTSD—if not through personal experience, then through media coverage of it. Even so, the concept of PTSD is still evolving and, in fact, continues to be hotly debated. The very definition of PTSD is constantly being reviewed as scientists struggle to understand what the difference is between someone experiencing a normal stress reaction and someone who has tipped over into an abnormal state of mind. While some experts consider this diagnostic category to be a useful way of recognizing the problems that people face, others believe that PTSD is now over-diagnosed.

For the media, and for many professionals, PTSD certainly provides a vocabulary for conveying the personal devastation that trauma can cause. Prior to the American Psychiatric Association's definition of PTSD in 1980, there was no formal psychiatric category for recognizing the effects of traumatic stressors. Of course, this isn't to say that people didn't experience the effects of trauma: Stories of trauma have always been with us in some form or another. In this chapter I will dig into the history of PTSD and discuss how the diagnosis came about in the latter half of the twentieth century.

Possibly the earliest description of trauma is one found in the Sumerian "Epic of Gilgamesh," written five thousand years ago. Inscribed on clay tablets, this tale tells of a Babylonian king who was distraught over the death of his closest friend, Enkidu: "I was terrified by his appearance, I began to fear death, and roam the wilderness. How can I stay silent, how can I be still! My friend whom I love has turned to clay! Am I not like him! Will I lie down never to get up again! That is why I must go on, to see Utanapishtim, 'The Faraway.' That is why sweet sleep has not mellowed my face, through sleepless striving I am strained, my muscles are filled with pain."[5] Many other descriptions followed over the centuries.

Homer's *Iliad*, for example, acutely depicts the experience of psychological trauma. During the siege of Troy, Achilles is betrayed by his commander Agamemnon. The betrayal shatters Achilles' world. Rage drives him until his psychological stress is compounded by the loss of his best friend, Patroklos, in battle. Achilles is now grieving and suicidal; stricken by bad dreams and a keen sense of guilt, he loses all semblance of self-control. The traumatic experiences depicted in this Homeric epic parallel those of soldiers returning from Vietnam.[6] Such reactions to trauma seem to be embedded in human nature.

Four hundred years after Homer, the Greek historian Herodotus related a new story about trauma. He described the Athenian warrior Epizelus who collapses in the midst of the Battle of Marathon in 490 B.C.: "Epizelus, the son of Cuphagorus, an Athenian soldier, was fighting bravely when he suddenly lost the sight of both eyes, though nothing had touched him anywhere—neither sword, spear, nor missile. From that moment he continued blinded as long as he lived. I am told that in speaking about what happened to him he used to say that he fancied he was opposed by a man of great stature in heavy armour, whose beard overshadowed his shield, but the phantom passed him by and killed the man at his side."[7] This narrative, in turn, has modern parallels in the experiences of soldiers in World War I.[8]

The famous diarist Samuel Pepys provided one of the best-known historical accounts of the emotional effects of trauma. Pepys lived through the Great Fire of London in August of 1666. The fire raged through a large portion of the old city of London, where most of the houses were made of wood. St. Paul's Cathedral was destroyed in the inferno. Six months later, in his entry dated February 18, 1667, he wrote of his "dreams of the fire and falling down of houses" and the terror he felt as it advanced toward his own home. Pepys continued to be troubled by problems sleeping. He wrote: "I did within these six days see smoke still remaining of the late fire in the City; and it is strange to think how this very day I cannot sleep at night without great terrors of fire, and this very night could not sleep until almost two in the morning through thoughts of fire."[9]

Two hundred years later, the experience of trauma took a new form with the industrial revolution and the invention of the railway. For the first time, people were witnessing the effects of accidents caused by high-speed travel. The early days of railway travel were marked by danger, with hundreds of deaths annually. A condition called "railway spine" was identified by physician John Eric Erichsen in his 1867 book *On Railway and Other Injuries of the Nervous System*. Also known as Erichsen's disease, railway spine collectively refers to the emotional and physical reactions of victims of railway collisions and other accidents. In his book he presented a series of case studies of railway-spine victims who had experienced memory problems, sleep disturbances, nightmares, and paralysis.

The author Charles Dickens was one of those victims. In 1865, he was a passenger on a train that crashed in Staplehurst, England. Physically unharmed, he remained on the scene to help tend to the injured and the dying. Hours after the accident, however, he described himself as feeling "quite shattered and broken up." Several days later, clearly overwhelmed by his experience, he complained of feeling "faint and sick" sensations in his head. In a letter to his daughter some years later, he wrote: "I am not quite right within, but believe it to be an effect of the railway shaking. I am curiously weak—weak as if I were recovering from a long illness."[10] Dickens believed this to be an effect of the accident and became phobic about traveling on railways. He died on the fifth anniversary of the disaster.

History shows us that people have always had nightmares, feelings of anxiety, and troubling images, and so on, but what these experiences mean, and how they are experienced, is culturally fashioned. Each generation and culture finds its own ways of understanding what these experiences mean. Today, we talk about such experiences as those described above—sleeplessness, upsetting thoughts, physical reactions—as symptoms of PTSD. Yet the history of trauma shows us that what these experiences mean is not a fixed truth: It is also a series of changing social constructions as each generation and culture grapples with the question of what trauma means for them and how best to make sense of these various experiences. The most pressing of issues shaping how we understand reactions to trauma is our understanding of the causes. Throughout history the pendulum of debate has swung between two opposite assumptions: on the one hand, that such problems arise from within the person as a result of psychological or physiological vulnerabilities and, on the other, that they arise from the overwhelming impact of an external force on the human mind and body.

Although railway spine was acknowledged as a disorder, its cause remained a topic of heated debate. Erichsen believed that railway spine was the result of concussion of the spine—a condition reflecting damage to the nervous system. At the time, however, little was actually known about the workings of the nervous system and others took a different view to

Erichsen about the cause of railway spine. In 1883, Herbert Page argued that railway spine constituted a psychological rather than organic disorder. According to his analysis, the symptoms associated with this condition arose from profound "nervous shock": "We know of no clinical picture more distressing than that of a strong and healthy man reduced by apparently inadequate causes to a state in which all control of the emotions is well-nigh gone; who cannot sleep because he has before his mind an ever present sense of the accident; who starts at the least noise; who lies in bed almost afraid to move; whose heart palpitates whenever he is spoken to; and who cannot hear or say a word about his present condition and his future prospects without bursting into tears," wrote Page.[11]

Railway spine faded from the textbooks, but debate over the causes of trauma continued. In the late nineteenth century, Freud was concerned with a disorder referred to as hysteria. The symptoms included physical incapacities (e.g., paralysis or blindness) and strange movements (tics) that made no physical sense. Prior to Freud, hysteria was dismissed as being of little interest to doctors, but Freud understood that the psychological suffering of hysterical patients was real in the sense that their lives were blighted by such suffering. For many centuries, the condition was considered a disease of women—the word *hysteria* is derived from the Latin for "wandering uterus." Originally, it was thought that the uterus became detached, rendering the individual unable to think clearly. Though questioned even in Freud's time, the notion that hysteria was something that women and not men experienced was commonly held. Freud initially developed his theory around the idea that traumatic experiences lay at the root of hysteria. The central cause, he argued, was always a traumatic secret—something locked within the unconscious mind.

One of Freud's most famous cases was Anna O, a young woman who suffered from seemingly physical symptoms, including paralysis, blurred vision, deafness, and mood swings, that seemed to have no biological cause. She was a patient of Freud's colleague Josef Breuer, who initially treated her with hypnosis. But at her request changed to talking through whatever came to her mind—the birth of what became known as "free association." Building on this work, Breuer and Freud published their influential psychological theory of hysteria in which neuroses arise from unconscious causes, and symptoms are resolved when these causes become conscious to the person.[12] Anna O (her real name was Bertha Pappenheim) went on to become a well-known social worker who described her treatment with Breuer as the "the talking cure."

Afterwards, Freud continued to develop his ideas on the causes of hysteria. His most controversial thesis, which led to disagreement between Freud and Breuer and the end of their collaboration, was that the fundamental cause of hysteria was the sexual seduction of a child by an adult. "I put forward the proposition, therefore, that at the bottom of every case of hysteria will be found one or more experiences of premature sexual experience, belonging to the first years of childhood," he wrote in 1896.[13] Freud speculated that childhood sexual traumas lay forgotten until puberty, when, with the emergence of adult sexuality, these early repressed experiences were recalled, causing hysteria.

At first, Freud fiercely defended his "seduction theory," as it was then known. But over time he began to question whether all of his patients had indeed been sexually abused as children. First he reformulated the theory, hypothesizing that hysteria could also arise from conflicts between sexual desires and psychological inhibitions. Then he retracted it altogether and turned his full attention to the idea of unconscious desires. Hysteria wasn't solely due to sexual abuse, after all. Freud ultimately replaced the "seduction theory" with theories about "fantasy," emphasizing not actual sexual experience but the repression of fantasized and instinctually derived sexual conflict. At the time, some critics of Freud saw him as having lost interest in the effects of real-life trauma, so immersed had he become in the inner world of unconscious motivations, but most psychoanalysts of the time went along with Freud's repudiation of seduction theory.[14] These latter theories about unconscious processes are the ones that Freud is known for today.

Freud's original emphasis on sexual seduction as the source of hysteria was largely disregarded throughout most of the twentieth century. This changed in the 1970s and 1980s after a reappraisal of his work by feminist scholars. These thinkers criticized Freud for retracting his sexual seduction theory, accusing him of running from the truth. Armed with new evidence of the damaging effects of early sexual abuse, they argued that he withdrew the theory because the notion of sexual seduction was just too controversial in Vienna in the late 1800s.[15]

The idea that sexual abuse is a cause of later psychological problems is of course no longer controversial; indeed, it is now readily accepted by psychologists and psychotherapists of all persuasions. But as Freud came to recognize, sexual abuse is not the only cause of such problems—and thus he was right to seek other explanations. In turning his attention to unconscious processes and the repression of sexual fantasies, Freud laid the foundation for the development of psychoanalysis. As an unfortunate consequence of this new emphasis, however, his attention was directed away from the real-life effects of actual events.

It was then that World War I opened up the topic of how real-life events affect people to psychiatric scrutiny.

The field of psychiatry was still in its infancy at this time, regarded as a fringe of medicine. But after the experiences of the war, it would soon be taken much more seriously. Historically, war has tended to play a crucial part in shaping the meaning of trauma.

During the war, young men enlisted to fight and were sent to the front with limited training and little knowledge of what was to befall them. Bombarded by exploding shells for months on end, they were entrenched in the terrifying sights and sounds of death. Wilfred Owen, in his best-known poem "Dulce et Decorum Est," describes the horror of seeing his companion dying in a gassing attack:

> As under a green sea, I saw him drowning.
> In all dreams, before my helpless sight,
> He plunges at me, guttering, choking, drowning.

The haunted men who returned from the front were sent to newly opened neurological wards for several days' rest, then expected to return to the front good as new.

For many of these young men, life at the front was too much to bear. Some tried to run away; others began to behave in erratic ways. Being unable to perform one's duty in war due to fearfulness was seen as cowardice. As a result, several hundred soldiers were court-marshaled for cowardice or desertion and shot by firing squad. But as the incidence of such behaviors continued to increase, it became clear that a full-fledged epidemic was under way. Back home, as soldiers filled more and more hospital beds, tormented by nightmares of what they had witnessed, it also became clear that their symptoms required treatment.

A major in the Royal Army Medical Corps, Arthur Hurst, described the case of a twenty-three-year-old soldier, Private M, who had lost the power of speech. Based in an England hospital, Private M had no idea of who or where he was and was behaving like a child playing with toys. Two years later, in the middle of the night, he felt something snap in his head, at which point his speech returned and he began to talk normally. For Private M it was as if he had been at the front only a few days before. He had no memory of the previous two years.

Besieged with many such reports, the war office was at a loss to explain this strange epidemic.[16]

In 1915 Charles Myers, a doctor in the Royal Army Medical Corps, coined the term *shell shock* in an article for the medical journal *The Lancet*. He was describing the cases of three soldiers whose injuries were sustained in close proximity to exploding shells. One of the three was a twenty-year-old private who had been caught on barbed wire. A shell had showered him with hot shards of metal but he escaped without injury, or so it seemed at the time: Weeks later he was found to be suffering from involuntary shivering, crying, and loss of memory. Myers concluded that the noise of the exploding shell had led to a sort of "molecular commotion in the brain."

Another medical physician named R. G. Rows further developed the concept of shell shock, speculating that it resulted from microscopic brain lesions caused by the atmospheric pressure of exploding shells. In a 1916 paper, he provided a description of battlefield reactions surprisingly similar to those associated with what we now call PTSD:

> The physical expression of a special emotion, such as fear or terror, persists for a long time without much change. This condition is usually associated

with an emotional state produced by the constant intrusion of the memory of some past incident. . . . [The soldiers] know they are irritable, that they are unable to interest themselves or to give a maintained attention to a given subject. . . . [A]ll this is very real to them and leads to a condition of anxiety which is increased by their not being able to understand their condition.[17]

The term *shell shock* spread like wildfire. Yet the cause of the condition continued to be debated, as had been the case with "railway spine." Whether shell shock was a physical or a psychological disorder remained unclear: Was it due to the physical effects of the concussion or to emotional factors like fatigue, hunger, and the stresses of war?

Row's physical explanation that shell shock was caused by atmospheric pressure soon came under fire. As more and more soldiers were diagnosed with shell shock, it became clear that many had not been exposed to exploding shells. A psychiatrist named W. H. Rivers suggested an alternative explanation. He concluded that the numerous civilians who had joined the war effort had been trained too quickly and, as a result, failed to build up sufficient psychological defenses against trench warfare. Rivers and a few other doctors advocated humane methods of treatment, but the prevailing view dismissed the soldiers as having weak wills or lacking moral fiber, implying that what these men needed was stronger discipline. Attitudes toward soldiers suffering from shell shock were generally unsympathetic, and treatments were harsh.

Nevertheless, the overwhelming number of soldiers suffering from shell shock forced reconsideration of the issue. Their symptoms could no longer be attributed to a deficiency of moral fiber. During the Battle of the Somme, as thousands upon thousands of men left the British trenches and walked toward the German lines, many were shredded by machine-gun fire, racked to death on barbed-wire fences, or blown to pieces by shells. In a matter of days there were 55,000 casualties and 19,000 dead.[18] As noted earlier, the atmospheric pressure explanation could no longer hold up; far too many of those admitted for psychiatric treatment had not been exposed to exploding shells. Attention now turned to psychological explanations.

By the end of the war, scientists generally accepted that battlefield reactions were a direct result of the extreme stressors of war and, as such, should be considered "normal" psychological reactions of men under great stress and not due to any moral failing.

Intrigued by trauma once again, a now-older Sigmund Freud was drawn back to the topic through his work with soldiers. Up to then, Freud had envisioned dreams as wish fulfillments related to the pursuit of pleasure. But as he listened to soldiers talk of their nightmares, he began to realize that his theories of psychoanalysis failed to account for what was then called war neurosis, marked by obsessive thoughts and nightmares about horrific battle scenes. Once again he was compelled to rethink his ideas to accommodate his new observations, marking a new shift in how trauma was conceptualized.

In his 1920 book *Beyond the Pleasure Principle*, Freud proposed that repetitive dreams represented attempts to achieve a sense of mastery over distressing memories. Such dreams, he argued, were a form of "repetition compulsion" in which the mind returned to the memories again and again—reworking them in order to transform the traumatic experiences underlying those memories.[19]

In a related vein, the eminent French psychiatrist Pierre Janet, a contemporary of Freud's, observed that healthy psychological functioning requires a unified memory of all facets related to an experience—actions, thoughts, emotions, and sensations.[20] His research suggested, however, that memories of traumatic experiences are different because they are split off from conscious awareness and experienced as visceral sensations of anxiety, nightmares, and flashbacks, which interfere with the consolidation of memories. Treatment therefore required patients to be able to transform their traumatic memories into autobiographical narratives. As we shall see, this idea remains at the heart of trauma theories today.

World War II saw the introduction of diagnostic terms such as *war neurosis* (noted above) as well as *battle fatigue, combat exhaustion, post-trauma syndrome,* and *traumatophobia*.[21] Around the same time, research was also documenting the adverse psychological reactions of survivors of civilian trauma. On November 28, 1942, a Boston nightclub called the

Cocoanut Grove burned to the ground. The deadly fire killed 492 people and injured hundreds more. In a study of the survivors, psychologist Alexandra Adler noted that, after one year, around half of them were still experiencing nightmares, insomnia, anxiety, guilt over survival, and fears related to the fire.[22]

By the middle of the twentieth century the negative effects of trauma were well documented, but there was no formal method for recognizing the effects of extreme stress on people's functioning. This was yet to come. It would take the devastation of the Vietnam War to create the kind of trauma for which such a method was needed.

The trauma of the Vietnam War could be extreme. Many of the soldiers were quite young, conscripted on their eighteenth birthday to swell the ranks of regular recruits. Having never left their hometowns before, they were now being sent away to fight a horrific war—one that divided the nation back home. Many veterans developed serious psychological problems as a result of their experiences. At the time, they were believed to be suffering from depression, anxiety, substance misuse, personality disorder, and schizophrenia. However, none of these diagnoses adequately encompassed the soldiers' symptoms, which included nightmares, emotional numbness, and hyperarousal—nor did they explicitly indicate that the roots of such symptoms lay in combat.

As the number of psychological casualties escalated, treatment providers faced mounting pressure to establish a formal diagnostic category. Throughout the late 1970s a committee of anti–Vietnam War psychiatrists and scholars in the newly emerging field of trauma psychology met to discuss the need for psychiatric recognition of war's damaging psychological effects.[23] Fueled by investigations into the psychological consequences of the war and by the advocacy of campaigners on behalf of Vietnam veterans, the American Psychiatric Association took the bold step of introducing the concept of PTSD into its third edition of the *Diagnostic and Statistical Manual of Mental Disorders* (DSM–III), published in 1980.[24] The term *posttraumatic stress disorder* was not immediately agreed upon; some psychiatrists preferred the more specific phrase *post-Vietnam syndrome*. Others on the committee persuasively argued that this new diagnostic category should be flexible enough to encompass other horrors of the twentieth century, such as the Holocaust and Hiroshima—events that had been documented as leading to similar psychological reactions.[25]

Unlike most other DSM categories, the PTSD label describes symptoms thought to arise as the *direct result* of a psychologically traumatic event. Indeed, with only a few exceptions, the DSM is agnostic about the causes of the disorders listed.[26]

This distinction was the key to PTSD: It signified the recognition that virtually anyone subjected to extreme events could end up with the disorder. For veterans, the PTSD label changed the entire conversation about war's effects.

The Vietnam War was reported in more graphic detail than any war before. Americans witnessed its horrors in their own living rooms, and thanks to the televised investigation of My Lai, they learned that some veterans had committed atrocities. Even as the war drew to a close, anti-war feelings continued to run high in the United States. Returning veterans were shunned by a society that had distanced itself from the war. The anti-war movement inevitably affected their morale. Arriving home, they were confronted by anti-war protests and an atmosphere of defeat, leaving many veterans feeling alienated, lonely, and abandoned. Blamed for the atrocities that had been carried out, they were labeled psychopaths and called names like "babykiller."[27] Not surprisingly, this reception took an emotional toll of its own. Indeed, one reason the Vietnam War had such a profound and long-lasting impact on veterans was the hostility they received on returning home.

The diagnostic label of PTSD provided newfound recognition for veterans. It acknowledged that what they had gone through was genuinely disturbing and, in doing so, helped pave the way toward a more sympathetic public attitude. It wouldn't be long before other groups joined Vietnam veterans in campaigning for further recognition through more widespread use of this diagnostic category.

Feminists were among these other groups. During the 1970s and '80s they sought to overturn elements of psychiatry that were biased against women, such as the use of what they viewed as pejorative psychiatric labels. Borderline personality disorder (BPD) was one such label. By emphasizing personality as the problem, BPD was criticized as a diagnostic category that stigmatized and discredited women. By drawing parallels between the symptoms of BPD and those of PTSD (and the fact that women with BPD often had terrifying experiences of abuse and neglect in childhood), some feminists hoped to develop an awareness of the psychologically harmful effects of abuse and attract public sympathy to the plight of women who had suffered domestic violence and childhood sexual abuse.[28] Indeed, what seemed so different at first—BPD and PTSD—now appeared to have core similarities, leading to the recognition that trauma at a young age affects people's ability to regulate and express their feelings and, ultimately, to find meaning in life.

In short, psychological suffering could now be viewed as arising through external events rather than from a person's "character." War veterans and abused women benefited from the new spotlight of PTSD and the resultant discussion of the various ways in which trauma could affect psychological functioning. But, equally important, the PTSD label itself consolidated the scientific thinking that had surrounded the concept of trauma throughout previous decades.

As should be clear by now, culture frames how we think about psychiatric disorders. What we define as psychological problems and how we deal with those problems are nothing more than contingent decisions made by society at some given point in history. They are decisions—not facts.

Psychiatric disorders are indeed products of their times. For example, forty years ago homosexuality was classified as a psychiatric disorder; almost overnight, many people simply ceased to be "ill" when this category was removed from the DSM. Clearly, psychiatric classification is not a neutral tool: The categorizing of human behaviors by a group of professionals takes the process of "naming" out of the hands of those who actually experience those behaviors.[29]

While it is likely that experiences of intrusive thinking, arousal, and avoidance occur in all societies throughout history because there is a biological basis for these (as we shall see in the next chapter), how we understand and make sense of these experiences is a product of our culture.

This debate over the causes of trauma continues today, shaping society's judgments of whether traumatized people are deserving of sympathy and help. Culture influences what we consider to be mental disorders and it shapes our beliefs and expectations about how to respond to traumatic life-events.[30] Differences in cultural beliefs about the expression of emotions, the role of fate, personal responsibility, human purpose, all influence how trauma is experienced and dealt with. As we move on to a discussion of PTSD's symptoms, this contingency is worth remembering. Ultimately the aim of this book is to argue for a change. My hope is that we can replace our current conceptualization of trauma in favor of a new understanding—one that allows us to see posttraumatic stress as a natural and normal process with the potential to lead to posttraumatic growth.[31] This alternate view of trauma not only resists the tendency to medicalize human experience but also, and more important, places responsibility for recovery back in the hands of those who have experienced the trauma themselves.

In the 1980 edition of the *Diagnostic and Statistical Manual of Mental Disorders*, the description of PTSD grouped problems into three categories: re-experiencing of the trauma, numbing of responsiveness, and a miscellaneous section that included impairment of memory, difficulty concentrating, hyperalertness, sleep disturbances, avoidance of reminders, and guilt. This grouping has changed over subsequent editions of the DSM.

In the most recent edition of the DSM, PTSD is characterized as consisting of three clusters of symptoms: persistent re-experiencing of the traumatic event, avoidance of stimuli associated with the event and numbing of responsiveness, and persistent symptoms of increased arousal.[32]

The first characteristic of PTSD is persistent re-experiencing of the traumatic event. In some cases, people re-experience a traumatic event through intrusive and involuntary recollections of what happened. Thoughts, feelings, images, and memories invade conscious awareness and trigger intense emotional reactions such as panic, terror, grief, or despair. Sometimes the trauma is replayed in the form of dreams and nightmares. Leon Greenman, who you may remember from the beginning of the book, wrote in his autobiography that even twenty years after the end of the war he dreamed of being back in Auschwitz, watching his comrades hanging by their necks and running from the SS officer who wanted to hang him, too.

In other cases, experiences are replayed through flashbacks and hallucinations when the person is awake. Flashbacks are characterized by the sudden and usually vivid feeling that the event is actually happening again. They are often accompanied by physical reactions such as a racing heart or sweating. Often the person is unable to recognize the experience as a memory and instead feels or acts as if it were happening "in real time." One man, David, was celebrating with friends on a riverboat when, late at night, the boat was sunk in a collision with a barge. David survived but many of his friends died that night. Afterwards he was wracked with guilt that he could have done more to save others. He found it difficult to sleep and was haunted by memories of what had happened. Months later, he was travelling by bus one night when the bus crossed a bridge over a river. Seeing the lights reflect in the water below, he immediately had a terrifying flashback in which he felt himself to be back on board the boat that fateful night. Only several hours later was he able to calm down and get back in touch with reality.[33]

External cues such as sights, sounds, smells, locations, or other people can call to mind the original event; internal cues such as emotions, thoughts, and psychological states can do the same. Witnesses on the scene at Lockerbie in the aftermath of the bombing of Pan Am flight 103 in 1988 remember the smell of airplane fuel in the air; more than two decades later, similar smells still evoke powerful memories of the devastation. Other reminders can also be very vivid. In a case study described by the psychologist David Murphy, one participant explained that whenever he was hugged by a man with a beard, the touch of the beard reminded him of the abuse he suffered as a boy in foster care. He called it the stubble effect.[34]

Ordinary memories tend to be forgotten over time—but not so for traumatic memories. Recollections of trauma take hold and become amplified, even imprinted, in the mind (see Figure 2.1). More than thirty years after returning home from Vietnam, one veteran recalled: "They're screaming and in pain and legs missing—bowels sticking out and eyes

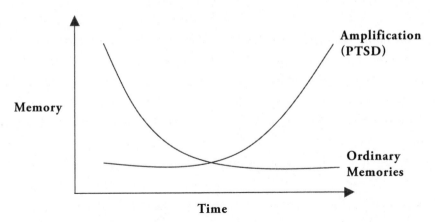

FIGURE 2.1 The Relationship Between Memory and Time for Ordinary Memories and for PTSD Memories. While ordinary memories fade, memories of trauma amplify. *Source:* Dekel (2009).

gone . . . 'cause it's life and death, it never leaves you, it's vivid in your mind all the time. . . . You leave it—leave it in the background and get on with your life the best you can but ah—but ah—it's always there."[35]

Bear in mind, however, that the presence of such thoughts and memories does not automatically mean that a person has PTSD. Throughout life, we are all bound to encounter horrors and tragedies that stay with us, but that fact alone does not signify psychiatric disorder. In fact, it can be beneficial to remember such events, as they are often turning points in our life stories that define the people that we are.

The second characteristic of PTSD, as noted above, involves the deliberate effort to avoid stimuli—thoughts, feelings, people, conversations, situations, or activities—that arouse recollections of the traumatic event. An inability to remember certain aspects of the event and deliberate attempts to block out memories are also aspects of avoidance.

Jan, pregnant with her third child, was rushed to the hospital when she began having contractions earlier than expected. During delivery she lost a large amount of blood. Drifting in and out of consciousness, she overheard a voice saying, "I think we are losing her." Unsure of whether that sentence referred to her or her baby, she finally lost consciousness altogether. Upon waking the following day, she was convinced that she had lost the baby until she understood that the baby was alive, and lying beside her.

In the following weeks she became highly avoidant, trying not to think about her experience. She steered clear of newspaper and magazine articles that mentioned pregnancy, switched off the television if an image on the screen reminded her of it, and even crossed the street if she saw a mother and baby.[36]

Individuals with PTSD may also experience emotional numbing, which is characterized by feelings of detachment or estrangement; a sense of being disconnected from others; a difficulty experiencing positive feelings such as happiness, love, and intimacy; and a loss of interest in usual activities. A woman named Maria who had been sexually assaulted told me that she felt numb in her body afterward, as if she were dead from her neck downward. She lost interest in sexual activity with her boyfriend. She called herself an emotional zombie. She would watch television but wasn't really watching, just staring at the screen, uninterested in what was going on.

The third characteristic of PTSD is persistent symptoms of arousal. This phenomenon results in bodily symptoms characteristic of anxiety, such as accelerated heart rate, rapid breathing, cold sweats, and heart palpitations. Some PTSD sufferers might also exhibit increased irritability, rage, hostility, or outbursts of anger. Many survivors of extreme trauma report difficulties controlling their temper as well as sleep disturbances—especially insomnia and night terrors. Such individuals tend to be hyperalert and hypervigilant, staying constantly "on guard" and scanning for signs of threat or potential danger in the outside world; in such cases, the threat associated with the original trauma has become generalized. They are also easily startled and often react with excessive fright. One man who had served as a soldier in the Falklands War told me that he would literally jump out of his seat if he heard a car backfire outside in the street.

Carol, a survivor of the London underground train bombings in July 2005, told me that even now, several years later, she is hypervigilant during her train rides to and from work. She makes sure that she sits either at the front or the back of the train, as she now knows that is where the rescuers will come first. She also knows which of the trains run on the newer lines with wider tunnels. The deeper tunnels, she explains to me, are smaller—and if a bomb goes off in a smaller tunnel, the train will implode. In the wider tunnels, however, the train will explode and she will have a chance of survival.

The ways in which these and other symptoms are grouped together continue to be debated in the field. Indeed, diagnostic criteria for psychiatric disorders are subject to constant revision and reformulation.[37]

The PTSD symptoms described above—summarized by the terms *intrusion*, *avoidance*, and *arousal*—can be deeply distressing and unpleasant. Nevertheless, all are natural and normal reactions to stressful and threatening events. They may even occur during everyday events. Taking an exam, being interviewed for a job, or having an argument with one's spouse can elicit any one of these reactions, albeit to a lesser degree of intensity.

The intensity of posttraumatic reactions ranges along a continuum from mild to severe. To address this continuum, we may find it more useful to use the term *posttraumatic stress*: Once posttraumatic stress reaches a certain level of intensity, the person experiencing it is said to have PTSD.[38]

There is a clear difference between individuals at one end of the posttraumatic stress continuum and those at the other. Most psychiatrists think of the people at these opposite extremes as two separate groups. The issue is more complicated, however, for people in the middle of the continuum. Many people who experience trauma fall just short of a full diagnosis of PTSD; for instance, they may have all but one or two of the characteristic symptoms. Such people are probably similar to someone with the diagnosis of PTSD, yet they would technically be grouped among those without this diagnosis. For this reason, talking about whether a particular person has PTSD can be confusing.

Further complicating the issue is the arbitrariness of where one draws the line above which someone is said to have PTSD. The diagnosis of PTSD remains targeted at intrusion, avoidance, and arousal— once such symptoms become so frequent and intense that they impair the person's functioning at home and at work.[39] But how should *impair* be defined? As the diagnostic category of PTSD has evolved over the years, this threshold has shifted. As with other psychiatric disorders, the point at which normal reactions end and abnormal reactions begin is not clear-cut.

One generalization can be made, however: What readily distinguishes those with PTSD from those without is that their lives revolve around it. Just controlling one's emotional states can be a struggle. One woman who survived a vicious attack described how she plans each day around "what ifs" to avoid shocks of any kind. She explained that these are strategies for getting through each day with the least likelihood of being startled. She feels on edge and hyperalert to danger, always suspecting that bad things are about to happen. Simply walking down the street provokes anxiety in her, for she is flooded with thoughts of the mishaps that might befall her. As a result, her life has become severely constricted. She cannot watch television because of her fear of violent images. She is troubled by upsetting memories—thoughts and images that come flooding back whenever something reminds her of what happened. And she avoids going shopping at busy times of the day because she becomes anxious whenever other people are around, particularly in places where she might run into her attacker.

It is hard to imagine the sheer terror and hopelessness of PTSD if you have never experienced it. But think of the expressionist painting *Angst* by Edvard Munch and the staring eyes of the people in that picture. Or *The Scream*, his painting of an agonized figure set against a blood-red sky. These figures are seeing not what is in front of them but images of something so traumatic and shocking that they cannot look away. From these pictures we get a glimpse of what it is like to live with PTSD.

The symptoms of PTSD can be so upsetting that thoughts of suicide arise. One man who had been subjected to a vicious assault feared his nightmares to the point where, night after night, he did all he could to stay awake. Eventually he would fall asleep against his will, only to wake up in the early hours of the morning drenched in sweat, terrified by nightmares in which he was being chased and then strangled. After several months of this he began to contemplate suicide and sought professional help. Fortunately he received advice that helped him to better understand what he was going through, reassured him that he was not "going crazy," and provided methods for dealing with his nightmares and for getting to and staying asleep.

Some people seek professional help only as a last resort. For them, seeking help is a sign of weakness, and they simply do not see themselves as the sort of people who need psychiatric assistance. Others may want to keep aspects of their trauma hidden. Sharon, a woman who had developed PTSD following a complicated childbirth, was for many years ashamed to talk about her difficulties. She believed that mothers should love their children but did not feel an affectionate bond with her own child and, as a result, worried that this meant she was a bad mother. But rather than seeking help, she attempted to lie to herself (as well her husband), pretending that everything was going well. She overheard a radio program one afternoon in which I was talking about this very topic—childbirth-related PTSD—and later told me that this experience gave her the confidence to approach a doctor: "When I realized I wasn't the only one who felt like that, it made all the difference."

The translation of traumatic experiences into symptoms is a process unique to every individual. Many PTSD sufferers seek to avoid reminders of their experience, but what serves as a reminder can be different for each person. For Sharon, it was a dread of future childbirth. Sharon said, "I would avoid childbirth again; if I accidently become pregnant I would want to die rather than go through that again." In this instance, avoidance became a larger problem—one that ultimately affected her marriage. Sharon never told her husband about the feelings she was experiencing, but she did all she could to avoid pregnancy. In particular, she began taking additional contraceptives and avoided sexual relations as much as possible. Over time, the relationship deteriorated and divorce followed. Sharon never explained to her husband what was going on with her—largely because she didn't fully understand herself. It is the nature of avoidance that people don't confront the issues that they should.

Posttraumatic stress reactions can manifest in other unique ways as well. One person may be reminded of a long-ago event by a particular type of bus; another, by a song on the radio; still another, by the sound of rain on the window. As long as such reminders evoke painful and upsetting memories, people will do what they can to avoid them. And, indeed, some people are so successful at avoiding reminders that they seem on the surface to have overcome the trauma they experienced. But life is unpredictable; if by chance they are confronted by the reminder they have so successfully avoided, memories may instantly come flooding back, leading to PTSD. One man who many years previously had been held captive as a prisoner of war and was kept in isolation in a single cell without windows, experienced full-blown PTSD many years later when he was moved to a windowless office at work.

It is important to understand, however, that many posttraumatic reactions subside after a period of days. It is only when such reactions are both *intense* and *persistent* that PTSD is considered the appropriate diagnosis: Specifically, they must be frequent and severe, and they must persist for several weeks after the traumatic event. Most people who experience a trauma will exhibit these reactions in the initial weeks afterward, so for this reason a diagnosis of PTSD cannot be made until at least a month has passed. Before that, someone might be described as suffering from *acute stress disorder*—the term used to describe posttraumatic stress reactions that occur between two days and four weeks following trauma.

The diagnosis of PTSD thus applies only to those whose problems have become relatively persistent and long term. Stress reactions are normal in the initial days and weeks after a traumatic event. The time frame of one month rests on clinical observations and research suggesting that this is the expected trajectory of recovery for most people who experience a traumatic event. I do not mean to suggest that such people are fully recovered after a month; indeed, many may still be experiencing several of the reactions associated with posttraumatic stress. Rather, my point is that these symptoms will not be as intense as they once were, and certainly not at the level equated with the diagnostic threshold for PTSD.

Among those for whom posttraumatic reactions do remain intense after a month or so, such reactions can last for many more months, and even for many years. Mary was a woman who, like Sharon, experienced PTSD after childbirth. After undergoing a complicated emergency Caesarean section following twenty-five hours of painful labor, Mary was in agony and absolutely terrified for her life. Seven days later her baby daughter died. Five decades later, Mary is unable to watch television shows in which someone is depicted as suffering. The sound of a baby crying can still start her heart thumping and set off a panic reaction. At the time of her difficult pregnancy in 1960, the diagnostic category of PTSD did not yet exist. Mary was merely reassured by the medical staff that she would soon feel better. Decades later she remains affected.

The case of Mary raises another question: How do we define what constitutes a traumatic event? This is a question of considerable importance because to be diagnosed with PTSD one first has to have experienced an event defined as traumatic by the American Psychiatric Association.

In 1980, when PTSD was introduced as a diagnostic category, *traumatic event* was defined in the DSM as a stressor that "is generally outside the range of usual human experience" and that "would evoke significant symptoms of distress in most people."[40] Immediately, scientists began to debate the types of events that could fulfill this criterion. Certainly, extreme events such as combat and disaster were understood to be traumatic events. But what about other events that caused stress? Could stressors include traffic accidents, life-threatening illnesses, the death of a close relative, or, as happened to Mary, a complicated and painful childbirth?

At the time, the majority of experts did not consider these four events to be capable of evoking "significant symptoms of distress" in almost anyone. A complicated and painful childbirth, for example, was not considered an extreme enough event for the diagnosis of PTSD even if the woman in question experienced such severe and chronic problems as intrusive thoughts and avoidant behavior for years afterward. As Mary explained to me: "I was told that there was nothing wrong, that I had only had a baby. Even my husband said, 'What's the problem? Thousands of women have babies every day.' He couldn't understand why I couldn't just get over it like all other women." In the past, women like Mary, if they sought help at all, were often diagnosed with depression and prescribed antidepressants. Many of the women who received this diagnosis felt that the message they were being given was that they were "imagining things," when all they really wanted was for people to understand what had happened to them—to understand that for them childbirth was as horrifying and painful an experience as torture, violation, or mutilation.[41]

In 1980, when PTSD was first introduced, someone like Mary would not have received a diagnosis of PTSD as what happened to her would not have been deemed outside the range of usual human experience and leading to significant symptoms of distress in most people. But since then the definition of PTSD has expanded beyond its original focus on combat, disaster, and the Holocaust. It now encompasses a range of other events, such as sexual assault, traffic accidents, criminal victimization, and life-threatening illnesses and medical procedures, in recognition that such events can also lead to the symptoms of PTSD. But the definition of a traumatic event had to change to make room for events which do not lead to significant symptoms of distress in most people. Whereas the 1980 definition emphasized the universality of human response to trauma, a new definition was needed that was able to recognize the differences between people. The definition of trauma had to accommodate the fact that people will often experience the same event differently, so what is traumatic to one person, is not to another.

A useful context for discussing this issue is provided by the eighteenth-century Scottish philosopher David Hume, who observed that it is not what happens to us that determines our reactions but, rather, how we *appraise* what happens to us. The rise of cognitive psychology in the late twentieth century helped to consolidate this extremely important notion.

It follows that *traumatic event* should be defined not in terms of external occurrences but in terms of survivors' perceptions of what has happened to them. This point is illustrated by an old German legend about a man who arrived at an inn on a cold winter evening. He was pleased to have reached shelter after riding his horse over a wind-swept plain covered in snow. The landlord viewed the man with surprise and asked him from what direction he had come. The man pointed, whereupon the landlord, in an awe-struck tone, told him he had just ridden across the frozen, vast Lake of Constance. Upon hearing this, the man dropped dead through sheer fright. In this story, the rider was traumatized not by what had actually happened to him but by his later realization of the danger that he had unknowingly confronted.[42]

Some events are so overwhelmingly terrifying that almost all who experience them would appraise them as traumatic. The Holocaust was certainly one such event. But other events are ambiguous in the sense that some people would appraise them as traumatic whereas others would not. Examples include diagnosis of illness, divorce, and involvement in a traffic accident; these are events that lead to PTSD in some people but not in others. And then there are events that most people would not consider traumatic even though a few do—for instance, viewing a televised report of a murder. For a minority, such events are traumatic.

In short, the effect of traumatic events is *mediated* by how one regards the event, either at the time or later on. We now know, for example, that people can develop PTSD following accidents involving head injury. Even if they lost consciousness at the time of the event and have no memory of it, as they begin to piece together the details from reports of what happened, like the rider across the frozen lake, they can become traumatized.[43]

Appraisal, then, is a function of both the objective nature of an event and the individual's perception of the event. Indeed, two people who experience the same event can be affected quite differently. The way they react to this event is ultimately the result of their perceptions of what has happened and what it means to them. If the rider in the German legend had not been told he had just crossed the Lake of Constance, he would not have dropped dead.

In recognition of this relationship between exposure to a traumatic event and perceptions of the event, the definition of PTSD was amended in the 1994 edition of the *Diagnostic and Statistical Manual of Mental Disorders* (DSM-IV) as follows:

The person has been exposed to a traumatic event in which both the following were present: (1) The person experienced, witnessed, or was confronted with an event or events that involved actual or threatened death or serious injury, or a threat to the physical integrity of self or others. (2) The person's response involved fear, helplessness, or horror.[44]

The implications of this two-part definition were profound. The phrase "outside the range of usual human experience" had been dropped and the emphasis shifted from an expectation of how most people would respond to how they perceived the event.

Someone like Mary—who after a horrific childbirth experience more than fifty years ago was merely told "that she would soon feel better"—would be diagnosed today as suffering from PTSD. Indeed, a study using the 1994 DSM-IV criteria of what constitutes a traumatic event found that 89.6 percent of adults in the Detroit metropolitan area could be classified as having experienced or witnessed a traumatic event. But in 1980, only 9.2 percent of these people would have been said to have PTSD. Comparing the 1994 diagnostic criteria with the previous criteria, the researchers concluded that almost 40 percent more people would now be diagnosed with PTSD than before.[45]

The 1994 definition introduced the idea that subjective appraisal of an event is more relevant than the event itself. In doing so, it characterized PTSD as a condition caused not just by external forces but also by the sufferer's perception of the event. This emphasis on how people experience events marked an important turning point in how PTSD was defined. It provided the basis for allowing the diagnosis to be given to people who previously would not have been diagnosed with PTSD. But widening the definition of what constituted a traumatic event was controversial, and still is.

How a traumatic event is defined is important, therefore, because it acts as the gatekeeper to the diagnosis of PTSD. If it is a broad definition, more people will have PTSD than if it is a narrow definition. The implications of this are profound and fiercely debated.

Many treatment providers saw the change as reflecting a necessary recognition that traumatic events could take many different forms. However, critics saw it as a dilution of the concept of PTSD—a tendency that has been referred to as "conceptual bracket creep." In the view of these critics, too many people who experience stressors that might previously have been considered ordinary—such as bereavement, marital breakdown, and illness—can now be diagnosed with PTSD. Moreover, before 1994 this diagnosis was restricted to people who had experienced an event them-selves, whereas now people could be diagnosed with PTSD if they wit-nessed an event. Thus, for example, some individuals who watched the 9/11 attacks—on television—were diagnosed with PTSD for their stress. PTSD symptoms have even been reported in people following the de-feat of their favorite football team.[46] Critics argue that such experiences are simply not comparable to surviving Auschwitz—the kind of trauma the term *posttraumatic stress disorder* was originally meant to encompass. The danger, they say, is that the concept of PTSD could lose its useful-ness as it becomes applied to more and more people and an increasingly broad range of accidents, illnesses, and injuries.

As usage of the PTSD label has widened to include events that not everyone experiences as traumatic, another question arises: Why do some people and not others develop PTSD? Traumatic events are still part of the criterion for this diagnosis—but if not everyone who experiences an event develops PTSD, then the events are not sufficient causes in them-selves. As we have seen, subjective perceptions play a role, but to fully understand the differences between people and how PTSD develops, we must also look inside the brain to see what's going on.

CHAPTER 3

The Biology of Trauma

DURING TRAUMA, things happen fast and unexpectedly—and the overall experience is not easy to comprehend. We can take in only so much information. Yet evolution has equipped us with the ability to react quickly and automatically to danger. Imagine that, while reading this, you hear a loud bang. Before you have time to think about what is happening, your body will react automatically, turning you in the direction from which the noise came. You are now in alarm mode; your body's automatic defense mechanisms have kicked in, ready for action.

The next action is to freeze.

When I was a boy, *Jaws* was showing in the cinemas. As a birthday treat, my father took me to the movie theater in the center of Belfast city. I was just old enough to be admitted to see the movie. Afterward, still excited by it, we had just stepped out into the street when we heard a loud crash. Startled, I turned to see that two cars had collided fifty yards away. Out of control, one of the cars was now hurtling toward me. I stood there frozen, watching it come nearer and nearer. Time seemed to move in slow motion. I remember thinking that the grill on the front of the car was like a mouth of dazzling teeth. The great white shark was coming straight for me. Within a split second, my father had grabbed me by the shoulder and pulled me out of the way. I could feel a rush of air; then the car smashed into the wall of the cinema.

I realize now, that when I stood outside that cinema, frozen to the spot, I was responding as dictated by millions of years of evolution. My reaction to the oncoming car was no different from the one I would have had if I was confronted by a real shark. And my experience was typical: For all of us, the immediate reaction in such situations is to freeze—to be motionless so as not to draw attention to ourselves—while we determine what the danger is and where it's coming from so that we can take whatever action is required to ensure survival.

Then we react with what is known as the *fight-or-flight response*— which prepares us to either protect ourselves or escape.[1] The Nobel laureate Hans Selye conceptualized the fight-or-flight response as a three-stage process: the *alarm* stage in which the organism freezes in readiness for flight or fight; the *resistance* stage in which resources— whether biological, psychological, or social—are mobilized to cope with the stressor; and, finally, the *exhaustion* stage. If attempts to cope with the stressor are unsuccessful, it is during this last stage that the organism collapses from physiological exhaustion and eventually dies.

To understand these bodily processes, we need to know how the autonomic nervous system (ANS) works. The ANS has two branches: the sympathetic nervous system (SNS) and the parasympathetic nervous system (PNS). The SNS can act as the body's accelerator. When we are confronted with extreme stress, various processes swing into action: The pupils of the eyes dilate, the heart beats faster, the rate of breathing increases, blood flow increases and is redirected to the muscles for quick movement, the skin becomes cold and pale, fat is made available for energy, hormones surge throughout the body, muscles tense, the bladder empties. Lighter on our feet and equipped with energy that has been diverted from ingestion and reproduction, we are now ready for action. We are ready to fight or take flight.

But when we can neither flee nor fight, we submit. In these circumstances, the PNS is aroused. Heart rate and respiration decrease, blood pressure lowers, the pupils return to normal, and the skin becomes warm and flushed. If the SNS is the body's accelerator, the PNS is the body's braking system.[2] What happened to me outside the cinema was over in seconds, as I was quickly pulled to safety. However, in situations where neither fight nor flight is possible, people submit by going into a stupor. In this state, though conscious of what is happening, they are able to observe the proceedings without sensation or emotion (much like patients partially under the influence of chloroform)—a phenomenon known as *tonic immobility*.

The explorer David Livingstone provided a vivid example of this phenomenon when he wrote about an experience he had while hunting a lion: "When in the act of ramming down the bullets I heard a shout, and looking half round I saw the lion in the act of springing upon me. He caught me on the shoulder and we came to the ground together. Growling horribly he shook me as a dog does a rat. The shock produced a stupor similar to that which seems to be felt by a mouse after the first grip of the cat. It caused a sort of dreaminess in which there was no sense of pain or feeling of terror, although I was quite conscious of all that was happening."[3]

Tonic immobility is a clever evolutionary innovation. It may seem self-defeating; but in actuality, if we put up no resistance and remain silent and motionless, it is possible that predators, such as the lion that attacked Livingstone, will be fooled into leaving us alone. At worst, they may shake us and drop us to the ground, thinking that we are already dead, and thereby give us the opportunity to escape. In our altered state of consciousness we don't feel fear, time moves slower, and pain is absent.

In fact, human responses to stress have been shaped by millions of years of evolution, most of which elapsed in a wilderness setting. After all, it is only comparatively recently that humans have lived in cities with populations in the millions. In 98 percent of human history the predominant way of life was the hunter-gatherer community, in which women gathered plants, collected firewood, and raised children while men hunted wildebeest, giraffe, and steenbok. In such environments, infectious and parasitic illnesses, high mortality rates, exposure to natural disasters, and attacks by wild animals were the forces shaping the evolution of our species. Accordingly, we are hardwired to adapt to these stressors: Our anxiety reactions are a legacy of our history. In a sense we are survival machines, programmed to react in ways that help ensure our survival.[4]

Although we are far less likely to be caught and shaken by large predators today, the same survival mechanism kicks in during times of stress. One woman I interviewed, Sarah, was caught up in a fatal shooting. It was a sweltering mid-August day, and she had just left the grocery store with her friend Dawn. Instead of going directly back to the car with their groceries, they decided to take a coffee break in a nearby shop; as a new mother, Sarah wanted to take this opportunity to catch up with her old school friend. Wrapped up in their conversation, they did not notice a man running toward them.

Two shots rang out.

Sarah was suddenly very alert. Other shoppers were shouting and running away. Dawn dropped to the ground a few yards from where Sarah stood. Blood seemed to be everywhere. Dawn lay on the ground motionless, covered in blood. Sarah was aware of drops of blood on her own dress, but she was frozen to the spot. A man was pointing a gun at her. Everything was happening in slow motion, as if in a dream. Looking directly at Sarah, the man moved his gun closer to her head. She stood motionless at gunpoint for what seemed like an eternity. A river of blood ran from Dawn's head. To this day, that is all she can remember: standing there as if in a dream, seeing her friend Dawn lying dead on the ground and thinking that she was about to be shot herself. What happened next she cannot say. All she remembers is being surrounded by police, who were asking her questions.

Sarah told me later that she had felt like a detached observer, looking down on herself from afar. She said that it seemed as though she was "standing there forever, but it must only have been a few seconds." Sarah's experience is not unusual. Following a trauma, many people feel as though they are outside of their bodies.

Indeed, a small percentage of the survivors of the *Herald of Free Enterprise* described entering such an altered state of consciousness. In our three-year survey we found that 11 percent felt that they left their body during impact, 12 percent felt that they entered a tunnel leading to a bright light, and 9 percent felt the presence of a spiritual being.[5] Research suggests that such experiences as these are a protective mechanism intended for use in dire situations where no options remain. It kicks in when the circumstances are such that struggling might only make things more dangerous. But as protective as tonic immobility might be in terms of enhancing physical survival, many people who experience this state undergo great mental distress afterward. Indeed, although tonic immobility is not the sole cause of PTSD, it does seem to add to the probability that PTSD will develop. One explanation for this finding is that people often feel shame or guilt for not "putting up more of a fight."[6] Sarah often wonders what she could have done differently; although she realizes from a logical perspective that there wasn't anything else she could have done, such thoughts still trouble her.

Tonic immobility is an instinctive response. As such, it is normal and adaptive, honed through millions of years of evolution. When faced with clients who blame themselves for the way they acted during a traumatic event, many therapists offer this as an explanation—as doing so will often lift their heavy burdens of shame or guilt. Such clients may also benefit from a discussion of what happens in the brain during a traumatic event.

The *limbic system* is the part of the brain that operates the autonomic nervous system. In evolutionary terms, it is the oldest structure in the brain—one that we have in common with our mammalian ancestors. The limbic system acts as a trauma control center; in this role, it regulates fear conditioning and memory storage, the two processes central to our reactions to trauma. The specific parts of the limbic center that operate these processes are the amygdala and the hippocampus.

The *amygdala* is the brain's gatekeeper for incoming emotional information. Located at the top of the brain stem, it controls a variety of brain functions—most notably emotional memory, fear, and anxiety. In particular, it assesses incoming information for its emotional significance. People whose amygdala is damaged lack the ability to judge the emotional significance of events. They remain as impassive when confronted with threatening events as when they are facing pleasant situations.

In everyday circumstances, information is passed from the amygdala to the frontal cortex, where higher-order thinking takes place. But under threatening circumstances in which speedy reaction time is essential for survival, the amygdala takes a "short cut" and alerts the hypothalamus directly. In response, the hypothalamus releases a chemical called corticotropin-releasing factor, which in turn stimulates the release of adrenocorticotropin hormone from the pituitary gland. This hormone in turn stimulates the adrenal gland's release of cortisol, which activates the sympathetic nervous system and gets the body ready for fight or flight. Conversely, in situations where neither flight nor fight is possible, the limbic system activates the parasympathetic nervous system and the body goes into the submission state known as tonic immobility.

The amygdala is like a smoke detector for the brain. In an emergency it runs the show, making decisions before they are filtered through conscious awareness, compelling us to respond before we have time to think. Responses triggered by the amygdala are automatic and reflexive: Soldiers who fall to the ground immediately upon hearing a car backfire are being led by their amygdala. Their training and battlefield experience has kicked in, beyond any conscious control.[7]

If the amygdala is to take center stage, however, it must "inform" other parts of the brain to shut down—specifically, brain structures such as the hippocampus (the part of the brain that stores memories of time and space, orders memories along our life's timeline, and makes connections between memories) and Broca's area (the part concerned with translating emotional experiences into language). These mechanisms are too time-consuming at a time when immediate reactions to the current situation are necessitated.

Under normal circumstances the hippocampus plays an important role in processing and storing memories. It is believed to act like a USB cable that transfers information from the right side of the brain (where information is held as it actively awaits processing) to the left side of the brain (where it is stored in memory). In contrast to the amygdala, the hippocampus is associated with a conscious, explicit, verbal route to learning and the storage of memories. When someone is rehearsing a talk or planning a travel route, it is the hippocampus that is responsible for transferring memories into long-term storage.

During trauma, however, the activity of the hippocampus is suppressed. Many scientists believe that this outcome is related to excessive stress, which kills neurons in the hippocampal pathway. It is as if a fuse has blown in the brain, shutting down the usual transfer of information. In these circumstances, memories lack detail. Sarah—who, as described earlier, was caught up in a fatal shooting—told me that the details of this event remain fuzzy in her memory. She can't recall exactly what happened but does remember the moment when she realized that the man had left the scene and that the police had arrived. Other than that, her memory of that afternoon is fragmented: being asked questions by the police—seeing faces peering down at her—realizing that someone had dressed her in something other than her own clothes—realizing that it was now evening and she was at home—becoming aware of her husband's voice. She has spent the last few years trying to piece together these fragments and to comprehend what actually happened.

In normal circumstances, memories are filed away as representations of past events. But following trauma, they remain in an active state—and thus seem to float in the present. At the same time, they are difficult to talk about coherently: An overload of information is associated with the traumatic experience, information that the individual is unable to manage. As Sarah put it, "It was like my mental filing cabinets had been toppled over." In many cases, traumatic memories are filed away over time. When this does not happen, the re-experiencing symptoms of PTSD are the result.

In short, PTSD is a disorder of information processing. The PTSD sufferers' traumatic memories remain active because the brain structures concerned with memory storage and language have shut down, leaving the individual "on alert" until these parts of the brain are reactivated. It usually takes around a month for the brain to repair the "blown fuse" in the hippocampal pathway so that the usual memory-processing mechanisms can come back online.[8] For some people, however, it takes longer. This difference could be due to a number of factors, including natural variations in the capability of the hippocampal pathway, the occurrence of other traumatic events that subsequently slow the repair process, or continued activation of the amygdala even though the danger has passed.

An intriguing possibility suggested by recent research is that vulnerability to PTSD has its roots in the early years of childhood. During a period when the brain is still forming, a lack of parental care or other stressors can alter the neural systems responsible for cognitive-emotional processing of traumatic information, leading to a reduced hippocampal volume.[9] One implication of this finding is that some people are more susceptible to PTSD than others because they file their memories away less efficiently. Another is that they have traumatic memories from early childhood that are reactivated by a later trauma, in which case the memories would be old ones that were laid down before language was formed. This would explain why some PTSD sufferers experience disorganized and distressing mental states that they are unable to meaningfully "pin down" to actual events in their lives, leading in turn to difficulty processing their current situation.

For such reasons the alarm stage of the fight-or-flight response may be prolonged in some people, leading to even further negative reactions that in turn cause physical, emotional, and mental fatigue. Since their "fear alert system" remains switched on for longer than usual, it may take more than the usual month to return to their previous level of functioning.

But while an excessive fear alert system may be maladaptive, since it causes more long-term damage, from an evolutionary point of view it actually makes sense that our fear alert systems do not switch off too soon. A fear alert system that is hard to switch on and that switches itself off too soon would not be of much use. Evolution has therefore selected for a system that is harder to switch off and stays on longer than necessary. It is better to have a hundred false alarms than to miss the one time that real danger is lurking; consider this the smoke detector principle.[10]

Given the argument that posttraumatic stress reactions represent evolutionary useful mechanisms for survival, it becomes understandable why a person experiencing a traumatic situation would experience intense bodily reactions. Accelerated heartbeat, cold sweating, rapid breathing, heart palpitations, focused concentration, hypervigilance, and a hairtrigger startle response are all likely to be adaptive in dangerous situations as they enable the person to react quickly to threat. Indeed, these reactions should be viewed as normal and natural adaptive responses that can mean the difference between life and death.

When these bodily reactions persist, however, they lead to other problems, such as sexual dysfunction, loss of appetite, and difficulty concentrating on other tasks. These outcomes, too, are understandable from an evolutionary point of view: When we are in danger, the last things we want on our mind are sex, dinner, and remembering to put the washing machine on. In cases of PTSD, unfortunately, the danger has passed, but the body continues to react for weeks or even months afterward as if the danger were still present.

Because the information processing and memory storage functions normally associated with the hippocampus have shut down in the face of the trauma, sights, sounds, smells, and tastes related to the traumatic event remain in "active memory." Though, again, this may seem maladaptive, from an evolutionary perspective it is actually useful for such memories to remain active.

This process in which memories remain active provides us with a way to learn from trauma. For example, if tens of thousands of years ago a lion jumped out of the bush and an ancestor of ours was able to escape, the trauma would have remained in his active memory, allowing him to recall that experience and thereafter stay away from lions. Indeed, doing so would have greatly improved his chances of survival. The implication is that retaining trauma in active memory is useful in an evolutionary sense, in that it keeps us on our toes and alert to danger. However, it can continue for only so long; eventually we need to file those memories away so that staying away from danger becomes automatic. In time, we know not to step out in front of traffic or to put our hands into the fire; such information has been filed away.

As we have seen, evolution has equipped us with an array of tools to meet the demands of our social and physical environments. When our ancestors were confronted with danger they needed to quickly freeze, fight, or take flight. There was a distinct survival value to remaining alert to danger and to remembering where it lurked. Thus the human brain became wired, so to speak, to make associations easily. Consider the experience of William, a Falklands War veteran I met when he returned to school in the early 1990s to continue his education. He was always on edge and easily startled. One day, during class, a bird hit the window with a sharp bang. William's military experience kicked in and he reacted in an instant, hitting the floor. Sarah, too, has told me that even the toaster popping up was enough to startle her and trigger memories of the gunman who shot her friend Dawn. In short, we are programmed through evolution to make associations that allow us to avoid future danger. Learning that certain sights, sounds, or smells are triggers for danger can help us survive. The startle reaction is therefore a product of fear conditioning.

The concept of fear conditioning is derived from the work of the famous Russian physiologist Ivan Pavlov, who is credited with the discovery of *classical conditioning* (sometimes called *Pavlovian conditioning*). Classical conditioning is essentially a process of learning by temporal association. Pavlov found that if two events occur in close succession, they can become associated with one another. He discovered this phenomenon in 1928 while studying the digestive process in laboratory dogs. As part of his research, he had given several dogs powdered meat. After a while he noticed that the dogs began to salivate just as the researchers were about to feed them. In time, the dogs began to salivate as soon as they heard the researchers' footsteps. Pavlov experimentally tested this observation by ringing a bell every time he brought food to the dogs. He found that the dogs quickly came to associate the sound of the bell with the food and began to salivate at the sound alone.

Since Pavlov's discovery, the phenomenon of classical conditioning has been confirmed in many studies. It is now a key theory for explaining post-traumatic stress reactions. If a rat in a box receives a series of electric shocks paired with flashes of light, it will develop a fear response to the light alone. For the purposes of this discussion, trauma can be likened to an electric shock; and the reminders of trauma, such as a car backfiring, to a flash of light. Noises, colors, smells—whatever details a person remembers from the time of the trauma—by association elicit the fear response even when the trauma is no longer present. For a Vietnam veteran it might be the background sound of a helicopter on television many years later. For a car crash survivor it might be the song that was playing on the radio immediately before the accident. Conditioned fear is a special type of memory, one that we do not have conscious access to. Specifically, it is a situationally accessible memory (SAM), which is created when the amygdala takes the "short cut" involved in alerting the hypothalamus to a threatening situation, thereby preparing the body for the fight-or-flight response.[11]

People who have been traumatized tend to avoid activating situationally accessible memories. Memories are outside conscious awareness but can be activated by reminders. This is one reason it can be so difficult for traumatized people to talk about their experiences. SAMs become activated leading to flashbacks and arousal but the person cannot describe in words what happened. For example, when Sarah told me her story, her voice slowed, became quieter, and eventually trailed off. It was as though the power had been cut off. She ground to a halt, with a terrified look in her eyes, and began to sway from side to side. She looked up at me but did not seem to see me. Then she slowly shook her head. She seemed absolutely petrified. Her mind was elsewhere.

It is important for therapists to work with clients at their own pace and not push them too far, too quickly. I assured Sarah that I could see how difficult it was for her to talk about her trauma, and suggested that she stop if she needed to. As if surfacing from a dream, she nodded, her eyes slowly coming into focus and her posture loosening. At that point she smiled, just to let me know she was back.

Triggers for the fear reaction can become generalized. Consider the case of Rebecca, a woman in her early twenties. For Rebecca, the color red was a reminder of a trauma. One day she was having lunch with her boyfriend in a fast-food restaurant. They were talking over the day's events. He picked up the ketchup bottle. The lid was loose and as he squeezed, ketchup spewed out onto the table. Rebecca froze. Then she burst into tears.

As a child Rebecca was subjected to sexual abuse in a room with red curtains. She recalls staring up into the curtains and losing herself in the swirls of pattern as her way of coping when her father would come to her room. Now, over a decade later, she generally manages well, having learned to control her emotions. But every now and then, as on that day in the restaurant, she is caught unawares. The color red has the ability to bring it all flooding back.

It is crucial for people to discern the point at which their conditioned associations are no longer helpful—a process called *extinction learning*. Over time they must realize that the familiar sights, sounds, and smells that once set them off no longer represent danger.

Many survivors of trauma feel compelled to take the extinction process into their own hands. Carol, for instance, told me that the day after the London bombings in July 2005, she went to an underground station platform and sat down: "I just wanted to feel normal again," she said. By engaging in such activities, traumatized people can extinguish their fear response. The reminders will eventually stop causing them pain. Indeed, over a period of months, most people habituate to triggers such that they no longer signal danger. But engaging in exposure of this sort is upsetting, and as already noted, it is common for people to want to avoid reminders.

The prospect of putting oneself back into a feared situation is so distressing that a person will avoid it at all costs—and fear does not diminish but builds. The normal evolved survival system fails to shut off once the threat of danger has passed and the body continues to maintain a state of high arousal.

The fear conditioning process accounts for the core signs of heightened vigilance and anxious arousal and provides the theoretical basis for extinction-based therapies. These popular therapies are founded on the idea that repeated exposure to feared stimuli eventually breaks the association.[12] Everyone has heard the old saying that it helps to get back on the horse after one has been thrown—and as we will see, there is truth to this. But as people often avoid reminders of feared situations, the task of therapists is to help them engage with such situations. What helped Carol was to return to the train station where the bombings occurred. Although her fear was not immediately alleviated by this single activity, it seems to have allowed her to resume her life to a larger extent than might otherwise have been possible. Doing so made it possible for her to return relatively quickly to using the underground trains again; however, as she explained it to me, she was still frightened and would shake uncontrollably, leading her to seek further support and more formal exposure therapy from a psychologist whose assistance ultimately proved beneficial.

Similarly, Rebecca now only very occasionally reacts to the color red; the association has become weakened over the years. When she was younger, it was a real problem. Luckily she found a school psychologist who helped her by using a process of extinction. First he repeatedly asked Rebecca to imagine the color red, stopping only when she was able to do so without panicking. Then he asked her to look at different objects in various shades of color fading into red; this, too, continued until Rebecca no longer expressed fear. In a sense, extinction is like rewiring the connections in the brain.

The reason some people continue to suffer from posttraumatic stress is that they do not get this extinction experience. They understandably prefer to avoid reminders of their trauma—but what they miss out on is the experience of learning that these reminders no longer represent danger.

Until their bodies' fear alert system is deactivated and their hippocampal pathways are reactivated, PTSD sufferers will probably struggle with upsetting memories. For this reason, before dealing with the issue of posttraumatic growth, therapists must reduce the symptoms of PTSD to a tolerable level, so that their clients can begin to talk about their experiences without becoming overwhelmed. This kind of talk is necessary to begin to make sense of what has happened. The foundation of modern trauma therapies is the notion of exposure to the feared thing, once the danger has passed. Such exposure is the most surefire way for the body's fear alert system to be deactivated.[13]

Yet even when fear reactions have been extinguished, PTSD symptoms may abruptly reappear. What happens in such cases is that the conditioned fear response becomes reestablished following a triggering event. Sometimes, however, people do not recognize the trigger event, so it seems as if PTSD has just reappeared at random. This is a puzzling phenomenon, but research suggests that even after extinction, a record remains in the brain. In other words, extinction does not eradicate the original learning but instead provides an overlay of new learning that inhibits the expression of the fear memory. Nevertheless, that overlay can be swept to one side if the danger appears to have returned.[14] This makes sense in evolutionary terms: "Wired up" in this way, the brain allows us to be prepared for danger when all seems safe yet not constantly on edge and alert.

From an evolutionary perspective, such heightened vigilance might be expected to continue until there is certainty that the threat has passed—and, indeed, people who have survived dangerous situations do tend to become more vigilant to future threats. Knowing that a threat has passed is not a simple matter. So it makes sense that over time the alarm system gradually switches off but remains easily triggered in case the same threat occurs again.

Like other evolution-based mechanisms, this one is characterized by individual differences: Some people's vigilance switches off more quickly

than others. After all, some of our hunter-gatherer ancestors needed to remain alert to danger so that others could return to their usual activities.
Such variability was necessary for the survival of all.

My own conclusion, based on my study of PTSD and posttraumatic
growth, is that although posttraumatic stress reactions can be long-lasting
and distressing, these reactions evolved for a functional reason: to allow
humans to respond quickly to threat, to be prepared for future threat,
and to learn about the environment they are in. The fact that they are unpleasant does not negate this evolutionary purpose.

The sensation of disgust is a good example. Let's say you come back
from a long holiday, open the fridge, and discover that you had left behind a dish of chicken, which is now covered in mold. You feel disgust.
Perhaps you vomit. These are functional reactions. They have evolved to
alert us to toxic substances and, when necessary, to clear our digestive
system of the poison. Disgust is indeed unpleasant, but that does not make
it a disorder. Rather, it is a result of the activation of a normal and natural process developed through evolution. Likewise, posttraumatic stress is
a natural and normal process signaling the activation of evolutionary-
based survival mechanisms and the need for cognitive processing of the
new trauma-related information.

For some, however, cognitive processing becomes impeded. The
process of extinction, so crucial to recovering from trauma, is believed to
happen when the hippocampus exerts an inhibitory effect on the amygdala. But if this connection between the hippocampus and the amygdala
is damaged, shutting down the fear alert system through extinction may
not be possible. Research suggests that this type of damage might occur in
people who experience traumatic events that last for considerable periods
of time. For example, individuals held in captivity, involved in prolonged
combat, or subjected to long-term sexual abuse all experience amygdala
activity at a heightened level for a considerable time. These forms of
chronic and intense trauma may lead to changes to certain regions of the
brain, particularly in people who experience the trauma during their early
development; in such cases, they may suffer long-lasting biological effects
that interfere with normal development and the ability to cognitively
process the trauma-related information. Similarly, extreme trauma might

affect the brain in such a way that switching the alarm system off becomes very difficult, inasmuch as the normal processes of the brain have been damaged. In light of evidence that PTSD is related to increased amygdala activity and decreased hippocampus activity, it has been suggested that PTSD is a stress-induced fear circuitry disorder whereby PTSD symptoms persist because of the malfunctioning of mechanisms that would otherwise shut down the brain's alarm reactions.[15]

The biology of PTSD is a fast-developing field—and rightly so. Identifying the minority of people who are truly suffering from PTSD, and whose ability to cognitively process trauma-related information is impaired, is an urgent matter indeed—not only because treatment procedures need to be improved but also because the PTSD label itself must be prevented from losing its force as a diagnosis and becoming merely a passing fad in psychiatric textbooks. Important therefore is the distinction between the minority of people who have an altered neural system that physically prevents them from cognitively processing traumatic memories and the majority of people who are able to process their traumatic memories and for whom posttraumatic stress is indicative of normal and natural processes of trauma resolution.[16]

There is no doubt that trauma can cut through people's lives, disrupting their everyday functioning at work and at home. Predicting exactly who will develop long-term problems is not possible, but therapists can certainly talk to their patients and evaluate whether they have social support available and are coping effectively. In this way, they can identify those who are more likely to have difficulty in the longer term and offer specific advice and guidance.

From a trauma perspective, one of the most pressing concerns of our time is the mental health of soldiers returning from combat—especially given the substantial research showing the difficulties experienced by many Vietnam veterans when they returned home—and for long periods of time thereafter.[17] Estimates suggest that soldiers returning from Iraq and Afghanistan could be similarly troubled. Also of great concern are the effects of war, terrorism, and potential climate change on civilian populations around the world. Nonetheless, we have to be careful not to set the expectation that most people will develop PTSD. On average, only 8 to 12 percent of people exposed to traumatic events—and around a fifth to a quarter of people involved in profoundly traumatic experiences—ever reach the diagnostic threshold for PTSD.[18]

Furthermore, only a minority of PTSD sufferers experience a long-lasting form of the disorder. Most people diagnosed with PTSD are relatively symptom-free within six months to a year. And for those whose problems do persist, various psychological therapies are available. Around 50 percent of people treated for PTSD no longer meet the criteria for diagnosis at the end of treatment.[19]

In sum, only a minority of people develop PTSD; of those, only a minority develop persistent PTSD; and only half of those whose problems are persistent do not benefit from treatment.

The fact is that most people are fairly resilient to what life throws at them. The term *resilience* was first used by psychologists in the 1970s to describe children who, though raised in poverty- and crime-stricken surroundings, were able to overcome their adversity and develop into well-adjusted young people. Since then, the term has become more widely used to refer to adults. Professor George Bonanno and his colleagues have taken the lead in drawing this issue to our attention. In one study, for example, they interviewed 2,752 New York residents by telephone in the six months after 9/11. Many media commentators had chattered about the likelihood that an epidemic of PTSD would follow the televised coverage of 9/11. It didn't. Bonanno found that "only one PTSD symptom or none at all" was reported by 65 percent of all the people interviewed, by 54 percent of the 22 people who were in the World Trade Center at the time of the attacks, and by 33 percent of the 59 people who were wounded in the attacks.[20]

These findings confirm that, contrary to what might be expected given the popularity of the PTSD label, this disorder is not the outcome for most people following trauma. In fact, research is beginning to tell us that, in most cases, trauma changes people in ways that are transformative and even positive—as we shall see. The majority of people were resilient and even in those groups that had experienced the highest of levels of trauma, the prevalence of resilience did not fall below one-third.

PART II

GROWTH FOLLOWING ADVERSITY

For winter's rains and ruins are over,
And all the season of snows and sins;
The days dividing lover and lover,
The light that loses, the night that wins;
And time remembered is grief forgotten,
And frosts are slain and flowers begotten,
And in green underwood and cover
Blossom by blossom the spring begins.

ALGERNON CHARLES SWINBURNE
(1837–1909)

CHAPTER 4

Transformation

IN THIS CHAPTER we will consider various forms of resilience to trauma, especially as these relate to the idea of transformation. People who report having been "transformed" commonly talk about how their views on life and their priorities have changed, or how they have developed a new sense of who they are and what they are capable of, or how they feel closer and more loving toward other people and have found that their relationships have been taken to a deeper level. The term that best describes such changes is *posttraumatic growth*. We will examine what research evidence tells us about posttraumatic growth, particularly in light of the remarkable assertion that posttraumatic stress is often the engine for posttraumatic growth. But first I want to show the different ways in which people respond to trauma, and for this I want you to imagine a tree on a hilltop during a storm.

The tree is buffeted by the wind, but it stands firm and unbending. When the storm has passed, it appears not to have been affected. Some people, too, seem to weather stressful events, emerging unscathed emotionally. They are like the tree that stands unbending in the wind. Such people are said to be *resistant*. (See Figure 4.1.)

Another tree bends in the wind. It does not break, and when the wind dies down, the tree returns to its original shape. In much the same way, there are people who bend with the strain of life adversity but quickly bounce back to their original state.[1] In other words, they *recover*. While we might admire people who are able to recover, ironically it is not these

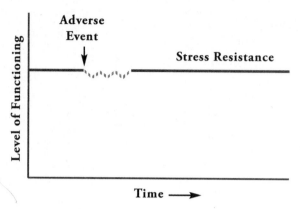

FIGURE 4.1 Resistance to Trauma
Source: Butler (2010).

people—nor is it resistant people—who are likely to experience post-traumatic growth.

A third tree bends in the wind. But instead of springing back to its original shape when the wind abates, it is permanently changed. Lashed by the winds, this tree has been altered, and its shape will never be the same again. In time, it grows around its injuries, and new leaves and branches sprout from the trunk where old growths were severed. Scars, gnarls, and misshapen limbs give the tree a unique character for the rest of its life span. It is no less of a tree than it used to be, but it is different.

There is a group of people who, like the third tree, grow following adversity. They may remain emotionally affected, but their sense of self, views on life, priorities, goals for the future, and their behaviors have been reconfigured in positive ways in the light of their experiences. It is to these changes that the term *posttraumatic growth* refers.[2] (See Figure 4.2.)

Posttraumatic growth encompasses many aspects of reconfiguration following trauma, but three in particular are most commonly reported: personal changes, philosophical changes, and relationship changes.

Personal changes may include finding new inner strengths, achieving greater wisdom, or becoming more compassionate. Consider the case of Marie, who was sexually assaulted on her way home from a nightclub early one morning. A man who may have been following her entered her apartment building after her. She let him in thinking he was a fellow ten-

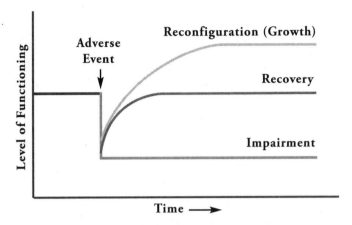

FIGURE 4.2 Three Trajectories of Adjustment Following Adversity. Posttraumatic growth means going beyond previous levels of functioning.
Source: Adapted from O'Leary and Ickovics (1995).

ant, and he followed her up the stairs to the second floor, where he grabbed her from behind and threatened her with a knife. Marie was able to get free of him long enough to smash the glass of the building fire alarm. As people began coming down the stairs, the man fled. The fire service and police arrived quickly, but the attack left Marie bruised, shocked, and in tears. In her mid-twenties, she was a quiet young woman who worked as a dental receptionist and was in a relationship of three years with plans of marriage. The senseless trauma she experienced that night seemed to tear her ordinary life apart.

Only now, seven years later, is she able to talk about what happened without losing herself in fury at her attacker and breaking down in tears. She still blames herself for letting the man into the building. But she is also proud of her quick thinking: Going for the fire alarm saved her from what could have been a vicious rape. In the immediate aftermath of the attack, she suffered from nightmares, and for a considerable time she was afraid to leave the safety of her home. When she did go out she locked the doors of her car. At home, she had all the locks changed and new locks fitted to her bedroom door. Her relationship did not survive.

Marie still gets angry about the assault. Yet she also says that, in a strange sense, it was a gift. People are usually shocked when she tells them this. But she explains that the trauma somehow helped her to change as a person. She believes herself to be much wiser now. Before the attack she lived her life as though she was asleep. "I've woken up now," she says. "I know what's important to me, what I want, who I am. Before it happened, I didn't know who I was or what I wanted."

Two years after the assault, Marie decided that she wanted to go to college and enrolled as a psychology major. She received high marks in her classes and says that her three years of college life were the best ones she ever lived. And it is a life she would not even have considered before.

She now feels that she has much to give to other people. After spending a year working for a charity, Marie began training as a counselor. Currently she works with women who have had experiences similar to hers. People who know her describe her as having a depth of maturity, wisdom, and compassion.

Marie expresses surprise at how life has changed for her, but she adds, "If someone had said to me the day after I was attacked that I would be able to do what I'm doing now, or that I would see the attack as a turning point in my life, I would have wanted to strangle them, but it *was* a turning point. I like who I am now and I'm doing things I never would have thought I was capable of. If I was to erase the past then I wouldn't be who I am today." Marie's story is a prime example of the life changes that many people undergo after trauma, changes that allow them the new freedom to finally realize a long-forgotten dream—to pursue an education, say, or embark on a longed-for career.

As noted, many trauma survivors also undergo *philosophical changes*. Like Marie, they find themselves unexpectedly gifted with a newfound sense of what is really important in life. An example is provided by Kevin, who recently had a heart attack. The doctors tell him his prognosis is good. But he remains frightened that he will have another one. His thoughts keep turning back to the original event: He can almost feel the shortness of breath and the tightness in his chest, and almost see the look of fear on his wife's face. Each time he has these thoughts, he feels a sense of panic rising in him, and he becomes frightened all over again.

Yet these recurring thoughts have a positive side. They have helped him to realize how much he values life. He strives to enjoy each day to the fullest now. For instance, Kevin was always an avid reader of history books, but he is even more so now. History gets him thinking, he says, and helps him to put things into perspective. He understands that each of us is just a dot along the line of history. As he puts it: "Here today and gone tomorrow. You never know what each day is going to bring. I don't waste my time worrying about the little things anymore. You get a new perspective. You don't need to have a lot of things that you thought you needed." Kevin says that he always knew this was so, but what the heart attack did was to bring the truth home to him. Before, he knew that it was "true in my head, but I didn't live it in my heart." He laughs, and tells me that he has realized that the heart attack was the trigger for a more heartfelt life.

Kevin's story illustrates the philosophical shift in values that can sometimes occur after trauma. It's a truism—one often repeated—that the best things in life are free. Yet, hackneyed as it may seem, this sentiment expresses something very real in the lives of many people who experience posttraumatic growth. For them, small daily pleasures are truly more important than expensive possessions and worldly successes. There is a Buddhist tale that illustrates this point.

A fisherman is relaxing on a beautiful beach. His rod is propped up, the line taut in the sparkling ocean. As he enjoys the day, a businessman comes along. "Why aren't you working instead of lying on the beach?" he asks. "Why would I want to work?" asks the fisherman. "So you can get more equipment and better nets to catch more fish," the businessman replies. "But why would I want to catch more fish?" the fisherman asks. Now irritated with the fisherman, the businessman replies, "You'll make money that you can use to buy a boat." "Why would I want to do that?" asks the fisherman. Exasperated, the businessman replies, "Then you can hire people to work for you." "Why would I want to do that?" asks the fisherman. "So you can buy more boats and hire even more people to catch even more fish and make a lot of money." "But why would I want to do that?" The businessman is by now infuriated. "It's obvious. You could become rich and never have to work again. You could spend your days lying on the beach, enjoying the sun, taking it easy without a care in the world." The fisherman looks up at the businessman and smiles. "What do you think I'm doing right now?"

Relationship changes also characterize Kevin's newfound enjoyment of life. He appreciates how caring his wife has been toward him—and has come to realize that in the past he had begun to take his marriage for granted. Now he feels he has woken up to his relationship, and the two are spending more time together. Recently they booked a holiday to Venice, a city they had always talked about visiting.

This third type of posttraumatic change occurs in the lives of many trauma survivors. Such people take a new approach to their closest relationships. Now that they are newly aware that human connection is one of the most important aspects of life, they begin to value their family and friends more than they did before the traumatic event. John and Julia's experience is instructive in this regard. Their son Benjamin, born with heart complications, died nine weeks later, despite his doctor's best efforts to save him. Emotionally devastated by the loss, and exhausted by two months of agonizing hospital visits, they shut themselves away from the world, tearful and unable to imagine their future. They were aware that their friends wanted to be supportive, but they felt that no one could really understand how harrowing it was for them to lose a child. After a while they didn't even talk to each other about what had happened. The grief was unbearable. John told me that it wasn't until after the first anniversary of Benjamin's death that they really began to pick themselves up and fully appreciate just how devastated they had been.

That was eight years ago. Now John and Julia have two little girls. Molly is one year old and still crawling, while Jessica, three years old, is beginning to talk and say her first words. "I am a different person now," John says. "Before [Benjamin died] I was quite arrogant, and wrapped up in myself and in my career. I don't know if it's just what happens when you have children anyway, but I think it's different when you lose a child; you learn the hard way that life is precious and to be savored. It made me aware of how short time is. I love my girls so much. It might sound stupid but it's like Benjamin taught me how to love." Julia echoes this, adding, "I think we love each other in a different way too now, like a deeper love that can only come from when you've shared something so painful together and come out the other side. There's a connection now between us that I don't think most couples have."[3]

John and Julia's story illustrates a common trend among survivors of traumatic events: After such events, people begin to appreciate their family and friends far more than before. Indeed, trauma victims often mention that their relationships have improved as they learn "who their true friends are" and that they honestly value friends and family and appreciate the joy of what relationships can offer. Many find themselves surprised by the helpfulness of others. Sometimes it is the most unlikely people who rise to the challenge of offering support. Friendships that were not close develop and deepen. And of course sometimes the opposite is true, as when friends who were expected to be supportive fail to meet the challenge of helping.

Many trauma survivors also discover that they have become more comfortable with intimacy. Indeed, their sense of compassion for others is heightened immeasurably. A woman whose son committed suicide put it this way: "One of the things that's come out of this for me is that I am very careful about my choice of Christmas cards and who I send what to. I now think very hard about whether they've had any sadness in their particular life that year—or you know, whatever—and send an appropriate card, because to me it was just unbelievable that somebody just knowing, fully knowing that we'd lost our son, just picked the next card out of the box without even so much as a cursory glance at it."[4] And as a Vietnam veteran said: "I feel grief for people. Anybody, anybody that has a tragedy in their life. I can feel their pain."[5]

In relating the foregoing stories, I have tried to provide a general sense of the forms of posttraumatic growth that scientists have observed thus far, and how the term refers to deep-seated changes in the person's sense of self, their views on life, priorities, goals, and their approach to relationships.[6] As the field continues to broaden, and research uncovers new elements, our understanding of such transformations will increase even further.

The new science of posttraumatic growth originated only about two decades ago and is thus still in its developmental phase. Yet I think it is one of the most exciting of all the recent advances in clinical psychology, because it promises to radically alter our ideas about trauma—especially the notion that trauma inevitably leads to a damaged and dysfunctional life.

Scientific interest in the topic of growth following adversity was sparked in the early 1990s, when researchers began systematically asking people about their changes in outlook following trauma. In one of the earliest studies to document such growth, people who had lost a spouse or a child in a motor vehicle accident were interviewed four to seven years after the traumatic event. They answered questions about what their life was like, whether they now did things differently, and whether the death had affected their life goals or philosophy of life. Most mentioned at least one positive change in their life: increased self-confidence (specified by 35 percent of the interviewees), a focus on enjoying the present (26 percent), an increased acceptance of mortality (23 percent), a greater appreciation of life (23 percent), an increased emphasis on family (19 percent), increased religiosity (15 percent), and increased openness and concern for others (7 percent).[7]

Following the initial focus on this topic during the 1990s, one event in particular led to a surge of new interest in posttraumatic growth: the terrorist attacks of September 11, 2001. The United States had experienced many disasters and been involved in many conflicts over the years, but the degree of anti-U.S. aggression behind the 9/11 attacks was unprecedented, ushering in a new era that demarcated history in terms of pre- and post-9/11. It was a challenge to the nation to make sense of what had happened.

In short, the events of 9/11 spurred the study of trauma, recovery, and reconfiguration. Research reported mild to moderate levels of positive changes in people's lives during the first few weeks following 9/11 as well as elevated levels of prosocial behaviors in the general population, including the finding that one in three Americans surveyed reported donating blood, money, or time.[8]

One particularly notable study begun in November 2001 examined the perceived benefits of the terrorist attacks. Over three years, it surveyed 1,382 adults who were representative of the general population. The researchers asked the following question: "Some people have reported finding unexpected positive consequences in the wake of September 11 attacks and their aftermath. Have you, personally, been able to find any positive consequences as a result of them?"

Respondents in the survey answered the question using a 5-point scale, where 1 = no, not at all; 2 = just a little; 3 = some; 4 = quite a bit; and 5 = yes, a great deal.

Those who said that they had found positive benefits (i.e., scored 2 or more) were then asked: "What positive consequences have you found as a result of the September 11 attacks and their aftermath?" What the researchers did next was to cluster respondents' answers into one of five categories:

- prosocial benefits (e.g., "most people are kinder and more caring to each other")
- philosophical changes (e.g., "life is precious, live every day like it is your last")
- increased religiosity (e.g., "more people praying and attending church")
- political changes (e.g., "increased patriotism, awareness of our government")
- increased national security (e.g., "heightened security at the airports and in general across the country")

Overall, the study found that 58 percent of the respondents reported benefits, sometimes of more than one type. The most commonly reported, as shown in Figure 4.3, were prosocial benefits (15.8 percent) followed by "other" benefits (10.7 percent), religious benefits (9.3 percent), political benefits (8.9 percent), security benefits (8.3 percent), and philosophical benefits (7.3 percent).[9]

Terrorist attacks have likewise prompted researchers to conduct similar research in other parts of the world. One study, for example, reported posttraumatic growth following the terrorist attacks in Madrid on March 11, 2004, when a bomb exploded on a commuter train.[10]

Similar surveys asking people to report whether they had experienced posttraumatic growth have now been conducted with a wide array of trauma survivors. Questions have been asked of people who have experienced the following: medical history problems (e.g., bone marrow transplant, breast cancer, testicular cancer, rheumatoid arthritis,

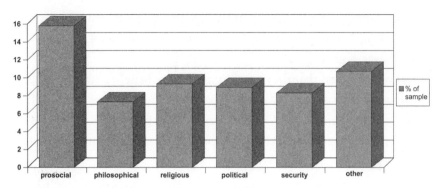

FIGURE 4.3 Percentage of Respondents Reporting Various Types of Benefits Two Months After September 11, 2001
Source: Poulin et al. (2009).

cardiac issues, mothers whose children have permanent physical disabilities); loss and bereavement (e.g., loss of a spouse or child, Israelis and Palestinians following the death of family members, widows in Iraq); adverse interpersonal experiences (e.g., rape survivors, survivors of childhood abuse, women who have experienced partner violence, community violence); and exposure to major accidents and/or disasters (e.g., Hurricane Katrina, the Southeast Asian earthquake-tsunami). The above include only a handful of the hundreds of studies that have now been conducted.[11]

Other surveys confirm that growth is not solely associated with recent, small-scale traumas. Indeed, posttraumatic growth is reported after events that occurred long ago—for instance, in prisoner-of-war or Holocaust circumstances.[12] Many types of events—but especially those that are perceived as life-threatening—have the potential to trigger posttraumatic growth.

Events that involve the suffering of others, especially people close to us, can also trigger growth. There are studies of daughters of women with breast cancer, husbands of breast cancer survivors, wives of former combat veterans and prisoners of war, and individuals whose occupations put them into contact with suffering such as disaster workers, funeral directors, and trauma therapists.[13] All of these studies indicate that people need not experience a life-threatening trauma themselves in order to experience posttraumatic growth.

What does seem to be an important factor accounting for posttraumatic growth is the occurrence of an existential wake-up call. After such an experience, people cannot avoid the realization that life is inherently uncertain, unpredictable, and uncontrollable—and that human beings are vulnerable and fragile. This realization may be the essence of posttraumatic growth in all of its forms.

It is not just adults who report such growth. Studies with younger people also find evidence of growth following life-threatening events, automobile accidents, and the deaths of family members.[14] Adults may also reflect on how early adversities have shaped them.

Professor John Harvey at the University of Iowa has analyzed interviews with hundreds of children following divorce. While his work testifies to the hurt and pain such children have experienced, it also demonstrates that many grow and learn. Here is how a twenty-two-year-old participant in Harvey's study described her experiences of the divorce of her parents: "I think that I did grow up emotionally faster than a lot of my friends, but I don't necessarily believe this is such a bad quality. I learned to do things on my own, and I learned that life does not always go the way that you expect it to go. Having to deal with the unexpected brings character, and it makes you see things for what they really are, not just what you see on the surface. So, I can honestly say that I have forgiven both of them and I don't place blame on either one of them."[15]

My own conclusion, after examining the many studies on this topic, is that between 30 and 70 percent of trauma survivors report at least some form of benefit following the events in question.[16]

This may seem an astonishing claim, one that may seem hard to believe, but it is quite valid, having been derived from studies involving interviews and questionnaires in which people are directly asked whether benefits have arisen from their experiences.

For some people there seems to be a sudden epiphany. The term *quantum change* has been applied to these sudden epiphanies of change.[17] One person who experienced a quantum change was a man named Robert. A keen gardener, Robert was out cutting his roses one Sunday. He felt a pain in his chest and within moments had fallen to the ground. Luckily his wife was home and was able to call for an ambulance. Robert recuperated over the next few days. He told me that when he was in the ambulance being taken to hospital, "I knew what mattered to me, my family, my friends, giving the children the best life I can. What I mean is being the best I can as a father, as a person, not wasting time. Everything was so clear to me when I thought that was it." While it seems possible that some people experience a sudden epiphany, it doesn't always lead to lasting change, and, in general, it is hard to imagine that posttraumatic growth usually occurs so abruptly.

Rather, the general pattern seems to be that growth emerges gradually over time. In one study, for example, 162 breast cancer patients were asked to complete the Posttraumatic Growth Inventory (PTGI), a twenty-one-item questionnaire developed by researchers Lawrence Calhoun and Richard Tedeschi at the University of North Carolina in Charlotte.[18] To statements such as "I developed new interests," "I developed a sense of closeness with others," "I developed a feeling of self-reliance," and "I have a stronger religious faith," participants are asked to rate the extent to which they have changed on a 6-point scale, ranging from "I did not experience this change as a result of my crisis" (given a score of 0), to "a very small degree of change" (1), "a small degree of change" (2), "a moderate degree of change" (3), "a great degree of change" (4), and "I experienced this change to a very great degree as a result of my crisis" (5).

Compiling answers to all twenty-one statements, the lowest score a person can get on the PTGI is 0; the highest is 105. The higher the score, the more the person perceives themselves to have grown. When analyzed across a number of studies, PTGI scores commonly range between 40 and 70, indicating that small to moderate amounts of posttraumatic growth are typical. In the study described above, the breast cancer patients completed the questionnaire three times: 4.5 months, 9 months, and 18 months after diagnosis. (The average age of the women was forty-nine years, and most were in treatment at the start of the study.) As

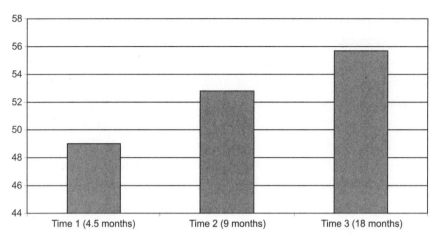

FIGURE 4.4 Posttraumatic Growth Inventory Scores Over Time
Source: Manne et al. (2004).

shown in Figure 4.4, their scores on the Posttraumatic Growth Inventory increased on average over the 18-month period.[19]

Given decades of research on posttraumatic stress, some commentators initially found it hard to take seriously the idea of posttraumatic growth. Do people really grow in the aftermath of adversity? We now know that such growth undoubtedly occurs, but we are dealing with a concept that can be hard to get hold of scientifically—as when we use a questionnaire such as the Posttraumatic Growth Inventory described above, we rely on people's perceptions of how much and in what ways they have changed. How can we be sure that what people say on these questionnaires is real?

One way of looking at this question is to examine people's perceptions of growth against what close friends and family say about them. One such study asked 61 trauma survivors to complete the Posttraumatic Growth Inventory. Another person who knew the survivor also completed the inventory independently, answering the questions in relation to the survivor. When looked at together, survivors' reports were corroborated.[20] This suggests that people's reports of growth are indeed real. But it's not a foolproof method. What if it's not only survivors who are biased, but also friends and family? To be sure that growth is real, scientists need to go beyond just asking people what changes they think they have experienced. Ideally, what they need to do is compare "how people are" after an event to "how they were" beforehand.

For example, we ask people who have not experienced trauma to rate how much they think their life has meaning on a 6-point scale, where 0 = my life lacks meaning and 5 = I feel that my life is very meaningful (with the numbers in between representing 1 = very little, 2 = a little, 3 = some, 4 = a lot). Then, once they have experienced a trauma, we go back to them and ask them to rate the same statement again. Imagine: At the first time a person scores 1, but at the second time they score 4. Subtracting the two scores, there is an increase of three points—evidence of actual posttraumatic growth.

Of course, this is hard to do because we don't know who will experience a traumatic event to be able to obtain a measure of their well-being beforehand. But sometimes this is possible. A study illustrating this principle, involving the collection of divorce data from all seventy-seven counties in Oklahoma between 1985 and 2000, showed that there was a decline in the rate of divorce following the Oklahoma bombing in 1995—a finding that is consistent with the idea that trauma strengthens relationships.[21]

There are of course other possible explanations. For instance, a general decline in divorce may have occurred over that period. On its own this study on divorce offers only weak evidence. More powerful evidence comes from a fortuitous study of over 4,000 people who completed an online questionnaire assessing their character strengths before the terrorist attacks of 9/11. The researchers had not intended to use these data to test for posttraumatic growth, but they quickly realized after 9/11 that if they could assess the same people a second time, doing so would allow them to find out whether these people had changed since the attacks. They were able to look at people's scores on character strengths two months after 9/11 and compare them to before the attacks.

If posttraumatic growth is real, they reasoned, then one would expect to see an increase in score totals on the character-strengths questionnaire. And that is exactly what they found. After the 9/11 attacks, the study participants scored higher on gratitude, hope, kindness, leadership, love, faith, and teamwork. And, importantly, these changes seemed to stick:

When the participants completed the same questionnaire ten months later, their scores were even higher.[22]

Before-and-after studies are difficult to carry out, because no one knows precisely who will experience adversity. Sometimes, as in the study described above, the unexpected happens, making it possible to compare how people are after an event to how they were before, but such studies are difficult to plan for obvious reasons.

But if researchers use a large enough sample of people, they can be fairly certain that a sizeable percentage of them will likely experience some form of adversity in the following months. In one such study, performed by Professor Patricia Frazier and her colleagues, 1,500 students were asked to complete an online survey about their psychological well-being. Eight weeks later they were contacted again. This time, they were also asked if they had experienced any major life-events in those previous eight weeks. Ten percent reported that they had experienced a traumatic event—such as a life-threatening accident, an assault, or an illness contracted by themselves or a close friend or loved one— that they rated as causing intense fear, helplessness, or horror. Would these students score higher on psychological well-being? The results showed that, yes, on average, those students who had experienced a traumatic event scored higher on psychological well-being than before: 5 percent reported an increase in the strength of their relationships; 12 percent found life more meaningful; 25 percent were more satisfied with life; 8 percent were more grateful; and 7 percent were more religiously committed than before.[23]

This before-and-after study and others confirm that actual positive changes take place after adversity. Even the harshest of critics do not now deny that people can grow following adversity.

But there is one further criticism that remains to be fully addressed. Because it is difficult to measure actual changes (for the reasons mentioned), researchers tend to rely heavily on questionnaires such as the Posttraumatic Growth Inventory, which asks people to rate how much they perceive themselves to have changed. To what extent do people's perceptions of how much they have changed actually mirror their actual change?

The ingenious twist in Patricia Frazier's methodology was that she and her colleagues asked the 10 percent of students who had experienced a traumatic event to complete the Posttraumatic Growth Inventory in order to assess the ways in which the students perceived themselves to have changed over the past eight weeks.

These ratings were then compared to the before-and-after results. The two sets of data did not correspond exactly. This study raises questions about the validity of people's self-reports. It may be that the results are at least in part explained by the choice of measures in this particular study, as other work has found stronger convergence between perceived and actual growth using different measures.[24]

Another possibility is that for some people, their perceived growth is consistent with their actual growth, but for others it isn't. Evidence for this comes from a study which found a high level of consistency in people who were less distressed, but not in those who were highly distressed.[25]

The conclusion? People do grow following traumatic events, but they are not necessarily accurate when it comes to recalling and reporting how they have actually changed and in what ways.

In short, people are not very good at recalling past states and making comparisons with present states. This is particularly true for people in a high state of distress. Recalling the details of personal change requires complex mental calculations, as survivors must not only evaluate their pre-trauma and post-trauma states but also compute the difference between them. Accordingly, they might inflate their perceptions of change. Research suggests that some people see the past as worse than it actually was. In such instances, when they perform a mental calculation in response to the question of how they have changed, they tend to see the present as brighter.[26]

Another reason for the discrepancy is that measures like the Posttraumatic Growth Inventory ask people to rate how much they think they have changed because of a specific event in their lives, but we are influenced by so many things that happen to us. Life-events that are independent of the trauma might also provoke growth. Perhaps the traumatized person was promoted at work and learned new skills that increased her sense of competency and mastery. Alternatively, a life situation indirectly related to the trauma could be responsible for growth, as when a survivor seeks support from his friends, takes a break from work, and so on—actions that might themselves cause positive changes. All of these other effects will be picked up by the measure of actual change but not necessarily by the measure of perceived change.

In addition, responses to posttraumatic growth questionnaires are influenced by the fact that some people may be inclined to say that they have changed more than they have. Some people deliberately exaggerate when asked how much they have changed as a result of trauma, often in an effort to present themselves in a positive light to others. In other words, they let on that they're doing better than they really are in order to avoid disapproval. As one woman who had been bereaved through suicide put it during an interview: "You can't actually say anything to other people because you don't want to shock other people, you don't want to upset other people, and you don't want to certainly lower the tone, because people like to hear about uplifting things. They don't want to hear about anything downbeat or depressing."[27]

This reason may explain why studies using direct questions seem to yield higher rates of reported growth than open-ended interview studies. By the same token, providing people with checklists about positive changes may artificially inflate reports of growth. Conversely, there are circumstances in which people might even downplay the amount of posttraumatic growth they have experienced because they believe it is inappropriate to talk about "benefits." In the same study of people bereaved by suicide, some participants said that they experienced benefits but that they felt that others would not understand this if they voiced it, so they kept quiet—only talking openly to the researcher who was herself bereaved through suicide.[28]

Such considerations may explain the discrepancy between how much growth people report and their actual growth. But a further explanation that is more troublesome is that some people may persuade themselves that something good has come out of their experience, but their growth is illusory.[29]

In a study of breast cancer patients, two-thirds of the participants talked about how their lives had been altered for the better. They spoke about how they had reordered their priorities, spending more time on important relationships and less time on mundane activities.[30] But there seemed to be a mild disregard for the truth in some of their accounts, especially those in which the women talked, unrealistically, about having a sense of personal control over the cancer and its recurrence. Even so, such illusory growth can sometimes be beneficial. In the same study, the researchers examined whether these seemingly positive but false beliefs were related to well-being. Using measures based on ratings by oncologists and psychologists, as well as on self-reports by the patients themselves, they found that these beliefs appeared to be beneficial to psychological functioning. Perhaps we can conclude that, when confronted with adversity, some people cope by using "positive illusions" as a way of maintaining their psychological functioning and bolstering their sense of self-worth.[31] In another survey of sixty-seven women who had sought help from a rape crisis program, all were asked if rape had caused any positive changes in their lives—a question put to them three days after the rape in each case. To the researchers' surprise, 57 percent reported some positive change.[32] In a later similar survey of 171 women, the same researchers found that 91 percent of women reported at least one positive change within two weeks of being assaulted.[33] Among their responses were "more concern for others in a similar situation" (80 percent), "better relationships with family" (46 percent), and "a greater appreciation of life" (46 percent).

Whether such results reflect posttraumatic growth or simply a way of coping is impossible to ascertain, but for the reasons outlined above, we might be more cautious about accepting people's self-reports of growth at face value in the immediate aftermath of traumatic events when they are most distressed.

As we have seen, there are a number of reasons why trauma survivors might report more or less growth than they have actually experienced, and as a result there are a number of pressing questions to keep researchers busy in the years ahead. Continued research will further illuminate this important topic—especially as psychologists begin accruing data from studies that follow people's posttraumatic growth trajectories over many years using both measures of perceived and actual change. In this way, we will get a better sense than we have now about the speeds and time frames of growth.

Even so, despite the fact that posttraumatic growth is a relatively new field of study, and many questions remain, a vast body of scientific research has now accumulated providing some intriguing findings. One of the most striking is that the people who report the most growth are not those who are resistant to the effects of trauma but, rather, those who are psychologically shaken up and who exhibit some degree of posttraumatic stress.

It is this fact that is beginning to change how we think about posttraumatic stress, from something which was previously considered as all harmful, to understanding it as the engine of posttraumatic growth.

A frequent misunderstanding about posttraumatic growth is that it is the opposite of posttraumatic stress, and that those of us studying growth are claiming naively that traumatized people do not suffer posttraumatic stress or any other psychological difficulties. But posttraumatic growth does not imply that the person is free from posttraumatic stress. Indeed, as already mentioned, posttraumatic growth seems to go hand in hand with posttraumatic stress.

People who report growth are often deeply distressed and also experiencing posttraumatic stress. Growth emerges through their emotional struggle. One is reminded of Bobby Kennedy, who, while giving a speech the night of Martin Luther King's assassination, quoted the poet Aeschylus: "He who learns must suffer. And even in our sleep pain that cannot forget, falls drop by drop upon the heart, and in our own despair, against our will, comes wisdom to us by the awful grace of God." Research backs this up. Studies have shown that higher levels of posttraumatic stress are often associated with higher levels of growth.[34]

Initially, some degree of posttraumatic stress is actually necessary for positive change to arise. Posttraumatic stress seems to be the engine that drives psychological growth following adversity—whereby recurring images, thoughts, and feelings signify that the person's mental world has been shaken up and that the person is actively engaged in cognitively processing the event.

In actuality, however, the equation is not so simple as that. The engine of posttraumatic stress turns over at different speeds for different

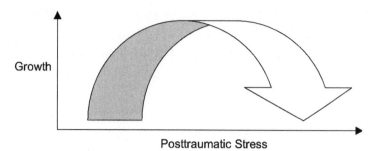

Growth

Posttraumatic Stress

FIGURE 4.5 Curvilinear Relationship Between Posttraumatic Growth and Posttraumatic Stress. As posttraumatic stress increases, so does growth—but only to an extent, at which point the growth begins to diminish.
Source: Adapted by author.

people, depending on a number of factors—what actually happened to them, how well they are able to cope, and how much support they have from others. For some people, the engine is ticking over: They might be distressed and troubled by their experiences but they are coping well enough. For others, by contrast, the engine is overheating: They are so completely overwhelmed by intrusive thoughts and avoidant of reminders that they are not actively engaged in cognitively processing the event. In such instances, posttraumatic stress seems not to trigger growth but to stifle it. This observation is supported by a study performed by Stanford University researchers after 9/11,[35] which found that those reporting moderate levels of posttraumatic stress showed the most growth.

When posttraumatic stress levels are too high, the possibility of growth diminishes. This relationship between posttraumatic stress and posttraumatic growth is represented by an inverted U-shape, as shown in Figure 4.5.

The point at which the engine overheats and the possibility of growth seems to diminish is approximately the point at which the experiences of posttraumatic stress become so overwhelming that a diagnosis of PTSD would be made. In a study of fifty homeless women with a history of trauma,[36] most were diagnosed with PTSD. For these individuals, there was no association between posttraumatic stress and growth. It is only at moderate levels of posttraumatic stress that the necessary cognitive processing can take place for growth to flourish.

In short, posttraumatic growth is not possible without some posttraumatic stress.[37]

There is an intricate dance between posttraumatic stress and posttraumatic growth. Once posttraumatic growth takes root, however, the relationship between posttraumatic stress and posttraumatic growth is reversed. As posttraumatic growth flourishes, it leads to an eventual reduction in posttraumatic stress. In another study, this one involving 195 survivors of disaster, those who reported benefits within four to six weeks of the event were less likely to be diagnosed with PTSD three years later than those who did not report benefits. In the Stanford University study following 9/11 noted above, those who reported growth in the initial few days and weeks experienced lower posttraumatic stress six months later. And in a hospice study that followed bereaved adults from three months before a loved one's death to eighteen months after, the researchers found that those who reported benefits from the experience exhibited lower distress at thirteen to eighteen months than those who didn't report benefits.[38]

What seems most important for mental health is that growth is consistently reported over time. The person who reports growth today and still does so several months later is the one who is most likely to find that it leads to better overall mental health. In a particularly sophisticated study, 171 rape survivors were asked to complete a questionnaire specially designed to measure positive changes two weeks after the assault and then, again, two, six, and twelve months later. Participants were categorized into four groups:

1. Those who reported low levels of positive change at two weeks and high levels at twelve months (the "gained positive change" group)
2. Those who reported high levels of positive change at two weeks and low levels at twelve months (the "lost positive change" group)
3. Those who reported low levels at both time points (the "never had positive change" group)
4. Those who reported high levels at both time points (the "always had positive change" group)

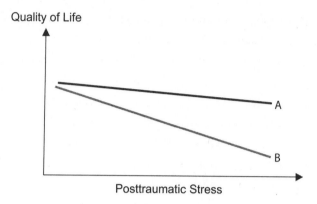

A = group with high levels of reported growth
B = group with low levels of reported growth

FIGURE 4.6 The Relationship Between Posttraumatic Stress and Quality of Life as a Function of Posttraumatic Growth. Reported growth attenuates the association between posttraumatic stress and quality of life. *Source:* Adapted by author from Morrill et al. (2007).

Those in the "always had positive change" group did the best, showing the lowest levels of posttraumatic stress.[39]

Research has also investigated whether more posttraumatic growth leads to better quality of life. The answer seems to be that it does. We know that people who experience posttraumatic stress report a diminished quality of life, but for those who also report posttraumatic growth, this stress is somewhat alleviated. In a study supporting this conclusion, investigators interviewed 161 women previously treated for early-stage breast cancer. Higher levels of posttraumatic stress were associated with lower quality of life as expected, but this association was weaker in those who reported high levels of posttraumatic growth. The results are shown in Figure 4.6. As levels of posttraumatic stress increase, quality of life decreases, but the decrease is much more evident among those with low levels of posttraumatic growth.[40]

Another study of 117 patients treated for cancer found that post-surgery benefit-finding was associated with greater quality of life and lower levels of both worry and depression one year after the treatment—and this held true even when depression, quality of life, and worry before surgery were taken into account. Overall, research shows that posttraumatic growth is related to fewer mental health problems, lower levels of depression and suicidality, and higher levels of positivity in a variety of trauma survivors, including people with HIV, women who have experienced sexual assault, bereaved family members, parents who have lost a child through suicide, victims of a tornado in Florida, a mass killing in Texas, a plane crash in Indiana, Hurricane Katrina, and following the aftermath of 9/11.[41]

The mental-health benefits of posttraumatic growth are now well-documented. Remember that when we talk about posttraumatic growth we are ultimately talking about an increase in eudaimonic well-being—which we know is associated with better long-term mental health. In one study published in 2010, investigators examined the results of a survey completed by 5,630 people when they were fifty-five to fifty-six years of age and, again, when they were sixty-five to sixty-six. Those who scored higher on a measure of eudaimonic well-being at the younger age were over seven times less likely to be depressed ten years later than those whose scores were lower.[42]

One possible reason for this is that as our eudaimonic well-being increases, we are able to engage in more approach-oriented coping. Studies show that people with greater eudaimonic well-being use more task-focused and emotion-focused coping, use less avoidance coping, and have more social support.[43]

But posttraumatic growth goes beyond repairing poor mental health. It also improves positivity and helps people flourish. In an Internet survey performed by Christopher Peterson and his colleagues, people with greater posttraumatic growth were found to exhibit more humor, kindness, leadership, love, social intelligence, teamwork, bravery, honesty, judgment, perseverance, perspective, self-regulation, appreciation of beauty, creativity, curiosity, enjoyment of learning, gratitude, hope, zest for life, fairness, forgiveness, modesty, and prudence.[44]

What about physical health? One study stands out in this regard: In interviews with 287 men who had recently experienced their first heart attack, over 50 percent reported some form of benefit, such as a positive change in their philosophy of life. But the main finding was that those patients who perceived benefits from their misfortune seven weeks after the attack were, eight years later, less likely to have suffered another heart attack or to have died and they were in better general health than the other survivors. This held true even after age, social class, and disease severity were taken into account.[45]

Another study—this time, one that examined patients with rheumatoid arthritis—found that those who engaged in benefit-finding as a result of their illness experienced physical improvement as well. One year later they were better able to perform various activities of daily living such as washing and reaching, and this held true even when disability was taken into account.[46]

These are striking findings. Some researchers have tried to investigate why this might be. Could benefit-finding be related to changes in immune functioning? Some intriguing studies suggest that it is. A study of forty HIV-positive men who had recently lost a close friend or partner to AIDS found that those who reported benefits showed not only a less rapid decline in their immune system over the subsequent two to three years but also a lower rate of AIDS-related mortality. Similar results emerged from a study of HIV-positive men and women showing that posttraumatic growth positively affects immune functioning, helping people to be more resistant to new stress.[47]

In pointing to the longer-term gains associated with posttraumatic growth, it is important not to lose sight of the distress often experienced by traumatized people, and the very real need they may have for psychological guidance and support to help them overcome any psychological roadblocks that they encounter.

Posttraumatic growth seems ultimately to lead to reduced posttraumatic stress, but it is posttraumatic stress that sparks the journey toward posttraumatic growth in the first place. But this is not an easy journey. Over thirty years of research into psychological trauma have shown us that people's reactions depend not only on what happened during the event, how they dealt with the demands of the situation, and what their immediate and early reactions were, but also on the ways in which they coped in the aftermath, the level of social support available to them, and other posttrauma life-events that they experience.[48]

People whose lives after a traumatic event are troubled by difficulties with family, loneliness, unexpected changes or upheavals, loss or bereavement, poor health, and economic problems—as well as by a lack of social support—may continue to be more affected than those whose life circumstances are more favorable. In addition, there may be secondary stressors related to the trauma—such as criminal proceedings, inquests, or media coverage—that conspire to keep the event alive in the trauma survivor's mind and thus become obstacles to finding the sense of closure that might otherwise have occurred.

People develop problems unique to their own situations. Survivors who feel that they have let themselves down, or let others down—or that they or others have behaved inappropriately—may experience intense feelings of guilt, shame, anger, fear, or rage. Yet these can be very useful emotions in terms of guiding people in their future actions—to avoid danger, to make reparations, to show remorse, or to seek justice. So it is not that these emotions are damaging "by definition," but they can be if they are felt too strongly for too long, or lead to actions that are misdirected.

Some people try to deal with their emotions directly, confronting them head-on by talking to others and seeking support. Others try to push their feelings "under the carpet" by keeping busy, using drink or drugs, or distracting themselves. Karen, for example, struggled with an obsessive need to keep things tidy. Some days, she would spend up to eight hours scrubbing the kitchen, often getting up in the middle of the night to clean. Karen was raped when she was fourteen years old. Cleaning helped her to switch off the horrible memories of that event and gave her a way to manage her emotions. Distractions of this kind may be helpful in the short term, but they are rarely so in the longer term. Like Karen, people who attempt to cope in this way can become more entrenched in such distractions. Eventually their emotions may intensify, resulting in uncontrollable levels of anger, irritability, fearfulness, sadness, sorrow, shame, or guilt.[49]

As with a row of dominoes, one problem leads to another. People's lives can simply begin to unravel. Problems in relationships develop. There are arguments. Marriages collapse. Friendships disintegrate. Work suffers. Unemployment results. Health problems develop. In all such instances, social support seems to be one of the most important factors in helping people psychologically.[50]

But social support is not always available. Indeed, there are times when traumatic events affect not only the individual but the family, the community, and society overall. Trauma can rip apart the social fabric of people's lives, destroying the social networks that are so important for healing. Alternatively, the social networks may simply not be able to provide the support that is needed. For example, soldiers sometimes find it hard to adjust after leaving the "family" of the army and entering into civilian life. In such cases, they may have difficulty finding the companionship and support from family and friends that they need.[51]

In short, growth will often arise out of the struggle with trauma. But that struggle is very real and it is vital that we do not romanticize the suffering associated with PTSD. Trauma survivors must acknowledge the struggle involved in managing the powerful emotions that arise and find ways of coping that allow them to navigate the journey toward transformation. Posttraumatic stress may well be the engine of posttraumatic growth, but survivors need to take control of the rudder and point themselves in the right direction. In subsequent chapters, we will take a more detailed look at this idea of posttraumatic stress as an "engine" and explore the different pathways that people can take.

CHAPTER 5

The Theory of
the Shattered Vase

TWENTY-SIX WILD-EYED dogs rage through the moonlit
street. People scatter in their wake. As the dogs gather under a window, you look out and see them staring up at you, ravenous, with bright yellow eyes.

It is a dream. It is also the opening of the award-winning movie *Waltz with Bashir*. Director Ari Folman portrays a night in a bar, where an old friend tells him about this recurring nightmare. The teller concludes that the dream is about his time as a young conscript in the Israeli army during the Lebanon war of the early 1980s. His superiors had ordered him to shoot dogs to stop them from howling warnings to the enemy. He killed twenty-six dogs in total. Now they haunt him, night after night.

The dream prompts Ari to wonder about his own experiences as a conscript. He cannot recall what happened to him. What is it that he has forgotten? The film tells the story of Ari's efforts to recover that time in his life. He sets off to meet with his old war comrades. They discuss their experiences. He listens to them describe their memories.

Slowly, Ari begins to remember: the shocking images of suffering. They were too much to bear—so painful that they had to be forgotten. Now, if Ari is to heal, he must remember them once again. The tension between remembering and forgetting, captured so well by this movie, is the essence of what it is to live with trauma.

Survivors of trauma often exhibit an inability to form coherent narratives about what happened to them. This begins at the time of the trauma and can persist for some time afterward. They struggle to tell a story that consists of fragments—bits and pieces of memory, isolated thoughts and feelings.

In ordinary circumstances, the brain processes memories in an orderly fashion. Through narrative processing, memory storage, and meaning making, memories are filed away in long-term memory. They maintain their sequence and internal logic—and can usually be recalled from start to finish without trouble.

However, during trauma those parts of the brain concerned with memory and language shut down. As a result, when we attempt to remember trauma, our memories are all over the place. They lack coherence and seem to be out of logical sequence. One man told me that, in his memories, "seconds, minutes, hours all ran together." Traumatic memories become fragmented, as they are held in what is called *active memory*, waiting to be processed after the trauma has passed. Thus, whereas normal memories fade over time, traumatic memories remain present in our minds.

Traumatic memory problems can last many years unless the memories are filed away. For this to happen, psychological alarm systems must first be deactivated—either through normal processes of learning that the threat has passed or through therapeutic interventions. At the same time, the parts of the brain concerned with narrative processing, memory storage, and meaning making need to come back online, allowing the memories to be filed away. These are the same biological processes involved in recovery and reconfiguration that we saw earlier. The coming decade will undoubtedly reveal much more about how these neurobiological processes underpin posttraumatic growth.

But neurobiology alone is inadequate to the process of describing how we deal with trauma. Important as our evolved responses and neural pathways are to dictating our life's course, there is another uniquely human element to posttraumatic growth—one whose absence makes healing far more difficult, if not impossible. It is our ability to reflect on, talk about, and ultimately comprehend what has happened and then to make sense of the significance of our experiences.

Understanding posttraumatic growth requires us to go beyond neurobiology and become aware of the roles that our own outlook and deliberations play in enabling posttraumatic stress to be the engine of growth.

Shifting the focus from neurobiology to observations of people's behavior, Mardi Horowitz, one of the world's leading trauma specialists, proposed that adjustment to trauma consists of five phases: outcry, numbness and denial, intrusive re-experiencing, working through, and, finally, completion.[1] These five stages are not set in stone. Not everyone moves through them in this sequence. Some people may skip certain phases or move through them in an alternative way. What is useful about Professor Horowitz's theory is that it provides an account of the mental processes involved in trauma recovery.

Immediately after trauma, many people go through what Horowitz calls *outcry*. This could be described as a period of stunned confusion. I once spoke to a woman named Lynne who experienced such an outcry. After a long day at work and a difficult commute home, Lynne found herself exhausted as she opened the front door of her house. She left her bags inside the door and went straight to the fridge to pour herself a glass of wine. Noticing that her husband was not yet home and that the house was cold, she turned up the heat. Something seemed odd. It wasn't until she returned to the kitchen that she realized there was a note on the table. She picked it up.

In the note, Lynne's husband had written that although he loved her he couldn't continue in the marriage. He had met someone else. He had already moved out earlier that day.

Lynne remembers that it felt like the floor gave way from beneath her feet. Her heart started to beat furiously, and she felt panic at the thought that she might be about to have a heart attack. Lynne spent the next few days curled up in a fetal position, crying and screaming. She simply could not believe that her marriage to Michael had come to an end. "I could hardly stand up, the shock was so great; and for days I was in a daze. It was unbelievable to me: I would be sitting staring into space, then I would remember—he's leaving me."

Following the initial outcry, trauma-related information in the form of thoughts, images, and memories can be overwhelming. So distressing is this information that the brain mobilizes defense mechanisms to force it from consciousness. There begins the second stage: *numbness and denial.*

Numbness and denial serve an important protective function. Some people feel as if they are acting in a play, watching themselves from a distance, or dreaming. Such reactions are ways of protecting oneself from distressing experiences. This protective state can also take the form of emotional numbness. As one woman said: "I had hardened. I had closed off. . . . I built the walls of Jericho around me—that's the only way I could deal with it."[2]

In some cases, the traumatic event can be so shocking that denial occurs ahead of the initial outcry. *I Am Alive*, written by Holocaust survivor Kitty Hart in 1962, describes the author's immediate onset of denial at Auschwitz: "All around us were screams, death, smoking chimneys making the air black and heavy with soot and the smell of burning bodies. . . . It was just like a nightmare and it took weeks and weeks before I could really believe this was happening."[3]

Yet denial and numbness (referred to more broadly as avoidance) can persist for only so long. Even when sequestered in active memory, where they cannot be processed, our memories are powerful and demand to be heard. If we shut out our memories and do not deal with them, they eventually come crashing in on us. Research has shown that deliberate attempts to suppress unwanted thoughts result in a paradoxical increase in the frequency of these thoughts—what is known as the "rebound effect."[4] In Horowitz's terminology, this is the *intrusive re-experiencing* phase of adjustment to trauma.

Researchers have compared this phenomenon to an unwanted roommate. Imagine a group of apartment sharers who decide among themselves that one resident is no longer welcome. Once day, while he is out, they change the locks. When he comes back, he can't get in. He bangs on the door. The others ignore him. He bangs louder. This goes on for some time, to no avail. Eventually, he gets tired from banging on the door and falls asleep on his own doorstep. All is quiet for some time and the other roommates think he has gone away. But then the banging starts up again, even louder. Eventually it stops again. This time, surely he has gone away, the other roommates think. All is quiet for some time. But then, suddenly, the unwanted roommate comes crashing in through the window.[5] Memories can be painful, but it is necessary for us to process them if we are to avoid this rebound effect.

Typically people go back and forth between these states of avoidance and intrusive re-experiencing. In most cases, they make a valiant attempt to integrate the new trauma-related information into long-term memory, but because it is distressing to remember, they do so only a bit at a time. They remember for a bit, and then they forget for a bit. This is the *working through* phase.

As they begin the working through phase, their feelings initially seem blocked off and the event itself is distant or dream-like—perhaps as a means of allowing the distress of the incident to be felt only slowly and gradually. Over time, as they continue to work through their trauma, the intensity of the denial and of the intrusions decreases. At the end of the process, they achieve a state of *completion*. The troubling memories that were stored in active memory have been transferred to long-term memory.

Typically, people move through these phases of avoidance and intrusion, but some people can get stuck in the outcry phase, or become frozen in avoidance, or intrusion, or in the oscillation between intrusion and avoidance. These phases are disturbing and frightening to people, especially if they don't understand what is happening to them. Sometimes people say they felt that they were going crazy. But, Horowitz's description helps us to understand the experiences of posttraumatic stress as a normal and natural process in which people are actively striving to work through their experiences and to integrate their memories.

To facilitate conceptualization of the stages of avoidance and intrusive re-experiencing that Horowitz describes, I sometimes explain to traumatized clients that their thoughts and emotions have been hurriedly "packed away" in a mental suitcase and removed from the scene of the trauma. However, this emotional luggage, because it was not well packed, may burst open from time to time, particularly when "knocked against" something. This manifests in distressing emotions, thoughts, images, and nightmares that traumatized people have tried to push out of their minds because they find them upsetting. They try to hold the suitcase closed; otherwise it bursts open and the contents spill out over the floor. But it is hard work keeping the case closed all the time.

To work through trauma, survivors must unpack and repack their emotional luggage, thereby helping themselves to come to terms with and make sense of their traumatic experience. Inevitably there are things they have to keep: They can't be rid of all aspects of the traumatic experience, much as they may wish they could be. But eventually they will be able to dispense with some items, such as feelings of guilt or anger, and to rearrange others so that they can be carried without rupturing the suitcase quite so often. Although the process of unpacking and repacking is painful, it becomes easier over time.

Eventually, survivors of trauma find that the suitcase can be carried without bursting open unexpectedly and that they can open it and view the contents at any time without experiencing undue distress. Because this "bursting open" occurs less and less frequently, the suitcase becomes increasingly less burdensome. Indeed, it is lighter and easier to keep shut now that some of the bulkier items have been dispensed with.

Metaphorically speaking, the items in the suitcase that trauma survivors need to unpack and repack are their thoughts, beliefs, and assumptions.

Traumatic events are by their nature unpredictable. Not only that, they run counter to the way we understand our world. Deep down we all tend to believe that nothing bad will ever happen to us, so when we are faced with the worst, our assumptions about what the world is like and our place in it come under fire. Anthony Browne, the British writer and illustrator of children's books, lost his father when he was a child. It was the greatest shock he had yet experienced in his young life. In his description of the scene, he recalls that "Dad was mending a plug when suddenly he fell, seemingly in slow motion, and started writhing around making these terrible noises. It went on and on: We didn't know what to do . . . and then he was just lying there: this great, god-like figure on the floor, amid this scene of total devastation. I'd thought he was invincible."[6]

What his father's death shattered was Browne's *assumptive world*—the fundamental assumptions that form the bedrock of our conceptual systems, which we begin to build as children. This idea draws on the work of child psychologist John Bowlby, who described how children build working models of themselves and the world through interactions with their caregivers.[7]

A simple example of an assumptive world is the belief of many children in the existence of Santa Claus. This belief provides children with a set of bedrock assumptions about the world and their place in it. Specifically, the children believe that if they are good they will be rewarded with presents and if they are bad they will be punished by Santa Claus, who, in turn, will strike them off his list for that year. It may be hard for adults to remember the power of this belief in Santa Claus and how it gave structure to our world as children. It is a belief we relinquish as we grow older and have more life experiences. Yet the kind of assumption embodied by the belief in Santa Claus persists.

Throughout our lives we are constantly revising our assumptions about the world. The process of revision is gradual and incremental. Most of the time, we do not notice it taking place. Although we no longer believe in Santa Claus, as adults we have cultural institutions such as government, education, and religion that, much like Santa Claus, offer us beliefs about justice, fairness, luck, controllability, predictability, coherence, benevolence, and safety—deep-seated beliefs that structure our world, provide rules for living, and establish the foundations for our goals in life.

Sociologists argue that culture was created to provide humans a sense of order and stability. It helps make sense of our experiences and allows us to function from day to day, while at the same time protecting us from the realities of human fragility. This illusion is a fundamental part of our assumptive world that trauma so cruelly shatters.

The truth is that we are frail biological creatures. Death lurks around the corner for each of us, but it seems to be human nature to fend off the knowledge of this fact, creating bulwarks against the terror that such knowledge brings. As Ernest Becker wrote: "The creatureliness is the terror. Once you admit that you are a defecating creature and you invite the primeval ocean of creature anxiety to flood over you . . . [you expe-rience] the anxiety that results from the human paradox that man is an animal who is conscious of his animal limitation. Anxiety is the result of the perception of the truth of one's condition. . . . It means to know that one is food for worms."[8]

The social psychologist Professor Ronnie Janoff-Bulman has described how in Western culture we grow up with three deep-seated beliefs. The first is a belief that the world is benevolent. We tend to underestimate the extent to which we are vulnerable to misfortunes such as accidents or disease and to overestimate the probability that good things will happen to us. We get up in the morning expecting the best rather than the worst to happen (Californians, for example, know that earthquakes are in-evitable but still head out to work assuming the ground will stay firm)—and we know that a large percentage of people will contract heart disease or cancer but believe that we are exempt. We lead our lives as if we are in-vulnerable to misfortune.

The second belief is that the world is meaningful, controllable, pre-dictable, and just: Good things will happen to those who are deserving, punishment will befall those who are bad—and if we work hard, do the right things, and eat healthy food, then all will be well.

The third belief has to do with our tendency to view ourselves in a positive light. We assume that we are worthy, decent people. So, when ad-versity strikes, the first question we ask is, What did I do to deserve this? If the world is just, then when something bad happens to me, I must surely have done something to deserve it.

These deep-seated, unquestioned beliefs form the core of our as-sumptive world even as adults. It isn't that we believe bad events will not happen; rather, we believe that such events are unlikely to happen to us. (In experiments in which people are asked to rate their chances of expe-riencing negative events, they consistently rate their own chances lower than those of others.)[9] On the whole, then, we are unrealistically opti-mistic about the future, see ourselves as relatively invulnerable, and have inflated perceptions of control and justice.

Not only that, but the assumptions underlying such beliefs can be very difficult to see within ourselves. Whenever I tell students about this theory, they admit that it might be valid but do not think it applies to them. So fundamental are these assumptions that even though we may "know" that bad things happen to good people, and so on, the assumptions persist at the very core of our being and affect the ways in which we live our lives. Unless we ourselves have encountered trauma and tragedy, it is nearly impossible to understand the power of our assumptions at a gut level.

Our deep-seated assumptions are the scaffolding of our lives. Trauma, Professor Janoff-Bulman argues, brings that scaffolding crashing down, exposing us to the stark realities of existence—namely, that we are frail and mortal. Trauma has been called the atom smasher of our belief systems[10]—whether belief in the invulnerability of our parents (as in the story told by Anthony Browne), belief in the justice of the world when confronted with injustice, or, as one man who had witnessed the horrors of genocide in Rwanda put it, "I had a relationship with God before Rwanda. After it I never will again. I think he's a figment of man's imagination."[11]

It is when this scaffolding comes crashing down that we experience outcry and then the other phases described by Horowitz as we move into the working through phase and the need to rebuild a new assumptive world.

These fundamental assumptions are just representations of the world—not reality. Most of the time our assumptions serve us well, but throughout life we are always making revisions to them. The majority of these revisions are relatively minor. For example, perhaps a formerly trusted colleague lets us down. So we make a note that in the future we need to be wary of this person. Such an experience does not usually challenge the fundamental integrity of our assumptions about people in general. All we need to do is to make a minor revision—"Don't trust that particular person again"—and move on.

But like the child who suddenly discovers that Santa Claus does not exist, we find that when trauma happens, our new experiences lie completely outside the boundaries of our existing assumptions. There is a profound shock to our mental system: Our cherished assumptions no longer help us to make sense of where we are in life, what is happening, and what it all means.[12] Perhaps confronted by the horrors of human suffering deliberately inflicted by one group of people on another, whereas before we changed only our approach to one untrustworthy person, now we are at a loss as to whom we *can* trust. It seems as though nobody can be trusted ever again! Or confronted by massive death and destruction that follows natural disaster, our sense of invulnerability is shattered. As Becker put it, "The real world is simply too terrible to admit; it tells man that he is a small, trembling animal who will decay and die."[13]

The important point to remember here is that trauma is not simply an external phenomenon. What qualifies as "traumatic" is defined in terms of our assumptions and beliefs about the way the world works. Everyone is different, which is why people react differently to frightening events. What is threatening to an inhabitant of London may be different from what is threatening to someone who lives in the Ganges. What is threatening to me may not be so to you. Indeed, this is why events that traumatize some people do not traumatize others.[14]

The way in which trauma affects a particular individual depends on the exact nature of the discrepancy between the new trauma-related information and that person's preexisting mental models. As with fingerprints, people's assumptive worlds are different. In this sense, no two people ever experience the same traumatic event.

These theories about trauma's effects on the assumptive world predated the idea of posttraumatic growth. Nevertheless, combining the two concepts gives us a new starting point for comprehending the process through which posttraumatic growth arises. Specifically, posttraumatic stress can be viewed as indicative of cognitive processes that kick in when our assumptive world comes under threat.

Most psychologists regard posttraumatic stress as symptomatic of disorder. But if we regard these cognitive processes from a perspective that encompasses their interaction with our assumptive world, we can understand them as steps in an adaptive process rather than as symptoms of a disorder. They are indicative of people's struggle to rebuild their assumptions about themselves and their relation to the world.[15]

If the foregoing claims are valid, then we can begin to embrace a new theory of posttraumatic stress reactions as a normal and necessary part of the psychological adaptation process, whereby posttraumatic growth is the natural and normal direction of this process.[16]

The tree metaphor in Chapter 4 may shed further light on this concept. For trees, the motivation toward growth is inbuilt. The same is true for humans: It's in our very nature to grow. Humanistic psychologist Carl Rogers illustrates this principle in his description of an experience he had overlooking one of the rugged coves that dot the coastline of northern California:

> Several large rock outcroppings were at the mouth of the cove, and these received the full force of the great Pacific combers which, beating upon them, broke into mountains of spray before surging into the cliff-lined shore. As I watched the waves breaking over these large rocks in the distance, I noticed with surprise what appeared to be tiny palm trees on the rocks, no more than two or three feet high, taking the pounding of the breakers. Through my binoculars I saw that these were some type of seaweed, with a slender "trunk" topped off with a head of leaves. As one examined a specimen in the intervals between the waves it seemed clear that this fragile, erect, top-heavy plant would be utterly crushed and broken by the next breaker. When the wave crunched down upon it, the trunk bent almost flat, the leaves were whipped into a straight line by the torrent of water, yet the moment the wave had passed, here was the plant again, erect, tough, resilient. . . . Here in this palmlike seaweed was the tenacity of life, the forward thrust of life, the ability to push into an incredibly hostile environment and not only hold its own, but to adapt, develop, and become itself.

Human beings, too, are always striving to adapt to their environments. But for people this also involves thrusting forward into the world of meaning. We are always trying to comprehend the world better than before and to understand the significance of events. Psychological growth arises whether or not we experience trauma.[17] But what trauma offers is the potential to heighten the process of growth. When we are confronted with trauma, it is in our nature to be driven to resolve the tension between preexisting assumptions and the new trauma-related information. Resolving this tension is not something we consciously decide to do (although the need to do so can become conscious); rather, it is an unconscious force rooted in our innate biological makeup.

To understand how this need to resolve the tension between preexisting assumptions and new trauma-related information plays out, child psychologist Jean Piaget distinguished between the processes of *assimilation* and *accommodation*. While Piaget's work was concerned with the ways in which children learn about the world more generally, the two processes he described also provide a way of understanding how adults engage with trauma. Piaget used the example of building blocks. Let's say a child learns to place one block on top of another. Playing happily, she builds a tower of blocks and then suddenly encounters a magnet. Never having seen a magnet before, she thinks it is another building block, and places it atop the tower. This is assimilation—the process by which a child takes in new information about objects by trying out existing assumptions on new objects.

But then, the child accidently discovers that this new building block attracts metal and begins to play with the magnet differently. This is accommodation—the process of modifying assumptions as a child encounters new information. Learning, according to Piaget, is a balancing act between assimilation and accommodation. Piaget was talking about how children learn, but the same process comes into play when, as adults, we encounter new trauma-related information. We try to place the new information on top of the old but discover that it does not quite fit—and that the new information needs to be handled differently.

Posttraumatic growth arises through the process of accommodation, during which our assumptions are modified so that they fit the new information, rather than through the process of assimilation, which involves our effort to make the new information fit our assumptions. I explain these processes using the theory of the shattered vase.

Imagine that a cherished vase sits on a table in your home. Perhaps it was a gift from a beloved relative or friend. One day you accidentally knock it off its perch. Luckily, there is only a little damage. It is easy to quickly glue the few broken pieces back into place. The vase looks as it did before and the mend is invisible to the eye. For some people, traumatic events are like this. Such events may dent or even break some of their core assumptions, but not to the extent that their overall worldview changes. It is relatively easy for them to assimilate the experience.

But imagine that the vase smashes into a thousand tiny shards. Devastated, you rush to collect the fragments. How to put them back together? In the disorganized confusion the vase seems beyond repair. Nevertheless, some people will try to put it back together exactly as it was before it fell to the ground. If they're lucky, the vase may look just as it used to. Closer examination will reveal the truth, however: It is held together by nothing more than glue and sticky tape. The cracks are still visible if you look carefully—and the slightest jolt could send the vase back into pieces once again. Likewise, those people who try to hold on to their worldviews following trauma are often more fragile, defensive, and easily hurt. Their wounded assumptions are subject to being shattered again and again.

But assimilation is not the only strategy: Some people will take up the pieces and build something new. They are sad that their prized vase is broken but accept that it can never return to its old form. The question now becomes, What to make of it next? Perhaps they can use the differently colored pieces to assemble a mosaic, finding a new and useful form to preserve their memories. This is the essence of accommodation.

The core of shattered vase theory is the notion that human beings are active, growth-oriented organisms who are—by nature—inclined to accommodate their psychological experiences into a unified sense of self and a realistic view of the world. But abandoning preexisting ideas about ourselves and our world can be painful: This is why we attempt to protect ourselves and our views of the world by trying to assimilate our experiences instead—even though doing so can often leave us defensive, vulnerable, and fragile. These two forces of accommodation and assimilation create a tension—the resolution of which determines a person's psychological outcome.

To genuinely move on from adversity, we must confront this new information and modify our perceptions. The shattered vase illustrates the extremes of accommodation versus assimilation. It is a useful metaphor, though in reality our growth after trauma depends on finding an equilibrium between the two processes. We must negotiate the tension between our defensive desire to assimilate new information and protect our cherished worldviews, on the one hand, and our biologically driven need to accommodate and learn from the new information, on the other. Our task in healing is to accommodate, but we strive to assimilate.

The most important thing we can do to avoid getting stuck in that tension is to actively process our memories. Survivors of trauma must be aware that moving on requires some degree of accommodation, even if it comes at the painful cost of abandoning previous worldviews and perceptions of themselves. People need to let go of old attachments, old ties of affection, old beliefs, old habits. If they can bring themselves to do this, equilibrium is theirs for the taking.[18]

Traumatic events impose great strain on our cognitive processing ability as we struggle to resolve discrepancies between our new memories and our old assumptions. Our tendency to vacillate between intrusion and avoidance is the concrete expression of that struggle to cognitively process the traumatic experience. The speed and depth of cognitive processing is affected by various factors; but, importantly, working through requires us to harness those uncontrollable intrusions into a force for positive change. We can accomplish this by ruminating on our experiences, whereby the thoughts, images, and new trauma-related information become the subjects of further conscious cognitive activity under our control.[19]

There are two types of rumination: reflective rumination and ruminative brooding. *Reflective rumination* is characterized by a purposeful turning inward to engage in adaptive problem solving and emotion-focused coping, whereas *ruminative brooding* is characterized by maladaptive thinking patterns. Research suggests that the quality of deliberation is important to cognitive processing, such that there is a greater frequency of reflective rumination than of ruminative brooding—indicating that the individual is seeking resolution, searching for meaning, and reframing and re-authoring his or her life.[20]

Accommodation calls for reflective rumination that actively seeks out new ways of looking at the world.

Resolving the disagreement between our meaning systems and the new information is the cognitive task all of us are faced with when we are confronted with trauma. Our success determines our subsequent trajectory. This can be a difficult and painful process, but at the end of it, we will be able to remember, think about, and talk about what happened without experiencing overwhelming distress.

Clearly, the human brain has been designed over millions of years of evolution to be sculpted through experience. Posttraumatic growth results from reconfiguration of our mental map to *accommodate* the new information. To fully work through trauma we need to redraw our mental maps to fit the new information we have gleaned about the world. The key to successfully dealing with adversity is to be able to revise and re-author our mental frameworks. But since accommodation requires that we let go of our previous assumptions, it can be a difficult and deeply distressing process.[21] After all, who are we if not the sum of our beliefs and assumptions? In a sense, accommodation represents the death of who we once were. So, understandably, our initial reaction is to try to hold on to our old assumptions despite the challenge—in an attempt to assimilate the new information.

Psychologists have found that we are biased toward assimilation and maintaining our worldviews. This phenomenon is known as *cognitive conservatism*. We seek out information that fits with what we already think, and we try to ignore, deny, and distort information that does not fit. An example would be the child who refuses to believe that Santa Claus doesn't exist even after finding his presents hidden under his parents' bed. We try to assimilate our experiences so that they fit with our old assumptions, much like forcing jigsaw pieces into spaces that do not match. As Ortega wrote: "Life is at the start a chaos in which one is lost. The individual suspects this, but he is frightened at finding himself face to face with this terrible reality, and tries to cover it over with a curtain of fantasy, where everything is clear. It does not worry him that his 'ideas' are not true, he uses them as trenches for the defense of his existence, as scarecrows to frighten away reality."[22]

Assimilation can take various forms. We may try to ignore what has happened and get locked into the unhelpful state of avoidance. Or we may deny and distort what happened. People often use the strategy of blaming themselves to protect their cherished beliefs about the controllability, predictability, and justice of the world. By blaming themselves they are able to hang on to their beliefs. (After all, if I am to blame, I could have prevented the traumatic event from happening. If I could have prevented it from happening, then my sense of control is maintained. And if I get what I deserve, then the world is still just.) In other instances, the traumatic event may threaten their self-worth. Many people often respond to such a circumstance by blaming others. Just as blaming themselves can restore a sense of control over their fate and a sense of justice in the world, blaming others protects their self-esteem. (If someone else is to blame, then I am not the one at fault and my self-esteem stays intact.) Nevertheless, there are costs associated with these assimilation strategies: Blame when inappropriately placed can be harmful.[23]

We can all think of people who cannot hear the truth about themselves and seem deaf to information that does not agree with their worldview. Think of your colleagues at work who do not admit their responsibility when things go wrong. Often, they lash out at others, defending their fragile sense of self. To some degree, we all do this, at least some of the time. It's how we are built. This strategy is understandable, to the extent that it reflects an effort to assimilate experiences (to glue the shattered vase back together again), but it is ultimately harmful.

As humans we are conservative when it comes to revising our mental models. We try to interpret new experiences within existing mental models. We continue to hold on to our existing models and to assimilate rather than to accommodate new information. Trauma simply amplifies this process. The new information is louder and more difficult to ignore, and we have to work harder to ignore it.

Trauma survivors who are caught up in their attempts to assimilate are characterized by increased defensiveness. Such people appear fragile. Like the shattered vase held together with sticky tape and glue, they are vulnerable to further trauma. Attempts at assimilation are like a game of tug-of-war against an elephant. We just cannot win.

Trauma challenges our global meaning system. It confronts us with existential truths about life that clash with this system. The more we try to hold on to our assumptive world, the more mired we are in denial of such truths. What we have to do is to accommodate the truths we have learned and change our assumptive world. We must accept that bad things *do* happen to good people and that most of us at some point or other will be forced to examine our beliefs in light of the fact that life is often arbitrary, random, and dangerous. Trauma survivors who are able to accommodate talk about their experiences differently from those who assimilate. They acknowledge the challenges in their life. They emphasize the mental effort involved in making sense of their experiences. They place their life story in a wider context, admitting to both the negative and the positive aspects of their transformation.[24]

Accommodation by definition entails modifying our assumptive worlds so that they are more in line with reality; however, some people take this too far. Necessary as accommodation is to growth, the danger occurs when victims of trauma overaccommodate, too readily abandoning their previous assumptions. Someone who is assaulted must learn whatever there is to be learned from her experience—for instance, that certain places and people are dangerous and to be avoided. All too often, however, the received lesson is that *no* place is safe and that *all* people are potential muggers. Perhaps in the short term such overaccommodation can be a useful protective mechanism that gives the person time to process the traumatic information. In the long term, however, it is maladaptive.[25]

Working through trauma requires the right balance of assimilation and accommodation. For this reason, growth can look very different from one person to another, and from one culture to another, depending on what the survivors' assumptions prior to the trauma were. For one person who was too trusting of others, accommodation might involve a shift toward becoming less trusting; another person might become more trusting. Both are trying to recalibrate their assumptive worlds in more realistic ways. In short, accommodation can occur in ways that are seen as either positive or negative—or, more frequently, as a balance between the two.

From this perspective, it is obvious that assimilation and accommodation processes are messy processes. People do their best to make sense of the world in light of their experiences. There is an intrinsic motivation to accurately reconcile their need for cognitive conservatism with their need to hold realistic views of the world and of themselves. What is important about getting this equilibrium between assimilation and accommodation right is that it is the route to increasing eudaimonic well-being—greater personal autonomy, mastery over the environment, meaning in life, positive relations with others, self-acceptance, and the ability to seek further personal growth.

The idea that human beings are constantly striving to increase their eudaimonic well-being as best they can is one of the biggest philosophical ideas in the history of psychology. We have already seen the example provided by Carl Rogers. Rogers used this example to convey the idea that there is a natural and inherent driving force within humans, a force that he called the *actualizing tendency*.

Indeed, the idea that people constantly strive toward their fullness of potential is the core of the new theory of posttraumatic growth. But by itself this does not explain why some people grow more than others. We have to take the theory further.

Just as people have within them the potential to become as fully human as they can be, an acorn has within it the intrinsic nature of an oak tree. Whether it will become the tallest, fullest oak tree that it can be remains dependent on the balance of sunlight and shade, moisture and nutrients. Given a lack of any such factors, an imbalance somewhere along the line, or disease or damage, its potential as an oak tree will be only partially fulfilled. Much the same is true of people, too. People are intrinsically motivated to grow and develop toward their fullest psychological potential—eudaimonic well-being—but only when their basic needs have been met.

Social psychologists Richard Ryan and Edward Deci have devised a theory of self-determination[26] that updates the idea that people are intrinsically motivated toward eudaimonic well-being. This theory emphasizes the central role of the individual's inner resources for personality development. It views the person as an active growth-oriented organism, maintaining that growth will naturally occur when the person's basic needs as a human being are fulfilled—specifically, the needs for autonomy, competence, and relatedness.

Building on the theory of self-determination, I propose that posttraumatic growth similarly requires that basic psychological needs be met in order to facilitate the accommodation process.[27]

The idea that that posttraumatic growth most readily takes place after such needs have been met is borne out by research. One study interviewed a group of people abused in childhood. Psychologists asked them to explain what had been the turning points in their lives that had helped them deal with the abuse.[28] The respondents highlighted certain experiences in their lives that helped them move forward. These included *genuine acceptance, feeling loved and nurtured,* and having a sense of *belonging and connection*—experiences that I would argue satisfied their basic psychological needs.

For one man, it was his wife and children who made such a difference—first through their acceptance and then through their love: "I was scared and I was alone," he said. "My ten-foot concrete walls of hurt made sure no one ever came close enough to making me bleed pain again. . . . I was able to say to a friend 'I was abused.' I expected to be rejected but I was not. . . . She accepted me and did not reject me. I was able to trust and love someone else; she is the keystone that had been missing in my life."

The respondents also talked about acquiring a sense of *liberation and freedom.* For Cathy, freedom came in the form of forgiveness: "I felt so burdened by the hatred and drive for revenge. . . . I gradually came to understand that if I really wanted to be free in my heart, I need to forgive my parents. . . . No other experience has been so life changing for me."

Others discussed feeling a new sense of *accomplishment and mastery.* For Susan it was getting top marks in her mathematics exam: "I went back to college to try to gain my G.C.S.E. in Maths. . . . This to me is a form of fighting against my parents, my ex-husband and plenty of others who have called me names over the years. . . . I now feel like I can take on the world and win, and no amount of being put down or bullying is going to affect me anymore!"

This is an important point: In order for people to move toward growth, these basic psychological needs for autonomy, competence, and relatedness must be met, so as to enhance and promote the natural tendency toward eudaimonic well-being. Further recent evidence for this observation is provided in a study by Marta Scrignaro and her colleagues, who asked forty-one cancer patients to rate the extent to which their needs for autonomy, competence, and relatedness were being met by their social support systems. Six months later, their posttraumatic growth was measured. These data indicated that those cancer patients who received support from family and friends that satisfied their psychological needs experienced more posttraumatic growth.[29]

Accepting the premise that people have a need to work through trauma in such a way that they resolve tensions between their preexisting assumptive world and new trauma-related information, we might speculate that this process is ultimately directed toward the development of eudaimonic well-being. Put simply, posttraumatic growth would therefore represent the natural and normal method of working through trauma. But even so, it can be a painful and long journey.

What I hope to emphasize here is that posttraumatic growth can be viewed as a *process* of change—not only as an outcome of change.

From an evolutionary psychology perspective it makes sense that human beings should be inclined to seek understandings of the world that maximize their fitness for survival. So the suggestion that there is an intrinsic motivation to perceive the world in such a way as to maximize one's personal autonomy, mastery over the environment, meaning in life, positive relations with others, self-acceptance, and the ability to seek further personal growth seems a reasonable prediction. All of these qualities would have served our ancestors well, and movement toward them is by definition growthful.[30]

Eudaimonic well-being is the natural and normal direction of trauma resolution, although the journey along this road can be slow and painful—and no matter how far we travel, the final destination is always over the horizon. There is no line beyond which a person is said to have achieved full growth. Growth is an ongoing process throughout life, so we grow in relation to our previous self, knowing that further growth is always possible. So while we might talk of people having grown following trauma, all this implies is that they are now higher on the eudaimonic well-being continuum than they used to be—not that they have reached a final fixed state.

One posttrauma phenomenon that is characteristic of growth is the reprioritization of values. In such instances, people look within themselves for clues to what really matters, having realized that their lives up to that point have been overly dictated by the demands of others and the expectations of society.

Trauma can leave people feeling less inclined to care what other people think about their successes and failures in life. They become less concerned with façades. They realize that what ultimately matters is what we think of ourselves.

As children we pick up messages from those around us about what is important. An example is provided by Jane, who, when she was young, picked up the message from her parents that to be loved she had to do well at school. It was not the message her parents intended; they were simply concerned about her future and assumed that good grades would give her more choices later on in life. She was a quiet, introspective girl whose inclinations were toward artistic and creative work. Like all children, Jane had a need to be loved and quickly learned that she received praise and affection from her parents when her grades were good. She internalized this message, put aside her inclinations toward creative and artistic work, and grew up learning to value herself only to the extent that she did well at school in more academic subjects. Following the early death of her father, she threw herself into her schoolwork as a way of coping and of holding on to a sense of control over her life in what seemed a very uncertain world. Now, many years later, Jane is an adult and has become a very successful lawyer. She no longer needs to do well to please her parents, but the message to succeed is so deeply internalized in her psyche that she accepts it as part of herself. Even so, she always had a sense of discomfort that somehow she was on the wrong track in life.

Following a battle with breast cancer, Jane began to listen more closely to herself and came to realize that deep inside, the values she was living were not hers but messages she had internalized as a young girl about what was important. Throughout her adult life she had tried to live according to the values she had internalized in childhood, and although she was successful in her career, her satisfaction with life was low. She was often irritable with those around her, and prone to depression. Prompted by active reflection on her assumptions, which she now questioned, and supported by those around her in her needs for autonomy, competence, and relatedness, she came to realize that what mattered most to her were things she had left behind in childhood: her freedom of expression and her creativity. Reflecting on the events of her life, she remembered the pleasure and fulfillment she had once achieved through drawing, and she began thinking about how to change the course of her working life to meet her need to express herself more creatively, and to find ways of living that seemed more true to who she felt she was rather than who she had become.

Many of us grow up internalizing the assumptions of those around us. Helping people to dig down into the values they took on board as children is one of the tasks of psychotherapy. Sometimes, as a way of helping people begin to explore the assumptions they have internalized, a therapist might instruct them: "Close your eyes, picture the house of your childhood, and imagine yourself as a child. You are standing at the front door. It opens. In your mind, walk into the home of your childhood. Your father is standing there. He turns to face you and he says to you, 'Whatever you do in life, you must always . . . ' Finish that sentence in your mind. Just say whatever comes to mind." Clients are then asked to imagine their mother speaking the same sentence. This helps people discover how early experiences with caregivers shaped their values. They often finish the "you must always" sentences with instructions like "work hard to succeed," "be nice to people," "do as you are told," "say your prayers," and "hide your tears." Many are surprised by what this exercise reveals to them.[31]

The values inculcated early on in life are so deep-seated that people barely realize how important such values are to them. And on the treadmill of everyday life, although we may feel discomfort that somehow things are not right, we rarely seek the opportunities to challenge the values, beliefs, or priorities by which we live our lives.

These are precisely the values that trauma challenges.

Trauma prompts us to reflect on our values, motives, and priorities in life. The consequence is often a letting-go of old ways of being and an embracing of new values, motives, and priorities. In this sense, the idea of growth following adversity is reminiscent of the Buddhist idea that those who have gone through hardships in life can stand more firmly in the face of new difficulties and that suffering teaches them lessons for life.[32]

Prince Siddhartha Gautama grew up surrounded by all the pleasures of life, and suffering was kept hidden from him. At age sixteen he married a beautiful princess and lived in his palace surrounded by comfort and luxury. But one day, now a young man in his late twenties, he left the palace and embarked on a journey, during which he glimpsed the suffering of ordinary people that comes with aging, disease, and hardship. First, he met an old man, exhausted by a life of toil. Next, he met a man afflicted with a serious illness. Then, he saw a corpse being carried in a funeral procession surrounded by mourners. Finally, he met a spiritual teacher who helped him realize that old age, sickness, and death are inevitable—even for those who have had the happiest and most prosperous of lives.

Newly aware that his life in the palace was not an answer to the problem of human suffering, Gautama left his kingdom. He studied for six years with spiritual teachers. Not finding the answers to his questions, he sat beneath a Bodhi tree and resolved not to eat or to leave until he reached enlightenment, even if death was the result. At the age of thirty-five, after deep and prolonged meditation, he eventually reached enlightenment and became the Buddha.

The term *Buddha* is not a name but, rather, a title that means "one who is awake." The Buddha claimed that he was merely a man who had achieved a greater understanding of human existence. He taught for the next forty-five years, traveling from town to town in India, and died at the age of eighty.

In a sense, trauma opens people up to their Buddha nature.

Specifically, it wakens people to the essential characteristics of existence. Buddhism holds that, in existence, everything is constantly changing and that suffering is inevitable. And as with Prince Guatama, who became the Buddha, people who have been traumatized embark on their own personal journeys to overcome suffering and find their own answers to the problem of suffering.[33]

In the next chapter we will look at the ways that people cope along that journey and how coping influences the development of posttraumatic growth.

CHAPTER 6

Paths to
Posttraumatic Growth

WE ALL HAVE OUR own approach to coping with stressful situations. Imagine it has been a difficult day at work. You feel stressed because you are not meeting deadlines. Tempers are beginning to fray in your team. Failure may damage your future chances of promotion.

What should you do? Look at the situation, as if from a distance, and work out your next move? Consult a colleague for advice? Gather more information so as to make a more informed decision? Take a walk to get some air—and possibly some perspective? Have a few drinks that evening to relax? Perhaps watch a favorite television show to help forget the problem altogether?

All of these behaviors are coping methods. *Coping* is broadly defined as the behaviors and thoughts through which people attempt to manage stressful situations. Psychologists have attempted to understand the different ways in which people cope, such as turning to others for advice, gathering information, going for a walk, using alcohol, watching television—the list of ways in which people cope with stressful situations is wide-ranging indeed. But whether any particular way of coping is helpful or not depends on the outcome a person is trying to achieve.

Broadly speaking, there are two methods of coping: *approach-oriented coping*, in which people concentrate their efforts either on changing the situation or on managing their emotions; and *avoidance-oriented coping*, in which people ignore the existence of the situation or their emotions.[1]

The question of how people cope following stressful and traumatic situations has been one of the most researched topics in psychology over the past thirty years. And the most prevalent finding, by far, is that avoidant ways of coping are the most problematic.[2] But as we have seen, the tendency toward avoidance is fundamental to posttraumatic stress.

Consider the case of Veronica, who was driving home from a shopping trip just before Christmas with her daughter Ruth in the passenger seat beside her. They were laughing and listening to one of Ruth's CDs. Suddenly, the car in front of them rolled over. As if in slow motion, Veronica watched it turn before crashing into the barrier, landing on its roof in the road ahead. Her foot hard on the brake, Veronica was not able to stop in time. She smashed into the back of the car. It seemed like forever, she said, but it was probably only minutes before people had gathered around the car. In a dazed state she heard voices asking her if she was all right and if she could move. Looking over she saw Ruth slumped against the door, which had caved in on her side. Blood was everywhere amidst the broken glass.

Ruth died two days later in the hospital with Veronica and her husband, David, by her side. They were overwhelmed with grief. As days and then months passed, Veronica became increasingly distressed, her thoughts churning over and over. She was troubled day and night, ruminating over the fact that she had been the one driving. Veronica tortured herself with "What if's." What if she had been driving more slowly? What if she had been paying closer attention? What if they had not stopped for coffee before leaving the shopping center?

Such questions in the aftermath of a tragedy are common. But when characterized by intrusive brooding ruminations, they are especially upsetting. People often use avoidance strategies to avoid the emotions generated by these ruminations. Over the next few months, Veronica immersed herself in work, which took her mind off how she was feeling. She managed to switch off during the day by distracting herself with tasks, meetings, and a busy work life. This brought her some relief.

The truth is, a little bit of avoidance can be helpful, protecting us until we are ready psychologically to confront a traumatic experience. Indeed, researchers at Stanford found that higher growth in the first months after 9/11 was related to higher use of denial as a coping strategy. Several months later, however, higher growth was reported among those who reported an increase in acceptance and positive reframing as their ways of coping. The researchers concluded that while denial is not likely to be growthful in the longer term, there is a difference between pathological denial and healthy denial. Early on, denial likely reflects the sheer incomprehensibility of what has happened: People know that the event actually took place, but they say things like "I can't believe this has happened" and "Surely this can't be real." Such moments of denial, they speculate, are healthy to the extent that they allow people to control the speed at which they face up to what has happened, thereby limiting the possibility of being psychologically overwhelmed. Elisabeth Kubler-Ross and David Kessler put it this way: "We experience our losses in our own time and in our own ways. We are given a beautiful grace in denial. We will feel our feelings when it's time."[3]

As noted, avoidance might even be helpful. Take the example of someone with cancer. Avoidance of thoughts about possible outcomes (such as death) might be adaptive if it allows the person to engage in practical behaviors such as seeking treatment. But avoidance of the fact of cancer itself—proceeding with life as if the cancer did not exist—can be detrimental as it might prevent the person from seeking treatment.

On the other hand, when avoidance is the only coping method for a prolonged period of time, problems begin to pile up. This is what happened to Veronica and David. David began to feel cut off from her, as she had started to stay late at work. And Veronica was not able to communicate to her husband what she was feeling. Distressed and confused, she avoided reminders of the accident and was unable to talk about her feelings of guilt and shame—feelings that she did her best to bury. As time passed, their relationship became increasingly strained. Veronica moved into a separate bedroom. David did not understand the process of avoidance that Veronica was locked into. He pleaded with her to talk to him. He wanted to understand what was going on, but his presence served as a continued, painful reminder to Veronica. The more he asked, the more Veronica withdrew into her own private world.

In the evening she would brood. She began to drink more than usual to numb her feelings, pouring herself two or three glasses of wine rather than the single one she used to have. On edge, she was always irritable and quick to cry. A year passed. Veronica and David were leading increasingly separate lives.

As more months went by, David was at his wits' end. He could not understand why Veronica was behaving as she was, and why she wouldn't talk to him. Now they were living apart. David eventually filed for divorce and began legal proceedings to end the marriage. For Veronica and David, the trigger was the death of their daughter—but it was their own avoidant ways of dealing with the situation that led to the breakdown of their marriage and to their increasing distress.

If Veronica had been able to confront her emotions earlier and replace her ruminative brooding with reflective rumination—and if David had better understood the process of avoidance that Veronica was going through—perhaps the outcome would have been different. Veronica and David were not aware of posttraumatic growth and the path one needs to take toward it, so they ended up only adding to their existing burden of distress.

This story is not unusual. Avoidance prevents people from dealing with their problems and working through their emotions. Veronica's experience demonstrates how prolonged avoidance can become a downward spiral. Avoidance is the major roadblock to recovery, slowing the process of posttraumatic growth. But as we have seen, avoidance is a common reaction to trauma.

Avoidance coping is most likely when a situation is highly distressing and the person perceives it to be both unchanging and uncontrollable. Trauma cuts us to the core, exposing the stark truth that we are fragile creatures who ultimately face death. Trauma also exposes us to ourselves, to our strengths as well as our limitations, and that, too, can be a shocking revelation that we do not want to face up to, and we seek to assimilate the new trauma-related information. Not surprisingly, people often deal with the realities that trauma reveals to them by avoidance.

Yet such avoidance is likely to lead to greater difficulties if it persists. It is all too understandable that people would seek to avoid reminders that are distressing and numb themselves from the emotional pain they are experiencing. But getting locked into the spiral of avoidance can preclude the possibility of moving on from trauma. This is precisely the stage when it is most important to move on to other, more approach-oriented coping strategies. Approach-oriented strategies involve facing up to what has happened, dealing with how we are feeling, and managing difficult situations differently.

There are two types of approach-oriented coping—task-focused coping and emotion-focused coping. *Task-focused coping* addresses the practical problems to be solved after trauma. *Emotion-focused coping* refers to a variety of strategies we can use to help us confront and manage our emotional distress.

One person who has mastered approach-oriented coping strategies is Michael Paterson. Three weeks after getting married, Michael, a member of the police force in Northern Ireland, was on duty in a high-risk part of Belfast. He was in the front passenger seat one morning when an Irish Republican Army rocket hit his Land Rover, followed by gunfire. Severely injured, Michael was rushed to intensive care. He survived, though his right arm was amputated just above the elbow, his left arm just below.

More than twenty-five years later, we sat together in a café in the university area of Belfast, surrounded by students lounging on sofas, working on their laptops, chatting, and drinking cappuccinos and lattes. Young people today live in a Belfast that is very different from the one Michael and I lived in decades before. Now, it is well-lit, with a vibrant nightlife. Although the sky is still often grey, we are both thankful that the truly dark days of political violence in Northern Ireland seem to have come to an end.

Michael can still recall his stay in intensive care back in 1981. He knew that he had lost both his arms but had already started planning how he would drive using his artificial limbs. In his mind he always knew he was going to drive again.

The same approach informed his life since then and his recovery as well. Once out of the hospital and in physiotherapy, he was determined to live again. He started circuit training, swimming to build up his muscles, and meeting with a psychologist who provided him with further support.

Michael's unique situation required that he use *task-focused coping* in order to learn to function again in the world. Researchers measure task-focused coping by asking people to rate statements such as "I concentrate my efforts on doing something about it," "I do what has to be done, one step at a time," "I try to come up with a strategy about what to do," and "I try to get advice from someone about what to do."[4] The important point to emphasize here is that this way of coping is associated with greater posttraumatic growth.

People's coping strategies vary according to their appraisal of the situation.[5] Those who believe that their situation will not change unless they do something about it, that change is desirable, and that they have control over the situation tend to deal with their trauma through task-focused coping, whereas those who believe that their situation cannot be changed tend to resort to avoidance as a way of coping.

Bear in mind that personality plays a strong role in determining how trauma survivors will appraise their situation. Some people are habitually avoidant in their ways of coping, while others are more inclined to deal with their problems head on.

Following trauma, people usually seek support from others. This tendency is probably hardwired into our evolutionary biology: When we are wounded, we retreat to the safety of our community for protection. In addition, people have a compelling need to talk after trauma. Psychologist William Stiles has described the need to talk when we are distressed as arising naturally, much like a fever does after physical infection. It is the mind's way of healing itself.[6]

Social support is critical, whether it comes from family, friends, or professionals. And the help it provides can be practical as well as emotional. Stressful situations call for both types of support: Every trauma survivor needs to talk with someone who is able to listen attentively, offer appropriate advice, and provide practical help when necessary—and, importantly, is able to do so in a way that meets the survivor's basic psychological needs for autonomy, competence, and relatedness.

Talking through experiences with supportive others allows us to convert upsetting traumatic experiences into posttraumatic growth. Like hands shaping a piece of modeling clay, conversation transforms the meanings that we make about our experiences. Through conversation, we are able to allocate blame and praise more objectively, seek new perspectives, correct incorrect perceptions, and find new insights.

The efficacy of this support matters. People with higher levels of social support, defined not by the number of people available to them but by the quality of their relationships—such that they nurture the survivors' needs for autonomy, competence, and relatedness—are more likely to report growth.[7] Social support is probably at its most valuable when it motivates people to take responsibility for their lives.

But while support of any kind is usually regarded as helpful, family and friends, despite their best intentions, may sometimes be unhelpful in terms of the way they provide support. They might offer us advice when all we want is to be listened to. They might encourage us to talk when all we want is to sit in silence. They might try to stop us from crying when crying is all we can do. Indeed, they might leave us feeling criticized when what we need is to feel accepted. In such instances, social support is less likely to help us on our path to posttraumatic growth.

The path can be damaged by social support that does not prompt survivors to take an active role. For example, researchers have found that HIV-infected men with a partner have a harder time adjusting than HIV-infected men without a partner. The reason, the researchers suggested, is that having a partner might encourage dependency and adherence to a "sick role," which in turn foster poorer social functioning and ill health.[8]

Seeking social support from others is an important coping strategy. It falls within the range of coping strategies that I earlier referred to as *emotion-focused coping*. Whereas task-focused coping is important when the situation needs to be changed, emotion-focused coping is what we need to do when our distress is overwhelming, as this form of coping helps us manage our feelings.[9] Various emotion-focused coping strategies can be useful, such as physical exercise, relaxation, talking things through with others, and actively focusing on the positive. Indeed, research suggests that exercises that ask us to deliberately think about the things in life that we are appreciative of can be helpful. People who are more appreciative tend to have more adaptive ways of coping.[10] Looking for the positives can allow people to gain a sense of control and mastery over their circumstances and help them restore their sense of self-esteem, thereby fostering a hopeful outlook.

Michael told me how he found hope in Douglas Baader's autobiography, *Reach for the Sky*. As a young man, Baader lost both his legs in a flying accident. Nevertheless, he was determined to walk again and sought to learn how to use his prosthetic limbs, persevering until he was able to walk unaided. But what was amazing was that he didn't stop there. He was also determined to fly again. Baader ended up becoming a top Royal Air Force fighter pilot in World War II. For Michael, he was a role model.

It was a combination of task-focused and emotion-focused coping that helped Michael deal with his loss and to move forward in his life. Today Michael has a doctorate in psychology, is a practicing clinical psychologist, and runs his own psychology business in the leafy suburbs of Belfast. He specializes in therapy for people who have experienced trauma. A few years ago, he was awarded the Officer of the Order of the British Empire (OBE) medal in recognition of his achievements. Michael's story reminds me of a well-known quote by Aldous Huxley: "Experience is not what happens to you; it's what you do with what happens to you."

Another specific emotion-focused strategy entails turning to religion. Evidence suggests that religion is often helpful to people. Those who are religious can find a deepening of their faith after trauma. In a study performed after 9/11, religious people reported an intensification of their spiritual growth.[11] Indeed, for such people, turning to their faith can be a helpful way of dealing with their emotions. One reason for this finding is that religion helps people elicit social support.[12] As Rosie, a survivor of breast cancer, told me: "As soon as I let someone at my church know of my illness, there were people praying for me. It is hard not to feel valued and closer to people who are showing so much care for you."

Another reason is that religion provides people with a sense of meaning. Rosie put it this way:

> Some people sent encouraging passages from the Bible. The one that kept cropping up was from Philippians 4: "The Lord is near. Do not be anx-

ious about anything, but in everything, by prayer and petition, with thanksgiving, present your requests to God. And the peace of God, which transcends all understanding, will guard your hearts and your minds in Christ Jesus." The bit about thanksgiving was what helped me to see all the things that I had to be thankful for. I thought hard about how I wanted to spend the rest of my life, which I now no longer took for granted. I feel as if I've had two lives, before the cancer, and after. I live for now. There is a saying that yesterday is history, tomorrow is a mystery, and today is a gift. That's why it's called the present.

A third reason is that religion provides people with rituals they can use to mark events in their lives—a process through which they can find both support and meaning. Rituals are very important when moving through trauma, whether they are personal rituals that are unique to us and our families or common rituals such as remembrance days.

Yet, to be most effective, emotion-focused coping strategies must utilize our emotional intelligence. *Emotional intelligence* refers to the ability to (1) perceive emotions, (2) access and generate emotions so as to assist thought, (3) understand emotions and emotional knowledge, and (4) reflexively regulate emotions so as to promote emotional and intellectual growth.[13] Indeed, the efficacy of our emotion-focused coping can be heightened if we know how to use emotional expression skillfully. When we talk to friends and family about how we are feeling, or seek support from them, we need to be able to express ourselves in such a way that we do not inadvertently drive them away. In short, we need to be emotionally intelligent about how we present ourselves to others and what we can expect from them.

A good example of this principle was provided by a study that surveyed a group of people who had encountered a variety of stressful and traumatic situations. They completed questionnaires that measured posttraumatic growth as a function of three variables: their use of emotional expression such as venting their emotions to others, their use of social support as a way of coping, and their emotional intelligence. The researchers found that those who scored the highest in emotional intelligence *and* who expressed their emotions exhibited the highest levels of growth.[14]

The lesson here is that we must use our emotional intelligence to determine which form of coping is best suited to our particular situation. For example, if we have supportive friends who are willing to listen to us, emotional expression might do us a lot of good. But if the people we are trying to talk to are judgmental or distressed themselves or simply not interested, we may come out of the conversation feeling guilt, blame, or embarrassment. Thus we need to be able to judge who we can confide in, what is appropriate to share, and when to hold back. This is particularly true in circumstances involving primal emotions such as fear, rage, anger, shame, and guilt. Such emotions need to be dealt with or, as we have seen earlier, they can lead to a downward spiral in which problems intensify. Sometimes, despite the damage we are doing to ourselves, we find it hard to loosen our grip on destructive emotions. Rage and anger can be particularly harmful. We need to know when to act on our emotions and when to loosen our grip on them. Michael, for instance, was actually forgiving of those who were responsible for the loss of his arms; he even took part in reconciliation meetings with ex-members of the Irish Republican Army. If instead he had become consumed with rage and anger, it is unlikely that he would have managed as well as he did.

But if some degree of emotional intelligence is an important prerequisite for successful emotion-focused coping, what about those who are at the opposite end of the expressiveness spectrum? Some people struggle to identify and describe their feelings, have difficulty distinguishing between feelings and bodily states, and suffer restricted imaginative processes. *Alexithymia* is the term that describes this condition. Derived from the Greek, it literally means "no words for feelings." People with alexithymia experience emotions but experience great difficulty explaining to others how they are feeling. They are unable to give depth and detail to their accounts beyond a feeling of being upset or bothered.

Alexithymia is not necessarily a problem in itself, but when paired with adversity it can lead to trouble. People with alexithymia are unable to translate how they are feeling into words. As a consequence, they often experience their emotional states as physical problems—as fatigue, unwellness, neck pain, and so on. Their ability to work through trauma is thus severely limited, and they struggle when trying to elicit support from friends and family.

Research studies show that, compared to people who have an avoidance coping style, individuals who use active task-focused and emotion-focused coping strategies generally do better. These are the people who are most likely to report posttraumatic growth.[15]

In short, successful coping requires flexibility. Like riding a bicycle, which involves knowing when to shift your weight, when to bear down on the pedals, and when to hit the brake, coping is a skill that can be learned.

For people who struggle to muster the appropriate coping skills, professional helpers can offer instruction in techniques such as relaxation training, identifying new thinking patterns, and monitoring and managing anxiety. A study performed in 2006 examined one such instruction program: a cognitive-behavioral stress management program for women who had recently been diagnosed with and treated surgically for early-stage breast cancer. A ten-week course, it aimed to reduce stress, teach cognitive and behavioral coping strategies, increase social support networks, disprove myths about the illness, encourage relaxation exercises, promote hope, and facilitate the expression of emotions in a supportive group atmosphere. On average, participants found the course useful. Nine months later, they reported that they were feeling less depressed and had begun to experience posttraumatic growth. The women who seemed to get the most out of the course were those who were less optimistic at the beginning.[16] One might imagine that it is the less optimistic people—who see the situation as outside their control and thus take less action to change it—who stand to benefit most from such training in terms of increasing their repertoire of coping skills.

Another group program for female breast cancer patients ran for twenty weeks. Each weekly session consisted of a ninety-minute session in which participants discussed their experiences, existential issues of threat and uncertainty, and problem-solving techniques and were taught new coping skills and relaxation techniques. At the end of the program, the majority of participants reported experiencing posttraumatic growth.[17]

Participating in physical activity following physical trauma such as cancer may also facilitate the growth process. Kate Hefferon is a researcher
who has studied the role of exercise with breast cancer survivors. She
found that exercise allows women to regain physical strength, gain a new
identity, achieve a sense of mastery over the body, and participate once
again in "normal activity," all of which were seen by the women themselves as important reasons for why exercise was growthful. She also suggests that exercise is helpful because it distracts attention and prevents
the person from ruminatively brooding on their illness.[18]

In the context of recovering from trauma, flexibility refers to a person's
ability to use different coping strategies in response to changing situations. Inflexibility, on the other hand, refers to the tendency to repeat
certain coping strategies regardless of the situation. We often get caught
up in patterns: It can be difficult to stand back from what we are doing
and reflect on how well our coping strategies match the intended outcome. To be flexible, we need to have a repertoire of coping strategies to
select from.[19]

As we have seen, coping strategies can take many forms: positively
reinterpreting a situation, distracting ourselves, venting our emotions,
seeking practical support, actively dealing with the problem, denial, religion, emotional support, planning what to do, blaming ourselves, accepting the situation, exercise.[20] But the healing value of any particular
coping strategy depends on its appropriateness to the task at hand.

To study this principle, psychologists use the Functional Dimensions of Coping Scale, a questionnaire that asks people to report what
activities and/or thoughts they have used to deal with their traumatic
event. The participants write down their answers, indicating whether
they, for example, turned to friends to discuss the nature of the problem, stepped back from the situation for perspective, used relaxation
or meditation, kept busy, and so on. Next, they answer questions about
whether their approach (1) helped them to manage the upset caused
by the event, (2) helped them deal with the problem, or (3) distracted
them from dealing with the problem. The participants then rate their
answers, providing a rare means of objectively gauging the usefulness of
various coping strategies.[21]

Whether a particular coping strategy is effective also depends on the fit between people's appraisal of the reality of their situation and their appraisal of their coping efforts. For instance, because religion can give people a sense of meaning, those going through divorce might find prayer helpful, whereas this strategy is not likely to be effective if they are out at sea and the boat is filling up with water. In the latter instance, a more task-focused strategy might prove more effective.

The key to successful coping is ultimately flexibility. It is by remaining flexible that we are most likely to find ways of coping that allow us not only to overcome our problems but also to deal with difficult emotions and to re-author our life stories. As noted, a wide range of possibilities is available to us: Talking things through, seeking support, turning to religion, and so on are helpful because they allow us to make sense of our experiences—specifically, by looking at them from different perspectives, seeking new solutions, and, ultimately, constructing a new understanding of ourselves that can accommodate what we have learned.

But people vary in their flexibility as copers. For example, some individuals hold rigid attitudes toward expressing themselves emotionally, even though doing so would be beneficial to them. A questionnaire that psychologists use to measure this trait is the Attitudes Toward Emotional Expression scale. Respondents are instructed to read four statements—"I think you should always keep your feelings under control," "I think you ought not to burden other people with your problems," "I think getting emotional is a sign of weakness," and "I think other people don't understand your feelings"—and then to rate how much they agree with them. Those who indicate agreement with such statements are less flexible in their emotional coping strategies and, as further research has shown, tend to have more psychological problems than those who indicate disagreement.[22]

All of us must explore our individual attitudes toward emotional expression. Becoming cognizant of our blocks may end up helping us later in life, when it comes time to contend with trauma.

Posttraumatic stress may well be the engine of growth, but in order to enable that growth to take place, survivors must steer themselves in the right direction using active coping strategies.

Doing so might seem easy, but in practice it is not. Trauma and stress often undermine our ability to think clearly. This is one reason people resort so frequently to avoidance. Clinical experience and research demonstrate the importance of intervening in the "avoidant spiral," so as to show people like Veronica new ways of coping and to give people like her husband, David, information about the consequences of trauma so they know what to expect. But no coping strategy can serve as a one-size-fits-all remedy. Rather, as I pointed out earlier, the key to successful coping is flexibility—the ability, in spite of the pressure and difficulty of trauma, to match the coping strategy to the demands of the situation and, equally important, to draw upon active coping strategies when it matters most.

First, however, trauma survivors must accept that the direction of their life is their own responsibility. One woman, for example, told me that she woke early one morning after a night of restless sleep and got up to look at a picture of her children.

> In the silent, wee hours of the morning, I sat staring at their picture and began to sob. Through my sobs, I heard the real voice of wisdom I believe we all possess. It was my voice, the voice that knows me best, but a voice that had become muted. Guess what. No one is coming to change the situation. No one will rescue you. No one can. It's up to you. Find your strength. I realized that as long as I remained a victim of this incident, I too made my family a victim. My anxiety could only teach them to be anxious. I was robbing them of happiness and a positive outlook on the world. I had come to the intersection of intersections. I could choose to end my life or I could choose to live. I needed to live for my family—and, later I understood most importantly, for myself.

Taking responsibility for the direction of one's recovery and growth is the most important first step in dealing with posttraumatic stress. Viktor Frankl thought that this was what made the difference between those who survived the Nazi concentration camps and those who did not—in other words, that survival was at least in part the result of the prisoners' inner decisions about their future. Thus, even under such dire circumstances as an extermination camp, we *all* have the power to decide what will become of ourselves; at the very least, we can choose to retain our dignity. As Frankl wrote:

> Man is ultimately self-determining. What he becomes—within the limits of endowment and environment—he has made out of himself. In the concentration camps, for example, in this living laboratory and on this testing ground, we watched and witnessed some of our comrades behave like swine while others behaved like saints. Man has both potentialities within himself; which one is actualized depends on decisions but not on conditions.[23]

What Frankl urges us to realize is that it is not what happens to us that determines our reactions but, rather, the meaning we make of what happens to us. Someone else who understands this is Terry Waite. In 1980 he successfully negotiated the release of several hostages in Iran as an envoy for the Church of England. In 1987 he traveled to Beirut, Lebanon, to secure the release of other hostages who had been taken by an Islamic Jihad organization. He agreed to meet the captors who promised him safe passage, but they broke their promise and took him hostage. It was not until 1991 that he was released, after spending four years in solitary confinement, chained, beaten, and subjected to mock executions. "I said three things on release: no regret, no self-pity, and no sentimentality. I tried to turn the experience around. Suffering is universal; you attempt to subvert it so that it does not have a destructive, negative effect. You turn it around so that it becomes a creative, positive force."

Meaning is not something out there that is given to us; it is something we give to ourselves. We do that through stories.

Human beings are storytellers. It is human nature to make meaning of our lives by organizing what happens to us into stories. We live our stories as if they were true. We tell stories to understand what happens to us and to provide us with a framework to shape new experiences. We are immersed in stories throughout our lives. We are told bedtime stories while we are growing up. Later on, we watch movies, listen to the radio, and read novels and newspapers. We also tell our own stories. We talk to our partners when we get home about the day we've had. We listen to their stories. Through interaction with others we confirm and disconfirm each others' stories. Our stories help us to construct self-understanding. They help us to bind together our thoughts, feelings, and behaviors in a way that is continuous with our view of ourselves and our past history. Stories surround us at the social level. Think back to how stories of Vietnam shaped the meanings of trauma for those returning from the war. Culture-driven stories shape how we all tell our own personal stories and influence our sense of what stories are legitimate to tell. Religion is a powerful force in this regard. And when trauma happens, the stories we tell have the potential to render our pain significant, and to give meaning to an otherwise meaningless experience.[24] A few words skillfully combined can be powerful enough to bring a nation together. One need only think of Winston Churchill's stirring speeches during World War II and how they undoubtedly shaped resilience in the population: "You [Hitler] do your worst, and we will do our best."[25] Or of John F. Kennedy's oft-quoted "Ask not what your country can do for you; ask what you can do for your country."[26] Likewise, each of us uses words to create meaning and a sense of purpose and direction in our lives.

As noted in the previous chapter, trauma creates a rupture in a person's life story. Assumptions about ourselves, our place in the world, and our expectations about the world are shaken, even shattered, leading to outcry. "Why me?" "How could this happen?" "I don't know who I am anymore." Indeed, trauma has the effect of rendering our life stories obsolete—and because we base our sense of who we are through the stories we tell, we feel that we are losing our very identity. Thus it is only through telling *new* stories that we are able to rebuild our sense of self—to reconstruct an understanding of who we are, our place in the world, and what our expectations of the world are.

The stories we tell reflect not only our personalities but also our cultural context. Different cultures have different ways of looking at the world: Some place importance on a sense of community; others value spiritual and religious views; still others emphasize personal responsibility. Our meaning making is inevitably influenced by this dominant discourse, regardless of what form it takes.[27]

When people experience trauma, they are troubled by their memories, but they do not recall events as if they were replaying a video. On the contrary, the process of recovering such memories has become disturbed and the contents of the memories are distorted. Rather than simply recalling what happened to them, they must first interpret it, and it is this interpretation that they will ultimately remember. Through *storytelling*, therefore, people first comprehend what has happened to them and then understand the significance of what has happened.[28]

Culture provides a forum for this kind of storytelling in the form of memorials such as Yad Vashem, the Holocaust Memorial in Jerusalem; and the Vietnam War Memorial in Washington, D.C. Indeed, this is why societies have days of remembrance and why rituals and ceremonies are so important for trauma survivors.

Ultimately, we seek meaning in our experiences. Once we find it, meaning provides us with the strength to move forward. Viktor Frankl discusses the story of one of his patients, an elderly doctor who, two years after the death of his wife, remained distressed. Frankl asked the doctor what it would have been like had he died before his wife. It would have been awful for her, the doctor replied, as she would have suffered terribly. Frankl then pointed out that her suffering had been spared, and that the cost of this was that the doctor himself had to take on the burden of suffering. This was a brand-new way of looking at what had happened. The doctor shook Frankl's hand and left the office with a new sense of meaning that allowed him to bear his suffering.

The stories we tell ourselves are the pathways through which we make sense of our lives, construct our identities, and establish why we choose to live our lives one way and not another. Through storytelling, we create understandings that increase our voluntary control over our memories and resolve the tension between preexisting assumptions and new trauma-related information. These outcomes can be accomplished either through stories of assimilation or through stories of accommodation.

Working through trauma takes place at three levels: first, in the stories that people tell in order to make sense of their experience; second, in the

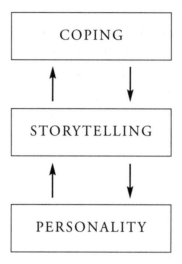

FIGURE 6.1 Relation Between Coping, Storytelling, and Personality. Storytelling provides the pathway to growth.
Source: Adapted by author.

ways that they choose to cope with these retold experiences; and, finally, within their own personalities, which both dictate their approach to coping and are changed as a result.[29] (See Figure 6.1.)

The psychologist Professor Donald Meichenbaum has shown that stories are the pathway through which coping exerts its influence.[30] He has explored what individuals tell themselves and others and how the way we choose to understand events in our lives shapes the way we behave. For example, stories that we tell which adopt the view that we are victims, that we are mentally defeated, and that the world is unsafe, unpredictable, and other people untrustworthy, are associated with higher levels of distress. But stories that construct meaning, in which we view ourselves as survivors and even thrivers and that establish hopefulness in us, will lead towards growth.

The stories we tell ourselves will "work their way down," transforming our personalities—first our autobiographical narratives (our life stories), then our personal goals, values, and priorities. Knowing this, we can choose to tell stories that are to our benefit.

Perhaps what is most characteristic of the process of posttraumatic growth is how it can bring about a realignment of our life stories, and our goals, values, and priorities, with our personality traits, such as extraversion and neuroticism, creating greater coherence across these three levels of personality.[31] Like Jane who we met earlier for whom the battle with breast cancer forced her to question the values by which she was living her life and to seek a new match between the various parts of her personality. She was able to reorder her interests and priorities in life in such a way as to be more consistent with her deep-seated personality traits. By this definition, posttraumatic growth is about becoming more authentic and true to ourselves.[32]

Seen this way, posttraumatic growth is not simply about coping, or about the things that people say about themselves: It refers to changes that cut to the very core of our way of being in the world. Posttraumatic growth has to do with the way we greet the day as we wake in the morning, the way we brush our teeth and put on our shoes; it reflects our attitude about life itself and our place in the world. Indeed, posttraumatic growth is deeply rooted in our personalities.

The process of posttraumatic growth arises out of posttraumatic stress and the resultant stories we tell ourselves. The speed with which this cognitive processing takes place is influenced by complex interactions between our personalities, our ways of coping, and our social context. For some, the process is impeded such that powerful emotions are channeled into destructive rather than constructive directions. Changes in personality can indeed be negative if the stories people tell themselves are overly dark in tone. And if feelings of anger, rage, resentment, or frustration are triggered by malicious or careless behavior on the part of others, such emotions can readily escalate into destructive behaviors such as seeking revenge, becoming overly hostile and defensive, or emotionally closing down.

Still, for most trauma survivors, there is at least a spark of growth. Coupled with the right coping activity, this spark can take the form of far-greater improvement of outlook and personality. The key to enabling such growth is to take control of the stories that survivors tell themselves, re-author these stories, value the positive changes that ensue, and begin to put these changes into action in their lives.

PART III

PUTTING THE GROWTH MINDSET TO WORK

Be who you are and say what you feel
because those who mind don't matter
and those who matter don't mind.

DR. SEUSS

CHAPTER 7

Nurturing Growth

ONCE A YEAR, those of us who teach in universities don our colorful academic robes for the graduation ceremony. It is a celebration, and a day full of hope for the future. One by one, the new graduates step up onto the stage to receive their degree certificates. Though most are in their early twenties, they represent a wide variety of nationalities and ethnic groups. Some shy students almost run past the podium, snatching their certificate as they go. Others are more leisurely, dramatically bowing and soaking up the applause of their friends and parents. It is a wonderful day for university staff members who have gotten to know these young people over such significant years of their lives.

This year, in the midst of writing this book, my mind wandered as I sat watching the procession of young people. I began to wonder about what will unfold in all of those young lives. What if each of us had an invisible mark on our foreheads, signifying the contents of our future—perhaps a green circle for a future absent of adversity and a red triangle for upcoming tragedy? Imagine we all knew that these marks were there from birth, though concealed from view. No matter how hard we strained to see the marks, they would remain obscure.

The real question is, Would we want to see the marks if we could? Would we want to know what will befall us in our own lives? What about the lives of our relatives and friends? And if we could see the marks of those around us, what would we do? If we knew that loved ones were marked for misfortune, and we had the power to change their red triangle to a green circle, knowing what we now know about post-traumatic growth, would we? When I ask people this question, without exception they say that they would choose to remove the mark and save their loved ones from a life marked by tragedy. As I would myself.

But unfortunately we do not have that choice. The one certainty in life is that things change. Adversity strikes unexpectedly. From personal tragedies of loss and illness to collective traumas of disaster and terrorism, all of us will at some point have to face the challenge of change.

As we have seen, trauma disrupts our personal stories. And when that happens, it can become the defining feature of our lives. So how do we deal with difficult events that change our lives?

Decades of research have shown that, when confronted by change, many people struggle to cope. They become distressed and have difficulties functioning at home, at work, and in their relationships—which brings us to the central message of this book: Although the road to posttraumatic growth may be paved with emotional pain, most people manage to adapt well over time and many go on to experience considerable benefits in terms of what they learn about themselves, how they relate to other people, and what life means to them.

The core idea of the theory of the shattered vase is that humans have a natural impulse to grow psychologically.[1] But this natural impulse can be thwarted; it can go into hibernation. Then, when adversity comes along, shattering the assumptions of everyday life and freeing up our natural motivations, can we begin to grow anew. Following trauma, it is this life force that needs to be harnessed.

If posttraumatic growth is to take place, we must be active agents in the creation of our own lives. It is through storytelling that we ultimately make sense of our experiences, piece together what happened to us, assimilate information that is concordant with our views of self and the world, and accommodate other information that is discordant—while at the same time rebuilding our worldview and our understanding of ourselves.

Posttraumatic stress is the engine of posttraumatic growth, but as we saw earlier, the engine can overheat. For those who are suffering from PTSD and whose lives are blighted by troubling intrusive memories, emotional numbness, avoidance behaviors, and an inability to concentrate and think clearly, it may be hard to imagine the *future*—much less the possibility of posttraumatic growth. The pathways ahead are overgrown. For such people, professional help can be quite beneficial. Indeed, there are therapies available that can help to clear those pathways ahead.

Trauma-focused cognitive behavioral therapy (TF-CBT) can help people deal more effectively with PTSD. TF-CBT draws from a variety of techniques to help people deal with their upsetting memories, avoidance behaviors and emotional numbing, and problems of arousal and anxiety. Generally speaking, it focuses on identifying the ways in which people's thoughts, emotions, and behaviors are interconnected. The idea is that how we think influences how we feel, and thus how we behave, so by changing our thinking habits we can change how we feel and behave. Likewise, by practicing changing behavior, we can change how we think and feel.

TF-CBT is conducted over a relatively short period of time, usually eight to twelve sessions over a few months. Someone who has experienced multiple traumatic events might benefit from a longer period of therapy. People suffering from PTSD can find it difficult talking about what happened to them and how they feel. In some cases the details are highly personal, perhaps embarrassing to the person, and it might take several initial sessions before the client feels comfortable enough with the therapist to talk in detail. The therapist's first step is to understand the patient's symptom patterns so as to formulate an understanding of what the blocks are in order to develop a treatment program. Often there is an educational component in which patients are given an explanation of PTSD to help them understand what they are going through. This can be useful as people with PTSD may be so overwhelmed with memories, images, and thoughts that they interpret their symptoms as signs that they are going crazy. Reassurance that it is common to feel as they do is welcomed.

For individual patients, treatment programs are tailored to their needs. For instance, people might be taught relaxation exercises to help them deal with anxiety, or they might be shown how to manage their upsetting feelings, or be taught new ways of coping. But there are broad similarities across treatment programs; commonly those with PTSD will benefit from facing up to their traumatic memories.

Memories that occur during trauma are stored differently from memories of everyday events. There are two memory systems: verbally accessible memory (VAM) and situationally accessible memory (SAM).[2] SAM is triggered by reminders but cannot be consciously accessed. And VAM contains trauma-related information that can be consciously accessed. Talking therapies can be useful in the treatment of PTSD because they help trauma survivors work through VAMs; however, until SAM-related problems are resolved, such people often find it difficult to engage in talking therapies. Resolving these SAM-related problems requires exposure therapies that can help extinguish conditioned fear responses among people who are stuck in heightened biological-alarm mode. Through exposure, they are encouraged to gradually begin facing their painful memories of the trauma in order to reduce fear and anxiety.

Exposure therapies are either imaginal (i.e., the patient talks repeatedly about the traumatic experience), in vivo (i.e., the patient is exposed to the situations or objects being avoided), or a combination of the two. Therapists may also use virtual reality (i.e., patients wear a head-mounted display that provides visual and auditory cues relating to the traumatic event). To avoid the risk of re-traumatization, it is important not to proceed too rapidly. The simplest way to do this is to gradually increase the frequency and duration of exposure to the feared situation. There are a variety of exposure techniques that therapists use. One of these, the rewind technique, requires patients to close their eyes and visualize two "films." First, they imagine watching the traumatic event unfold as if they were observing themselves from a third-person perspective, starting at a point in time before the traumatic event, when they were safe. Second, they imagine the first film being rewound back to the safe starting point. In the second film, however, instead of observing themselves from a third-person point of view, they imagine themselves in the film. Completion of the two films in sequence is indicated by the reopening of their eyes. Patients do not speak during this process, nor do they relate any details of the traumatic event to the counselor.[3]

Imagery rescripting is another technique in which patients are encouraged to think of their memories as "ghosts from the past" that can be creatively transformed into less distressing images. For example, they might be asked to imagine watching their traumatic event on TV, making it smaller or dimmer or further away, and then switching off the TV.

One of the most controversial techniques is known as eye movement desensitization and reprocessing (EMDR). EMDR is often included as part of TF-CBT. It is very popular among counselors and psychotherapists who work with traumatized people. EMDR literally owes its beginnings to a walk in the park. Its founder, Francine Shapiro, based it on a serendipitous discovery she made in May 1987: While walking through a park, she noticed that she was troubled by some disturbing thoughts, which "suddenly disappeared." She also noticed that when she tried to recall these thoughts, they were not as disturbing as they had been previously. Upon closer inspection of this phenomenon, she realized that during her walk her eyes had moved from side to side—and she speculated that this might have been a key factor in her ability to process the disturbing memories. Following experimentation with more than seventy subjects, she published her first paper on EMDR in 1989. In a typical EMDR session, therapists pass their hand back and forth across the patient's field of vision. Alternatively, they might tap the patient or use flashing lights or some other stimulation.

In essence, EMDR involves pairing memories/disturbing thoughts and the resultant emotions with repeated saccadic (rapid and rhythmic) eye movements, resulting in desensitization, or reduction, of the distress caused by the memories. During this process, the therapist asks questions such as "Have you noticed the image change at all?" "Has it become blurred, sharper, or more vivid?" "Has it moved further away?" "Has it changed color?" "What bodily changes do you notice, compared to when we started?" and "Has your anxiety decreased, remained the same, or gotten worse?"

EMDR appears to be most useful in cases of "single-episode trauma," such as a car crash or an assault, but it has also been used successfully with survivors of longer-term accumulative trauma such as sexual abuse. Although the reason it works is not fully understood, research suggests that EMDR is often very helpful for people suffering from PTSD.[4]

At first patients may find exposure therapies distressing. The therapist will guide them through the exercises, ensuring that at each step patients face up to their memories enough to be helpful, but not so much that it makes the problems worse. For example, for someone troubled by several different upsetting memories, the therapist may inquire which is the least upsetting and make that memory the focus for the first few sessions. Then when the patient is able to talk about that memory without being emotionally overwhelmed, the procedure is repeated with the next most upsetting memory. Over time, the patient becomes able to talk about, be reminded of, and visualize the trauma without undue emotional distress.

It is common for people who have been through a traumatic experience to want to avoid thoughts, places, activities, or people who remind them of their experience. Given the wide range of traumatic experiences that a person may encounter, attempts to cope through avoidance can amount to an extensive list. Avoidance behaviors stop patients from getting on with their lives and if left untreated can lead to further problems later on. A particular exposure procedure often used by psychologists to help people who are avoidant is *desensitization*, whereby patients are exposed, a little at a time, to the thing that triggers fears in them and that they are avoiding. For example, someone who is afraid to use public transportation might first be asked to imagine stepping onto a bus. Over one or two sessions, she might mentally visualize herself walking to the bus stop, seeing the bus coming closer, and getting onto the bus. Then, in subsequent sessions, the therapist might accompany the person on an actual bus trip. Over time (assuming that these trips are uneventful), the associations in her mind between bus rides and danger are extinguished.

Consider the case of Susan, who was driving home from work when a speeding car collided with a heavy truck behind her. In the subsequent chaos, her car was spun across the highway into the path of oncoming cars. Though not injured, she had to be cut out of her car by emergency workers, a process that took almost thirty minutes.

After a few days of recuperation, Susan returned to work using a company car. Over the next few weeks, although she was driving more cautiously than usual and avoiding highways as much as possible, she found herself becoming increasingly anxious while inside the car, even as a passenger. By the fourth week she had almost stopped driving altogether.

This inevitably affected her work and social life. She avoided talking about the accident and gradually cut herself off from friends and relatives. Susan's avoidance and anxiety were adaptive in the short term. In the longer term, however, her avoidance only worsened her problem. Realizing what she was doing, but finding it hard to do otherwise, Susan sought professional help.

For Susan, recovery entailed, first, just sitting in a car. Once she was comfortable doing this, the next step was to sit in a car with the engine running; then to drive very short distances in familiar settings; then to increase her driving time and distances in unfamiliar settings, building up to driving on unfamiliar roads in quiet times and, eventually, to driving on familiar roads at busy times.

Desensitization can be very helpful to people with PTSD. Sometimes it can be performed by patients themselves, without any professional help. An example is provided by Patricia, a trauma survivor who developed a fear of going outside that was interfering with her life. She knew she had to confront this fear, and she did so gradually, working up to it in stages. First she stepped out into the garden; then she walked to the end of the street; then she made it as far as the local shops; and, eventually, she was able to take the train to the city for the day.

Through desensitization, patients can set small goals that allow them to avoid overwhelming themselves. They overcome the first goal, and then move on to the next goal—each one representing a manageable step toward overcoming what they are frightened of. Patricia, for instance, read up on trauma and made the decision to do only those things she knew she could accomplish, one step at a time, gradually building up to making a trip into the city. The old adage about "getting back on the horse after being thrown" comes to mind here. Yet it can be difficult for some people to do this for themselves.

TF-CBT can help people deal with the problems of PTSD, but it is not designed to facilitate posttraumatic growth. As people become better able to manage their distressing emotions, to confront their memories without becoming emotionally overwhelmed, and released from the downward spiral of avoidance, they often become more interested in understanding the significance of their experience. Once the problems associated with PTSD have diminished to the point where patients are able to think more clearly, it is likely that those parts of the brain concerned with making sense of what has happened will come back "online." They may still be considerably distressed, but they are less troubled psychologically than before and more capable of functioning in their daily life. Now, it will be increasingly important for them to search for meaning. Something more than traditional TF-CBT is needed at this time.

At this point there is a shift from thinking about how to help alleviate PTSD to how to facilitate posttraumatic growth. The American Psychological Association has created educational materials that provide advice for people who have encountered adversity on best ways of coping:[5]

- making connections with others
- avoiding seeing crises as insurmountable
- accepting that change is part of life
- moving toward goals
- taking decisive actions
- looking for opportunities for self-discovery
- nurturing a positive view of oneself
- learning from the past
- maintaining a hopeful outlook
- self-care

As we have seen, more active ways of coping are beneficial. Therapy can be helpful in teaching new coping skills—but therapists cannot teach people meaning. Meaning is unique for each person. What they *can* do is to support patients in their own search for meaning. What people need are companions alongside them in their journey to rebuild their lives.[6]

All therapists agree that it is important to develop a healing relationship, but approaches on how to do so differ. Therapists using TF-CBT often take a doctor-like stance in which their role is to correctly diagnose the disorder so as to be able to prescribe the correct treatment. The relationship is seen as a means to an end, and the responsibility for a cure is held by the doctor. They believe that a healing relationship should have a utilitarian function in order to gain rapport with the patient so that the patient will be more able to engage with the treatment program. In contrast, when we are considering posttraumatic growth, my view is that the relationship itself is also an important vehicle for healing.

Therapy for posttraumatic growth is seen not as a doctor-patient relationship but, rather, as a new journey undertaken by two people—a journey in which the therapist serves as an experienced guide and the client is ultimately responsible for what route is taken. Clients are their own best expert on what direction to go in.[7]

It is this latter position that I advocate—the therapist as experienced guide—as most effective in aiding posttraumatic growth. This view is influenced by the core idea of the theory of the shattered vase—that people are intrinsically motivated toward posttraumatic growth—and supported by decades of psychotherapeutic research showing that what benefits people seeking help is not so much what technique the therapist uses but, rather, the quality of the client-therapist relationship that develops.[8]

Most crucial of all is the extent to which clients perceive themselves to be valued, listened to, and understood—in such a way as to support their basic psychological needs for autonomy, competence, and relatedness. A therapeutic relationship that meets this objective provides clients with a forum in which their intrinsic drive toward growth is given free rein.

My role is to help clients to explore the meaning and purpose they attach to their lives. One of the most important aspects of recovery from trauma is recognizing that life has changed and that old ways of looking at the world no longer seem to make much sense. Survivors have to rethink the ways in which they live their lives and rethink what is important to them. They need to take time to reflect on what they have learned from their experiences.

Attempts by the therapist to push the process of posttraumatic growth along can actually derail it. Indeed, since part of the posttrauma recovery process is to be avoidant of reminders, therapists who pressure their clients to remember can inadvertently drive the clients away. It is not uncommon for trauma therapists to open their waiting-room door to greet their clients for morning appointments and find the waiting room empty. By definition, traumatized people are at times avoidant of therapy. For this reason, they must be gently led to believe that they, and only they, are responsible for their own journey toward reconfiguration.

People who feel valued, accepted, and understood are more likely to open up, to honestly discuss their difficulties, and to feel capable of re-authoring their stories than those who keep their inner worlds hidden for fear of being judged. And those who are locked into negative emotional states such as anger, shame, guilt, or envy are especially unlikely to arouse compassion in others. The challenge of being a trauma therapist is to be able to offer such people a relationship in which they feel safe enough to open up. If they are going to reveal their darkest secrets and their most hidden feelings, they have to feel very safe indeed. In some cases I have met with clients for months and even years before they opened up about what was really troubling them.

I worked with Anna for two years. Together we explored many issues having to do with her relationships, her childhood, and the divorce of her parents. She was very angry. We did some anger management and discussed new coping skills for dealing with situations that triggered her anger. However, although I thought there were probably other issues beneath the surface that needed to be confronted, I waited until she was ready to introduce them. I felt sure that doing otherwise would be counterproductive—that it would damage the trust we were building together. On the anniversary of our first meeting, Anna was silent for the first twenty minutes of our session. Then she told me, through tears, about how her stepfather had sexually abused her throughout her childhood. It was a secret she had kept all her life, and this was the first time she had told anyone—and it was not something she was going to talk about to anyone at the first meeting. It would take time for her to feel safe and to be able to trust.

In my own clinical work, I think of myself as someone who helps to facilitate growth, not as someone who creates growth. Therapists cannot tell people how to make meaning out of what has happened. This is an important point. Seeking meaning following adversity might be a universal human characteristic, but the meaning a person finds must be unique to that person and his or her situation. Therapists cannot provide the meaning. It is up to trauma survivors themselves to move toward new understandings. After all, it is their experience, not mine—and I am in no position to say what meaning they should make of their life. On the contrary, people need to be open to the range of meanings a situation offers them and to select the one that seems most truthful to them.

We know that actively approaching difficult situations and emotions is helpful. Yet therapy does not usually proceed in an orderly fashion. In many cases, clients will express some of their feelings but then find that the intensity is too much for them. They may retreat until they are ready to express their feelings again. Such fluctuations are normal. Indeed, therapists must remain aware of these fluctuations so as to let the clients take the lead, directing their own rate of progress.

Research also shows us that major factors in successful psychotherapy are the qualities of the clients themselves—their resources, coping ability, sense of control, self-determination. Thus, therapy is at its best when it empowers people to take responsibility for their own recovery and helps them realize that the tools necessary to undertake the journey are in their own hands. For professionals accustomed to thinking of clinical success in terms of helping people reduce their distress and become happier, this shift in mindset can be difficult. Therapists must adopt a broader view that encompasses the idea of growth as an important clinical process in its own right, not as a utilitarian marker for some other criterion such as an increase in emotional well-being or a reduction in posttraumatic stress.

Survivors of trauma need to find a therapist who is able to sit with them and listen to their accounts of trauma and their struggles to move forward. Most of all, they need a therapist who will listen compassionately. Rather than pushing the idea of growth, therapists must allow clients to notice it in their own time. Otherwise, they risk placing a burden of expectation on themselves and their clients. That is not what this is about.

No one who is going through a crisis wants to hear that they should look on the bright side—or feel blamed for not taking a more positive attitude. That is simply not the message of this book,[9] and no serious psychological therapist would ever promote such a perspective to their clients in the midst of their distress.

Matt is a man in his late twenties. It was his first day of holiday vacation from his job as an executive in a large company. He and his wife were preparing for a relaxing long weekend at home before their trip away to visit friends, when his mother called with the news that his brother had been found dead. He had hanged himself. Matt went into a state of shock. He recalls driving to the family home that afternoon with his wife. She drove. "I couldn't drive," he told me. "My legs were like jelly." For the next few days, his family gathered together to make arrangements. But a year later, he still has a moderate level of posttraumatic stress. He feels that somehow he should have been able to prevent his brother from killing himself.

Although he did not see his brother hanging, he can picture it in his mind. He tries to push the image away, yet it still haunts him. "You can't make it not happen, it's always there," he said. "It's part of your life now." One thing that makes this difficult for him is trying to understand the significance of what happened. His brother left no note behind, and even today Matt struggles to understand his brother's suicide.

Matt has undergone changes as a result of this experience, and some of these changes have left him stronger as a person. And I can see that he has become more capable of dealing with life. His priorities have shifted too. He now visits his aging parents more regularly, despite it being a long drive, as he realizes that he probably only has a few years left with them. His relationship with his wife has deepened too. But these are observations I make in the midst of what he tells me about how he is struggling.

I am interested to hear him talk about his sense of having become stronger as a person, but the emotional pain is still too real and he has no "space" yet in which to acknowledge his posttraumatic growth. In no way would I want to diminish the significance of his experience by pushing him to accept it as "growthful." There is no need for me as a therapist to label it, or to explain that some positives seem to have come out of the experience. He will not be able to take that message in until he is ready—and then he will tell me about what he is doing differently in light of his trauma.

Sensitive therapists know that life is hard, that moving on after adversity is a struggle. They know that their task is to be patient, to let people move at their own speeds and in their own directions. They follow where the clients go—and if the clients begin to notice growth, and to label it as such themselves, then the therapist may shine a light on it so the clients can pick it up, look at it from different angles, and make their own decisions as to what to do with it.

Sometimes, in the midst of the struggle, people will report posttraumatic growth that seems illusory to the therapist. At that point, therapists might sometimes feel tempted to step in to correct the client. Yet even growth that seems illusory can, as we have seen, be a helpful way of coping. It is not growth in the sense of a genuine personal transformation, but it may nonetheless be helpful to the client at that time in bolstering their sense of self-esteem, fostering a sense of control, and giving hope for the future.

Positive illusions are not the same as the genuine personal transformations that arise through the resolution of discrepancies between preexisting assumptions and new trauma-related information. People seem best placed to achieve such transformations when they are able to reflectively and nondefensively engage with their experiences. The therapist who creates a safe space for the client where they do not feel judged but valued is more likely to facilitate this process in the client. By correcting the client whose reports seem illusory, this very process may be disrupted.

Mild positive illusions are common and are known to be related to healthy psychological functioning. So while positive illusions need not be encouraged by therapists, there is no reason to challenge the validity of clients' reports of growth; rather, therapists should simply acknowledge the clients' experience. The exception to this may be if the illusions are extreme and have the potential to lead to harm.

Used within the broad framework described above, the Psychological Well-Being Post-Traumatic Changes Questionnaire (PWB-PTCQ) can be used to check on a client's therapeutic progress (see Appendix 2).

The PWB-PTCQ is a new questionnaire designed to overcome some of the problems inherent in previous questionnaires.[10] It can be used to assess the ways in which people experience themselves as having changed. It includes eighteen statements divided into groups of three to measure self-acceptance, autonomy, purpose in life, relationships, sense of mastery, and personal growth. The highest that people can score on the PWB-PTCQ is 90, indicating that they experience themselves as having become much more self-accepting, autonomous, purposeful, relationship-focused, masterful, and open to new experiences and the possibility of growing even more. In general, scores over 54 indicate the emergence of posttraumatic growth, and scores over 72 indicate high levels of growth.

Of course, few people score at the very top of the scale. Sarah, for example, received an overall score of 74, which suggests that she has experienced a great deal of positive change. Her strongest subscale scores were related to self-acceptance, purpose in life, autonomy, relationships, and personal growth, while her relatively low score on sense of mastery indicated some room left for improvement. Michael, whom we met in Chapter 6, had a similar overall score of 76 but a different pattern of scores on the subscales. The PWB-PTCQ is a helpful tool for tracking positive change in clients. It is also useful for unobtrusively opening up conversations with clients about how they have changed.

To illustrate, during therapy, I usually ask clients to complete the PWB-PTCQ at two-week intervals alongside a standard measure of posttraumatic stress.[11] I explain that we are required to monitor our work with clients and that is why I will ask them to complete questionnaires regularly.

One man, George, was overwhelmed emotionally with memories of a traumatic event that had occurred when he was caught up in a violent demonstration as an overseas AID worker in Rwanda. When we met, he was on sick leave from work. At the first session, George's scores on the posttraumatic stress measure were high (scores above 35 are taken as indicative of PTSD) and his scores on the PWB-PTCQ indicated an absence of growth (see Figure 7.1).

We met for another fourteen sessions over seven months, during which questionnaires were generally completed every two weeks (we missed session seven). The first few sessions we focused on techniques to help him manage his emotions better when reminders would trigger his memories and on coping skills to combat avoidance. Gradually, as he became less avoidant, he engaged in exposure exercises to confront his memories. By the ninth session, he was functioning well enough to engage more fully with other issues, and we began to discuss many of the benefits that he felt had arisen due to his experience as an AID worker.

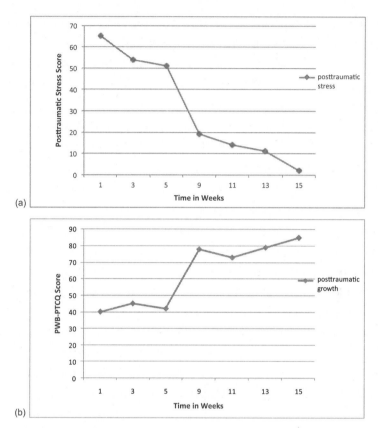

(a)

(b)

FIGURE 7.1 (a) Decrease in posttraumatic stress over time.
(b) Increase in posttraumatic growth over time.
Source: Adapted by author.

By the thirteenth session, scores indicated that dramatic changes had occurred on the PWB-PTCQ. He had also returned to work at this point. Several weeks later we met for a final session to check in with each other about how things were, by which point the changes on the questionnaires had been maintained and he was still at work and doing well.

What is also illustrated by Figure 7.1 is the changing relation over time between posttraumatic stress and posttraumatic growth. Early on, the pattern shows very high levels of posttraumatic stress accompanied by an absence of posttraumatic growth. Toward the end of the sessions, the pattern switches and there are very high levels of posttraumatic growth accompanied by an absence of posttraumatic stress. But what is interesting is that near the midpoint in our sessions, when George was still suffering from moderate levels of posttraumatic stress, the posttraumatic growth begins to be seen. This pattern is consistent with the evidence we reviewed earlier—showing that in the midst of working through trauma, moderate levels of both posttraumatic stress and posttraumatic growth may co-exist.

New ideas and a number of therapeutic techniques are developing about how to facilitate posttraumatic growth.[12] One of these is *compassionate mind training*, which promises to be particularly helpful for individuals who have difficulties with self-criticism and feelings of shame—a common occurrence among traumatized people.[13] It is important for clients to take time to reflect on how they are overly self-critical and to learn how to be more compassionate toward themselves. This therapy involves asking clients to compare how they respond to themselves with how they would react to a friend or a relative in the same position. By doing this, people recognize how they are much harsher toward themselves than to others. Then, through practicing responding to themselves in the same way they do toward others, people learn to be more compassionate toward themselves. Self-directed compassion can have a tremendously beneficial effect on their well-being.

Narrative exposure therapy is another relatively new therapy. First developed for use with refugees, it involves exposure coupled with testimony therapy. The idea is to help trauma survivors construct a chronological account of their biography, which includes the trauma, and then to transform this fragmented report into a coherent narrative. Narrative exposure therapy is increasingly being used in other contexts, and research suggests that it is able to facilitate posttraumatic growth.

Therapy is usually conducted one-on-one between therapist and client, but group approaches can be helpful too. In a study of parents who lost a child through suicide, participation in support groups was found to be related to personal growth among those whose loss happened at least five years before.[14] But whether participation led to personal growth, or personal growth led to participation, is not conclusively known: Longer-term survivors often assume caregiving roles at support groups. Perhaps "giving back" becomes a concern of survivors who are further along in the grieving process.

As we have seen, support groups and these other types of therapy can help us understand how previous experiences have shaped us as people—

and that by making sense of our past we can take more control of our future. Indeed, it is often through therapy that we become aware of things we were not previously aware of before. Whether through individual therapy, or through group approaches, one of the ways that change arises is through the stories that people tell.

At the heart of the stories we tell are metaphors. The American Psychological Association guidelines also encourage people to think in terms of metaphors, such as imagining one's recovery as riding a raft down a river.[15] I think this is a particularly useful metaphor, as it subtly conveys the message that there is no going back to life exactly as it was.

People can get stuck in the desire to go back to how things were. As one woman told me, "It's like I was on a train and the train had stopped. Instead of staying on the train I had got off and was waiting for another train to take me back. But the thing is, I realized that there was no train that went back. There is no going back. When something happens like what happened to me, things can never be the same again. They just can't. Life is different. You change. You have to stay on the train. When we try to go back, that's when we get stuck. You can't escape things happening to you in life. What we have to do is confront our experiences, and learn from them."

The metaphor of the train is useful, too. It deftly converts discussion of "wanting to go back" to discussion of more productive hopes for moving forward. I often share this metaphor with clients—although I warn them that it might not fit their situation. I am cautious because metaphors are powerful medicine. Therapists have to be wary of the subtle dangers of their profession—of how easily vulnerable people can be influenced.

A more useful approach is to help people find their own metaphors. Mary, for example, wrote about how having her own home allowed her to nurture herself and helped bring about change:

> Something else that has had a big impact is owning my own home. I bought my house about 18 months ago. It is a 3 bed mid-terrace with 3 floors (4 including the cellar) and a south facing yard at the back which produced some great sunflowers this summer! Having a home has given me a great sense of stability and security. . . . In a way I see it as a

metaphor for my life. When I bought the property it was very run down and neglected. Every room needed total renovation. . . . It's while I'm fixing up my house, I'm fixing up myself too.[16]

Another example is provided by Sarah, who grew up in a mountainous region where forest fires are common:

I saw them [the fires] only as destructive and unfortunate, but later was educated about the benefits of them. Believe me, when you see one in full flame, the word *benefit* does not come to mind, nor does it in the immediate aftermath. In the midst of trauma there is rarely benefit derived from the trauma itself, hence the word *trauma*. Yet forest fires serve as catalysts for new growth. The new growth occurs amongst the destruction. [This destruction] doesn't serve or benefit fauna or flora in the short term. Animals and their habitats are destroyed as are people and their homes. Yet it is only through the natural forest fire that some trees proliferate and habitats can rebalance. Just as the forest fire catalyzes growth, so does trauma. However, growth takes place along with consequences. A forest fire spurs growth in a positive direction (new flowers and trees) but also causes consequences such as mudslides. The PTSD symptoms—reliving sounds, tastes, and other sensations—are the mudslides. The meaning and strength derived from the struggle [are] the new flora and fauna.

In sum, metaphors allow people to regain a sense of control over their lives. They provide a way of constructing meaning around a traumatic event—a meaning that links the event to their past and to their future. Metaphors provide the essence of the script for trauma survivors' new stories that will enable them to re-author their lives. One way to explore the metaphors we use is through the expressive writing techniques that have been extensively developed over the past two decades, and which offer people a valuable way to work through trauma.

It was in the late 1970s that Professor James Pennebaker began his research on the healing value of emotional expression.[17] He carried out a random survey of 800 people. One question he asked was whether they had a traumatic sexual experience before the age of seventeen. Fifteen percent said that they had. This was an important finding in itself, but Pennebaker also found that those with traumatic sexual experiences before the age of seventeen were more likely than the other respondents to have physical health problems. Intrigued, he wanted to find out more.

He took an opportunity offered to him by *Psychology Today* magazine to conduct a survey of its readers, developing new questions for this purpose. Twenty-four thousand people answered the survey. Traumatic sexual experiences prior to age seventeen were reported by 22 percent of the women who responded and 11 percent of the men. These people were more likely than the remaining respondents to be admitted to the hospital and to have high blood pressure, ulcers, and a host of other physical health problems. Now he was on to something. Why should this be? Over subsequent years Pennebaker did more and more surveys. Consistently, they showed that having a trauma is a bad thing for people, but—and this was the turning point in his research—it was when people kept the trauma secret that it was toxic to health.[18]

As an experimental psychologist, Pennebaker wondered whether it was possible to bring people who are keeping secrets into the laboratory and get them to talk. This is how he did it: Students volunteered to come to the university to take part in an experiment. By the flip of a coin, students were divided into two groups. Those in the first group were asked to write about something that troubled them emotionally—just to "let go" and write about their deepest emotions. Students in the second group were asked to write about a non-emotional topic, such as what they were going to do over the next few days—but just the facts. For fifteen minutes at a time, for four consecutive days, students had to write about their topics. They were told that their writing was confidential and anonymous, that they had to write continuously, and that they did not need to worry about spelling. Just write. Pennebaker was able to access university health service records as part of the study. What he found out when he did so was striking. Those who were in the emotional group were much less likely to visit the university's medical clinic over the next six months than the control group. Evidently, writing about one's emotions is a healthy thing to do.

This really was an amazing finding. How could writing about one's emotions for fifteen minutes a day make such a huge difference? In a further study, blood samples were taken from participants and sent to the lab to be examined for immune markers. This time, Pennebaker found that those who were allocated to the emotional writing group had far more aggressive immune systems than those in the control group. One possible explanation is that emotionally expressive writing helps people sleep better, which in turn boosts immune functioning. Over the next twenty years, evidence of expressive writing's helpfulness continued to pile up. Studies have found that it leads to reduced absenteeism from work, improved grade-point averages, and decreased respiratory problems. Similarly, research that has tested the effects of experimental disclosure in real-world settings has found that it helps unemployed engineers find jobs faster, reduces posttraumatic stress among female caregivers, leads to fewer trips to the infirmary among incarcerated men, reduces distress among migraine sufferers, and decreases cancer-related doctor visits for breast cancer patients.[19]

In one experiment, breast cancer patients were divided into three groups. Those in the first group were instructed to write for twenty minutes a day for four days over a period of three weeks about their deepest thoughts and feelings regarding their experience with cancer (the expressive group); those in the second group were asked to write about the positive benefits that had accrued from their experience with cancer (the positive group); and those in the third were instructed to write about the facts relating to their cancer and its treatment (the facts group). Three months later, both the expressive and the positive groups were found to have had fewer cancer-related medical appointments than the facts group. There were also psychological advantages. Those in the expressive group showed lower levels of psychological distress—particularly those women who were low on cancer-related avoidance. (It makes sense that asking those who avoid exploring their deepest feelings to do just that is probably threatening. For this reason, we might expect expressive writing to be more useful for those who are low in avoidance.) For those who were avoidant, positive writing seemed beneficial—perhaps because it is less difficult than asking them to engage in full-blown emotional expression. In short, expression of emotions and benefit-finding seem to be effective ingredients for better health in cancer patients.[20]

One explanation for these findings is that people get distracted when they try to think through problems in life that affect them emotionally, whereas writing compels them to stay on track (as well as to dig down deeper into their emotions). Yet this benefit is related not to the act of expressing emotions per se but to how it is done. What seems to be most helpful is the use of positive words such as *love, happy, care,* and *good.* There is a big difference between saying "I'm not happy" and saying "I'm miserable." Using too many negative words is not beneficial. Nor is using too few such words. Rather, trauma survivors should use a moderate amount of both negative and positive words. Generally, studies have shown that those who express a positive-negative ratio of around 3 to 1 do indeed benefit psychologically.[21] Another important factor is using words that express causality and insight. Causality words include *because, reason, cause,* and *effect.* Insight words include *meaning, know, consider, understand,* and *purpose.* Both sets of terms help people construct stories that allow them to find meaning.

In writing this book I have used the stories of people I have met to illustrate my points, changing their names and details to make them anonymous. In some cases I have asked them to read extracts of what I've written. A few have said to me that they found it interesting to see their stories related as if written by someone else, and they began writing about their experiences as if they were that someone else. And for Sarah, in particular, writing in the third person allowed enough distance to actually look at some of the words she had avoided for years:

Creating a story seemed to help relieve me of concern over perfect accuracy, seeing as how my memory of the event is obviously not completely clear. I dissociated during the event . . . and it all gets very confusing. There are parts I am very clear about and parts—especially my orientation to time—I only know from reports. I still tend to dissociate if I am asked what happened. . . . It seems I can't speak about it without reliving it. However, this is the first time I have written about it and the third-person format seems to be helpful and quite a release.

Yet Sarah also found third-person writing very tiring: "It does take its toll. I was very tired after writing just that little bit and I expect it will proceed slowly. But worth keeping at it as long as it isn't overwhelming and interfering."

Indeed, people need to approach such tasks in their own way and at their own speed. But regardless of how they proceed, it is vital that they find a way to construct meaning in their experiences through the stories they tell and the metaphors they use, whether through professional therapy, talking things over with friends and family, keeping a written diary of their reflections, or taking part in rituals and ceremonies.

Psychotherapeutically, building on the knowledge presented here, we are now in a position to help people to foster growth. But we must be careful not to be narrow-minded when it comes to defining what that growth should look like. Growth may lead to a more fulfilling and meaningful life, but it is not the same as simply being carefree and feeling good. Indeed, it is about living life at a deeper level of personal, interpersonal, and existential awareness.

An important finding from the research literature is that posttraumatic stress and growth can co-exist, and that posttraumatic stress itself appears to be the trigger for growth. Professionals who work with trauma survivors need to understand this point, as it has many implications for the different type of therapy they must provide.[22]

Successful clinical work involves understanding distress as the signpost for change, so that posttraumatic growth can remain the focus of the therapy. But this is a subtle process. The aim is not to "cure" trauma survivors but to grapple with existential issues alongside them.

On the one hand, such people are motivated to hold on to the stories that have served them well up to that point and that define who they are. On the other hand, they need to reconfigure their stories in order to accommodate the new trauma-related information. This can be a long and painstaking struggle. Through talking, people gain the experience of being heard and accepted by others, which is very important if what is being told has previously been a secret. People also get to learn that their story resembles that of others who have had similar experiences and who have survived—thus giving them hope.

Psychotherapists know this. One of their tasks is to provide people with a safe environment in which to tell—and retell—the story of their troubles without being judged. In the relationship that develops, clients are able to generate new meanings; in a very real sense, they become the authors of their own lives. This is the essence of therapy: deconstructing the story of one's life while simultaneously reconstructing a new story. It is also the essence of growth following adversity. Growth is the process of constructing a new narrative understanding of how adversity has shaped and transformed us, such that it becomes fundamental to our life story and defines who we are.

The healing forces of storytelling play themselves out not just at the individual level but at the community and even national levels as well. As just one example, consider how beneficial the PTSD diagnostic label has been for Vietnam veterans, survivors of sexual abuse and sexual assault, and victims of the Holocaust. In validating their "stories" this label has provided important social recognition as well as relief from the conspiracy of silence that surrounded them.[23]

Hence processes such as "truth commissions" and "war crime tribunals" are powerful tools for healing. As vehicles for the establishment of justice, they help to restore the dignity of trauma survivors and to reintegrate them into society.[24] Here, too, what is important is that people have the forum to re-author their stories in such a way as to make the events in their lives meaningful in some way.

What has become clear to me is that we cannot force people to grow. As a therapist I know that I cannot change other people. I can help my clients learn new things about themselves. I can share some of my own experiences. I can make suggestions. But ultimately they have to decide for themselves that they want to change. The point is that the driving force for change needs to come from the client, not from the therapist.

Trauma survivors may struggle with this notion, particularly if they have adopted an illness mindset and expect their therapist to "cure" them of a lack of meaning. Therapists working from a growth mindset can thus be faced with a paradox: In order to maintain a working relationship with their clients, they need to be perceived as operating from an illness mindset; otherwise, the clients feel shortchanged. The task of such therapists, then, is not to step into the illness mindset but to subtly and over time let the clients become the agents of their own change.

Generally speaking, the job of psychotherapy is to provide people with a space in which they can slowly dismantle their beliefs and goals and over time build new mental maps. It is also about helping people confront truths about themselves and the world. But in contrast to psychotherapy, which people enter into by choice, trauma comes out of the blue and abruptly shatters their mental maps. This "new information" is too vivid, powerful, and discrepant to be ignored, and survivors are essentially forced to change.

Thousands of professionals' livelihoods now depend on the PTSD diagnostic label. Clinicians use it to be able to obtain payment for their services, researchers study it, and the pharmaceutical industry develops new drugs as treatment for the psychological problems associated with it. One of my arguments in this book is that, on the one hand, the diagnosis of PTSD has been useful in terms of providing recognition of the extreme suffering that can be caused by trauma, but, on the other hand, the concept of PTSD has diverted attention from the fact that trauma can also be a springboard toward a transformed life. Both sides of the coin deserve attention.

For those who are struggling with posttraumatic stress, professional help can be vital to getting them back on track. It can teach new coping skills, ways of managing anxiety, and methods for dealing with the psychological effects of trauma. In fact, professional help is often the only option for people who are locked into a state of avoidance that prevents them from dealing with issues they need to deal with. Such people may also have difficulties concentrating, leaving them unable to think clearly enough to work out what actions to take. But while professional help can be valuable in helping people cope and manage their emotions, when it comes to transforming trauma and understanding the significance of it in their lives and how to move forward, people have to take responsibility themselves for the direction they will take.

CHAPTER 8

Conclusion

IN THE STORY OF the Wizard of Oz, Dorothy, the Tin Man, the Scarecrow, and the Lion defeat the wicked witch and return to the Emerald City. The Great Wizard has promised to fulfill their wishes if they defeat the witch. Dorothy hopes to return to Kansas. The Tin Man desires a heart; the Lion, courage; and the Scarecrow, brains. Cowering before the booming voice of the Wizard, Dorothy and her chums ask him to fulfill his promise. But by accident, the curtain falls away. The Wizard is revealed as a small old man speaking into a megaphone and pulling frantically at levers. It is all smoke and mirrors.

The Wizard realizes that his deception has been revealed. I'm not a bad man, just a bad wizard, he says. But Dorothy's chums insist he keep his promise. The Wizard presents the Scarecrow with a certificate, the Tin Man with a clock, and the Lion with medals. He is a wise man who knows that the human qualities of brain, heart, and courage cannot be given. As such, he offers his gifts allegorically. In giving these gifts he acknowledges that, through their trials and tribulations, what Dorothy's companions are seeking was always within themselves. During their adventures, the Scarecrow had admirably shown his brains, the Tin Man his heart, and the Lion his bravery. Not realizing that the gifts are only allegorical, Dorothy's chums dance with delight.

Too often we act like tin men, scarecrows, and cowardly lions, blithely expecting others to provide the solutions to our difficulties. These solutions are actually within us. When we struggle emotionally, professional helpers can aid us by offering advice, teaching new coping skills, and listening attentively. They can be experienced guides. But they cannot tell us what meanings to make or re-author our life stories for us: That has to come from us.

Many of the problems we face in everyday life require help from someone more expert than ourselves—from fixing the plumbing to getting medical treatment. But the mere fact that we rely on experts in other areas of our lives does not mean that the same is true for understanding how to move forward psychologically. Psychotherapy researchers know that at least as important as anything else is what the clients themselves bring to therapy—their motivation for change, the extent to which they keep on practicing what they learn in therapy when they leave the therapy room, and their effort to actively cope with their difficulties rather than avoiding them.

Ultimately, people benefit from taking responsibility for their decisions. As we have seen, Viktor Frankl believed that this attitude helped make the difference between those who survived the Nazi concentration camps and those who did not. Although the conditions were horrific for all, not everyone reacted the same way:

> In the final analysis, it becomes clear that the sort of person the prisoner became was the result of an inner decision and not the result of camp influences alone. Fundamentally, therefore, any man can, even under such circumstances, decide what will become of him—mentally and spiritually. He may retain his human dignity even in a concentration camp. . . . [I]t is this spiritual freedom—which cannot be taken away— that makes life meaningful and purposeful.[1]

The notion of growth following adversity has attracted the attention of scientists across the world.[2] The challenge is to understand that trauma paradoxically encompasses both shadows and light. Indeed, the dialectical forces of positive and negative, loss and fulfillment, suffering and growth often go hand in hand. The approach to trauma that I have developed embraces aspects of positive psychology that are designed not only to help people deal with their distress and difficulties but also to provide guidance in becoming more optimally functioning and leading more fulfilling lives. Indeed, as I suggested in Chapter 1, my aim is to move trauma survivors' outlook not just from −5 to 0 but from −5 to +5.

Yet the positive psychology approach has been disparaged by critics who misunderstand it as encouraging people to deny reality, to submit cheerfully to misfortune, and to blame themselves if they do not recover.[3] When applied to much of the popular self-help literature, this criticism has some validity. On the other hand, the ideas in the present book are based on scientific evidence. Studies show that, in dealing with adversity, people need to (1) confront reality rather than denying it; (2) accept that misfortune has occurred rather than submitting to it cheerfully; and (3) take responsibility for how they live their lives in the aftermath rather than blaming themselves for their fate.

Someone who illustrates these principles is Thomas Buergenthal. Here he writes about arriving for the first time in America to begin his new life:

> But as I stood at the ship's railing, fascinated by a sky drenched in the reflected colours of the myriad lights that illuminated the city, I was transported back to Auschwitz and the reddish-brown smoke bellowing from the crematorium chimneys. Suddenly, the life I had lived—Kielce, Auschwitz, the Death March, Sachsenhausen—flashed before my eyes. Right then and there I knew that I would never quite liberate myself from that past and that it would forever shape my life. But I also knew that I would not permit it to have a debilitating or destructive effect on the new life I was about to begin. My past would inspire my future and give it meaning.[4]

Thomas Buergenthal became an expert in international law and human rights. In his book *A Lucky Child: A Memoir of Surviving Auschwitz as a Young Boy*, Buergenthal describes his formative experiences as a child in the concentration camps. In 1939, as he and his family were fleeing Czechoslovakia for England via Poland, the train they were on was bombed by the Germans. Prevented from escaping to England, they joined other refugees who were walking to Kielce; it was here that they lived until they were later deported to Auschwitz. When the Soviets invaded Poland, the Germans evacuated Auschwitz. Separated from his parents, Buergenthal, along with two other boys, joined the infamous death march from that camp. By mere chance, these three were separated from the other children who were taken away to their deaths. Buergenthal survived the march and made it to the new camp, Sachsenhausen. Two of his frostbitten toes were later amputated, but he survived this camp as well, living there until the end of the war owing to the kindness of others. After liberation, he was mistaken for a Polish Christian and given shelter by the Polish army until he eventually reached a Jewish orphanage.

From these experiences, Buergenthal learned valuable lessons about humanity. He was able to redirect his emotional pain into action, becoming a member of the United Nations Human Rights Committee as well as a judge at the International Court of Justice at The Hague, where he worked against genocide in countries such as Rwanda and Bosnia. In *A Lucky Child*, he wrote:

> My childhood experience has had a substantial impact on the human being I have become, on my life as an international law professor, human rights lawyer and international judge. It might seem obvious that my past would draw me to human rights and to international law, whether or not I knew it at the time. In any event, it equipped me to be a better human rights lawyer, if only because I understood, not only intellectually but also emotionally, what it is like to be a victim of human rights violations. I could, after all, feel it in my bones.[5]

The message of this book is that we must seek the right balance between the light and the shadows of trauma.

On the one hand, in moving on from trauma we need to be wary of the tendency for diagnosis of PTSD to engender fixed ways of thinking. This embrace of PTSD can stop recovery in its tracks. Therapists have to be skillful in recognizing it among their clients, as months can go by without progress. In such instances the therapists are puzzled and the clients go away dissatisfied and disappointed. Yet, deep down, the clients are relieved. Diagnostic labels can become part of people—and the truth is, many people are reluctant to give them up. Unfortunately, the dominant professional discourse of trauma tends to position people as "helpless victims with a lifelong condition," so it is not surprising that many people latch on to this way of thinking. It is what they have been told is true. But the diagnosis of PTSD does not describe a lifelong condition. It describes a set of problems that a person experiences at a specific point in his or her life—one that, when understood properly, can be the engine of posttraumatic growth. But this "engine" can over-heat. And when it does, we need to stop and check the radiator, ther-mostat, pump, and antifreeze. The point I'm making metaphorically here is that, when confronted by adversity, we need to actively search for new emotion-regulation and self-soothing strategies so as to get our-selves running smoothly again.

The idea that posttraumatic stress is the engine of posttraumatic growth is all the more intriguing when we realize that treatments to alle-viate posttraumatic stress might inadvertently be thwarting the develop-ment of posttraumatic growth. Such a thought is highly speculative, but it deserves serious attention—particularly given the pharmaceutical in-dustry's interest in developing pills that diminish the symptoms of PTSD. Given the possibility that posttraumatic stress is a prerequisite for post-traumatic growth, it is an especially important question—one that de-serves concerted philosophical thought.

Which is preferable: going through the pain and discomfort of post-traumatic stress knowing that it is an existential journey to a richer life; or swallowing a magic pill that takes away your memories and leaves you with a life free of pain and discomfort, but at the expense of riches that might otherwise be gained?

But on the other hand, it is important not to place a burden of expecta-tion of posttraumatic growth on ourselves or others. People who are going through a crisis do not want to hear that they should "look on the bright side." Sensitive therapists would never promote such a perspective to clients who are in the midst of distress.

I do not mean to suggest that clients have somehow failed if they do not feel that positive benefits have accrued. After all, people don't live in a vacuum where their thoughts and behaviors have nothing to do with the world around them. I strongly believe that it is natural and normal for people to move in growthful ways following adversity, but I also realize that this is not an easy process to deal with on one's own.

Indeed, what we also need are social, political, medical, and legal institutions that recognize the paradoxical nature of trauma. It is of great importance to humanity in general that we learn more about what leads to resilience and growth at the level of societies and nations—and, equally important, how governments can most effectively intervene following mass disasters, accidents, and terrorist attacks to foster resilience and growth in large social groups.

Growth from adversity not only benefits individuals but can be transformative for entire nations. Nelson Mandela spent twenty-seven years in prison before going on to become one of the world's most revered statesmen. In his book *Long Walk to Freedom*, he wrote:

> The policy of apartheid created a deep and lasting wound in my country and my people. All of us will spend many years, if not generations, recovering from that profound hurt. But the decades of oppression and brutality had another, unintended, effect, and that was that it produced the Oliver Tambos, the Walter Sisulus, the Chief Luthulis, the Yusuf Dadoos, the Bram Fischers, the Robert Sobukwes of our time—men of such extraordinary courage, wisdom and generosity that their like may never be known again. Perhaps it requires such depths of oppression to create such heights of character.[6]

As individuals and as members of communities and societies, we must learn that life invariably brings trauma and adversity. Understanding how to foster resilience and growth must surely be subjects of urgency in the coming years. The reality is that we are all haunted by the ghosts of our past. Our memories shape us, and the powerful emotions sparked by the past resonate, signaling new meaning to us. This is a natural state of affairs.

Thus we need to learn to lead our lives knowing that adversity is always around the corner. When trauma strikes, we must be ready and resilient, prepared to confront stark realities, open to change, and oriented toward using our suffering wisely.

THRIVE:
Six Signposts to Facilitating Posttraumatic Growth

When we are no longer able to change a situation—
we are challenged to change ourselves.

—VIKTOR FRANKL

THIS POSTSCRIPT IS designed to offer readers guidance in managing their emotions and taking the first steps toward seeking growth. It is also intended to be useful to the relatives and friends of people who are in need of support following trauma. Included in the information presented here are some common reactions to trauma, the changes that people might experience, and exercises that might be helpful along the way toward posttraumatic growth.

Posttraumatic growth does not imply the absence of emotional distress and difficulties in living; indeed, such difficulties are common among people who have suffered trauma or adversity in their lives. What this term does imply is that it is possible through the struggle with adversity to come out on the other side, sometimes stronger, and more philosophical about life. Quite simply, life shapes us. Or, more accurately, what we *do* with what life throws at us shapes us.

Three key messages are especially helpful. The first is that you are not on your own. The second is that trauma is a natural and normal process. The third is that growth is a journey.

MESSAGE 1: YOU ARE NOT ON YOUR OWN

Everybody encounters adversity in life. Whether it is experienced personally or vicariously through the suffering of a relative or friend, there's simply no way to go through life without hitting an emotional wall at some point. Trauma happens to all.

Yet people often convince themselves that they are on their own.

There's no question that every kind of distress is unique. Everyone has their own story: the respected married doctor in the community who no one knows is having an affair with a man fifteen years younger and who is tearing herself to bits emotionally because of guilt; the young teacher in the car in front of us who is driving home from a consultation with his doctor, having just learned that he has a potentially fatal tumor and will be going in for a serious operation within the week; the quiet middle-aged woman at the checkout who was raped twenty-five years ago and still has nightmares about it; the older woman who for over fifty years has been haunted by memories of her child being stillborn; the man next to you in line at the bank who can't shake off the memories of what he saw and what he did while in combat five years ago. Yet, individual as every story is, what they all have in common is trauma itself.

One of the first and most important messages for survivors of adversity is that they are not alone. It's not at all uncommon to feel confused, disorientated, and chaotic. It's okay to seek help. More often than not, once we begin to share with others, we realize that they too have their own stories to tell.

MESSAGE 2: TRAUMA IS A NORMAL
AND NATURAL PROCESS

People may feel very frightened and confused following trauma and adversity. They may experience posttraumatic stress. Upsetting and intrusive thoughts and images may become an issue. They might also become emotionally detached and avoidant. Anxiety and depression may be a part of this experience.

Yet it is common to feel this way after trauma. Indeed, for most people it seems to be part of the healing process to go through this. Feelings of anger, shame, guilt, grief, sadness, and sorrow are also common. Related to these feelings are thoughts and images about what happened, what we or others did, and what we or they could have done; they run through our minds, sometimes just seeming to pop up out of nowhere. These intrusive thoughts and images can be deeply upsetting and hard to shake off. But just knowing that they are common reactions—and that over time for most people such feelings, thoughts, and images will subside—can be a comfort.

MESSAGE 3: GROWTH IS A JOURNEY

Sometimes it is useful to think of healing from trauma as a journey. Each step might be painful, but it can be more painful not to keep moving. Sometimes people begin to report posttraumatic growth along the way. Those who have confronted tragedy, horror, and adversity often emerge as wiser, more mature, and more fulfilled people, sometimes despite great loss and sadness. But in making the journey, people must be careful not to place too heavy a burden of expectation on themselves.

THE ROAD AHEAD

In the following pages I will explore these key messages and, along the way, offer some exercises and guidance that might be useful. There will be much to consider, and a number of activities to try. A caveat: Some people may be afraid of the consequences if they are asked to think too much about their traumatic experiences. As with any journey, when you know that the weather might turn, it's a good idea to bring along warm clothes, a number to call if you get stuck, a flask of hot coffee, and a spade to dig yourself out. So before I go any further, you might want to pack a few things.

The first thing is a rule: Don't do anything that you think you might not be able to handle *now*.

Sometimes the memories of trauma are overwhelming. If you experience intense emotions, become physically upset, or begin to panic, my advice is to stop reading this postscript. Then, when you come back to it, move forward at your own speed. Think about the issues being raised and how they relate to your own life, and if that becomes overwhelming, just stop, set the book down. You are in control. Take your time to try out the exercises and absorb the ideas in the book. Remember, having a sense of personal control over your recovery is important. There might be some things you do not feel ready to handle now, but in time, as you discover new strengths and develop new coping skills, this will likely change.

One particular tool you can use on your journey is *safe place imagery*. Think of an image that makes you feel safe and calm—as safe and calm as you can imagine. It can be somewhere real or imagined, indoors or outdoors, with other people, or on your own. Focus your mind on this image. Then focus on your body and your feelings of calm. Concentrate on your feelings of calm. Finally, think of a single word that captures this image—a word like *beach*, *trees*, or *mountains*. Practice using the word to bring up the image and your feelings of calm.

Often when I introduce clients to this method, they are a bit skeptical. "How can imagining I'm on a beach help me?" I tell them that each exercise is a building block in your recovery. By itself, imagining a safe place won't solve everything. However, until you can calm yourself down you won't be able to take on the next challenges. By learning to find a safe image for yourself, you will learn to calm your body down and take control of your thinking.

So, practice safe place imagery. Try it out a few times when minor irritations occur—when the printer stops working halfway through, when you can't find a parking space, when the train is delayed. Get used to your safe place before you tackle the bigger things. If you find your mind wandering when you try this technique for the first few times, don't worry: With some practice it will become easier.

Another useful technique for the journey ahead is to *ground yourself*. If you find yourself becoming anxious—overwhelmed with thoughts and emotions of what happened—and feel that you are losing touch with what's going on around you, you need to learn to ground yourself, so that you can bring yourself back to the present. One way to do this is to put your weight forward so that your feet are flat, pushing firmly against the ground. Feel your weight pressing down. Be present in this moment. Notice your surroundings. Listen to what's going on around you. Either out loud, or just to yourself, describe what's around you and what's going on. "I can see a cup in front of me. It's red with a picture and writing on it. It's sitting on a table covered in a black-and-white cloth. The table is in front of the window. Outside the window is the garden." Tell yourself, "I am here in this room. Those are memories from the past, about something that once happened but is over now. This is now."

As you practice these exercises, you will find your own words to use that work for you—and you will be ready for the journey.

SIGNPOSTS TO SELF-HELP: THE THRIVE MODEL

The THRIVE model consists of six stages, or "signposts." These are arranged in a logical sequence, moving from an awareness of your readiness to change all the way to actually changing your thoughts, behaviors, and emotional states. The key as you move from one signpost to the next is to keep doing the new things you have learned at each of them, so that you build up your repertoire of new activities. Each of the six signposts offers exercises that might be useful, but they are only suggestions for things you might do.

SIGNPOST 1: *Taking Stock.* Signpost 1 refers to the process of finding out which "goods" are on the "shelves" and which ones are missing and thus need to be obtained.

SIGNPOST 2: *Harvesting Hope.* At Signpost 2, you find the hope within yourself. Being hopeful about the future will give you the ability to see further down the track.

SIGNPOST 3: *Re-authoring.* At Signpost 3, you listen to the stories you tell yourself and open up to new ways of looking at things. It is here that you begin to move from thinking of yourself as a victim to thinking of yourself as a survivor, and then as a thriver.

SIGNPOST 4: *Identifying Change.* At Signpost 4, you monitor the changes as they begin to appear. To build up steam, you need to begin noticing positive changes as they occur within you.

SIGNPOST 5: *Valuing Change.* At Signpost 5, you nurture the positive changes you are experiencing. You might notice strengths, abilities, or interests that you were not aware of before—and as you do so, you need to value these changes for what they are, not for what else they might bring you.

SIGNPOST 6: *Expressing Change in Action.* Signpost 6 encourages you to begin to put the changes you experience into action and to begin making them part of your life.

That's THRIVE in a nutshell. You are now able to see what is ahead. Next, I will discuss each of the signposts in detail and show you how to put into practice the lessons you have learned.

Remember, if you begin to feel uncomfortable or anxious, use your safe place imagery, and stay grounded.

Signpost 1: Taking Stock

In the immediate aftermath of adversity you might feel overwhelmed by the prospect of being unable to handle your feelings. You might feel numb, empty, tense, confused, exhausted, or troubled with thoughts and recollections of what happened. You might have upsetting dreams and poor sleep. Maybe you feel distant from family and friends and disconnected from the world around you. Maybe you find yourself drinking to help you cope. Your work may be suffering, and you may find that you've lost interest in the usual things.

At a time like this, if people were to say to you that you ought to "look on the bright side," you would probably chase them out of the room! Looking on the bright side is the last thing you feel like doing. It might even be disrespectful for someone to suggest there is a positive side to what you have gone through. In addition, something inside you may resist the idea of healing or growth.

People need to take whatever time is needed to make their own sense of things. Toward this end, taking stock is critically important. After all, people move at different speeds. They have different circumstances, personalities, and ways of coping. For some people, processing grief, loss, and trauma lasts a few weeks; for others, months or even years. Those who have experienced a personal loss as a result of their trauma may need the most time of all to work through what they need to.

Trauma activates the part of the brain concerned with threat and thus blocks us from being able to think things through. Until we have calmed ourselves down physically, we will find it hard to mentally engage with our recovery. It is important that we first seek emotional equilibrium and distance ourselves from what has happened. Family and friends might rush in to offer support—and, indeed, this might be appreciated. But those offering help have to be aware that what people need above all is quiet, a sense of safety, and a feeling of being protected.

During trauma and the immediate aftermath, many people go on "automatic pilot," attending to everyday details—paying the bills, making sure that dinner is prepared for the children, and so on. In other words, they may be focused on tasks rather than on themselves. As one woman told me after the loss of her husband, "The sun still rises every morning, breakfast still needs to be made, and the work has still got to be done. Life doesn't stop for you." Traumatized people often feel as though they have only enough fuel to do the most urgent errands and that there is no capacity to do the extras. Their emotional state is one of those extras. It has to wait.

If this describes you, you need to redirect your focus to yourself. And to do that, you must first deal with the basics of taking stock. Let us consider each of these basics in turn.

Check that you are physically safe. You need to make sure you are physically safe. Are you in physical danger? Sometimes people feel so chaotic in the aftermath of adversity that they put themselves in danger by leaving appliances switched on, driving carelessly, crossing the road without looking both ways, and so on. Often it's because they are distracted. But in some cases that risk may be deliberate.[1]

In the words of one survivor of trauma: "I knew I was driving too much and I was still tired, but at times I just didn't care. I thought if I do kill myself, all this will just go away." If that describes you, take a moment right now to think about how you can remove yourself from danger and from being a danger to others. Would it be useful to take time off? Can you stay with friends or relatives? Is it possible to change your routine for a while? If you can't come up with a solution yourself, you need to seek professional help.

Check that you are getting medical, psychological, and legal help if you need it. Everyone's circumstances are different, but when people are vulnerable they need to have people around them who can protect them and shelter them in some way. In addition to emotional issues, trauma often leaves people with a long list of other problems to sort out. Family and friends might be able to help with some of these, but professional help may also be required. Seeking help is not a sign of weakness. People need to be able to reach out for help when they are vulnerable and lack the resources or expertise to help themselves.

Check that you are eating well. Good nutrition is important. Make sure you don't eat too much, but also make sure you get enough calories. Emphasize fruit and vegetables, drink lots of water, and avoid processed foods as these often contain too much salt and sugar. A good breakfast is important, and it's better to have several small meals throughout the day than one big meal at night.

Check that you are getting enough sleep. Getting to sleep and staying asleep can be difficult for people who have experienced trauma. A few tips: Avoid coffee in the late afternoon and evening, make sure not to eat too much in the hours before bedtime, do not watch TV in bed, and make sure the bedroom is completely dark. If you don't have curtains that thoroughly block out the light, obtain eye shades. Some people also find calming music helpful.

If you've followed these tips and are still struggling to sleep, try this: Make a list of ten things you need to do but keep putting off—such as completing your tax return, cleaning the bathroom, or tidying the back of the kitchen cupboards. Then, once you've gone to bed, give yourself thirty minutes to fall asleep, and if at the end of those thirty minutes you are still awake, get up and do whatever is at the top of your list. Or, if you fall asleep but wake up during the night and can't get back to sleep within fifteen minutes, get up and do whatever is at the top of your list. And, when necessary, do the same thing on subsequent nights. After a few weeks you should be sleeping soundly. If not, seek advice from your medical practitioner.

Stay physically active. The mind and body are intertwined. Your physical state affects how you feel. For that reason, it's important to stay active. You needn't go to the gym every day, but you do need to make sure that your body is active during each day. Can you walk instead of driving? Can you take the stairs rather than the elevator? Do think about engaging in exercise, depending on your physical condition.

Exercise is healthy in itself, of course, but it can also provide a distraction and free up your mind when it most needs a break. As one woman told me, "Just keeping fit gave me a focus and helped take my mind off things." But remember: Exercise should leave you feeling refreshed, not exhausted.

Make sure you keep pleasurable things in your life, and try to maintain your routines as much as possible. Though you may feel tired or unmotivated, as is common among people with posttraumatic stress, take time to do the things you used to enjoy, such as reading, gardening, listening to music, eating out with friends, or soaking in a luxurious warm bath. Perhaps you can even try something new occasionally. You might not be able to maintain your routines at the same level as before, don't let them slip altogether.

Practice learning to relax. All too often, people forget to breathe. Breathing is the key to relaxation. Take a moment to focus on taking slow, steady breaths. Your out-breath should be longer than your in-breath. As you breathe out, count to 11; then as you breathe in, count to 7. When you first get into your car in the morning, take a few minutes to relax before setting off. Also schedule regular times during the day to check in on your breathing.

Another technique for relaxation is the *body scan*, which is used by yoga practitioners. You can use it yourself to help you fall asleep. Sitting or lying comfortably, pay attention to one part of your body at a time. Starting with your toes, ask yourself: How do they feel? Pay attention to each toe in turn. Take your time. Move up to your ankles. How do they feel? Keep moving systematically around your body. Stomach, chest, arms, fingers, neck. Remember to take your time. Be aware of the sensations in each part of your body, then move on to another part, and notice how relaxed you begin to feel as you do this. You might find it helpful to tense each part of the body for a few seconds as you move through the scan.

Some people feel more comfortable with *mindfulness* practices, which, in contrast to relaxation exercises, do not call for deep or patterned breathing. For five minutes, simply focus on the air going in and out as you breathe. Notice how it feels and where in your body it is coming from. Don't try to change it; just appreciate how your normal breathing functions.

Another way to relax is to sit and focus your attention on one thing. Then note three things you can see at the periphery of your vision. Just note them. Take your time. Don't look directly at these three things. Then close your eyes and note three things you can hear. Then open your eyes and note three sensations in your body. Repeat these steps a few times.

And don't worry if you find that your mind is wandering at first. It's understandable. And, in any case, relaxation is a skill that comes with practice. Instead of berating yourself, simply notice that your attention has wandered and return to the exercise.

Practice self-compassion. After trauma, people may become critical of themselves, agonizing about what they should have done. They need to think things through, of course—but endlessly brooding over things doesn't help. If you find yourself doing this, practice some self-compassion instead.[2] (Consider putting yourself in a state of relaxation first.)

People often find it easy to imagine being compassionate toward others, but when it comes to themselves it's more difficult. Begin by thinking about how you would feel toward loved ones who are suffering. Imagine that they are feeling as you do right now. How do you feel toward them? Try to actually experience the kindness, warmth, understanding, and wisdom that you have to offer them. Now imagine looking at yourself as if you were in a picture. Imagine the look on your face as you feel compassionate toward your loved ones. Imagine the tone of your voice. How do you sound? Try speaking out loud as if you were talking to them, and listen to your compassionate voice. Now think about what you would say that expresses your concern and warmth for those individuals; imagine that you are helping them think about ways to move forward without judging. What is it you would want to say? Take some time practicing this compassionate image of yourself, rehearsing the words that you would use to express yourself.

When you are ready, introduce that "compassionate you" to the "suffering you"—the self-critical, avoidant you. Practice offering yourself the same compassion you would give to someone else. When you notice yourself lurching into being self-critical, shift back into your compassionate body state and offer yourself the same understanding, warmth, kindness, and wisdom.

By learning to be compassionate to ourselves, we give ourselves the ability to soothe ourselves and to calm our rattled threat systems. This ability is vital to our moving on. But it requires practice. Whenever you have five minutes to spare, picture yourself as the compassionate person of your imagination.

Some people feel the need to be deliberately tough on themselves. For them, being compassionate would be a means of lowering their standards. But, in truth, being compassionate is nothing more than offering yourself the same warmth, wisdom, understanding, and kindness that you would give to someone else.

These basics will give you a foundation to build on, allowing you to begin to move on from adversity. But remember the rule: You are in control of your own rate of progress, so if doing any of the things described here begins to feel overwhelming, just stop. And when you start up again, always move forward at your own pace.

Once you feel that you are ready, you will need to begin to confront your memories and to deal with your emotions. Here are some guidelines for taking this next step.

Be aware of triggers. Many things can serve as triggers for your emotional reactions. Anniversaries can be particularly upsetting. Christmas, birthdays, and other memorable occasions can also be distressing, as can anniversaries of bereavement. Another form of anniversary is the day that people reach the same age as when a parent died, or, for parents, when a child reaches the age at which they themselves experienced trauma.

Unless a person is aware of the possibility of anniversary triggers, such emotional reactions can seem to come out of the blue. If, however, one reflects on what kind of triggers may be looming in the future, the inevitable emotional reactions will be less frightening and more controllable.

Avoiding avoidance. Switching off can be useful; sometimes it is calming to avoid talking about or being reminded of what has happened. The danger is when too much switching off for too long leads to a downward spiral, where it becomes harder to talk about or confront the situations that have been avoided. In such situations, people become more withdrawn and less capable of confronting what's troubling them so as to deal with their emotions.

One way in which people avoid dealing with emotional issues is to turn to alcohol or drugs. This may help them feel better in the very short term, but people who do this are storing up problems for later and very often creating new problems.

The ancient Chinese sage Chuang-tzu (369–286 B.C.) wrote:

There was a man
Who was so disturbed
By the sight of his own shadow
And so displeased with his own footsteps
That he determined to get rid of both.
The method he hit upon was to run away from them.
So he got up and ran.

But every time he put his foot down
there was another step,
while his shadow kept up with him
without the slightest difficulty.
He attributed his failure
to the fact that he was not running fast enough.
So he ran faster and faster, without stopping,
Until he finally dropped dead.
He failed to realize
that if he merely stepped into the shade,
his shadow would vanish,
and if he sat down and stayed still,
there would be no more footsteps.[3]

In the end, avoidance is like running to get away from our own footsteps: It just doesn't work.

Observe your reactions without judging. When people have distressing feelings, they often try to shut them away—but it's nonetheless important to be aware of these feelings. Rather than shutting them away, try to observe and acknowledge them. Ask yourself, What am I feeling right now? If you are able to recognize and acknowledge your feelings, you can begin to do something with them.

This is harder than it might seem. People often confuse their emotions, or don't have the right words to describe them; indeed, it takes patience and effort to understand emotions. When people judge their feelings instead of just observing and acknowledging what they are, they end up rushing to conclusions, wishing they weren't feeling them, or blaming someone else for making them feel as they do. The more you can simply observe and acknowledge, the more you can begin to understand yourself.

Confronting traumatic memories and emotions. It is understandable that memories and emotions can become overwhelming, causing people to want to switch off. But if they are to move forward, at some point people need to begin to confront their traumatic memories. Everyone is different; everyone does things in his or her own time. Maybe you need to go to a particular place or relive a particular situation. Whatever is necessary, it is important not to avoid the traumatic memories.

One useful self-help technique can be to close your eyes and imagine watching the traumatic event as if it was a film. To do this, imagine observing yourself as if you were on-screen, performing in front of the camera. It is important that the film starts off before the traumatic event happened—when you were in a place of safety. For example, if you were in a car accident, watch yourself in the time leading up to the accident and then as the accident unfolds. Next, watch the film again but this time as if it is being rewound from the end to the beginning at a faster speed. This time see and feel the event as if you are in the film while it is being rewound back to the safe starting point. Once you have completed this process, open your eyes.[4]

Connecting with others. Take time to be with family and friends. This can be difficult—the first reaction to trauma is often withdrawal from others. So, you might have to resist this first reaction and make sure that you mobilize your social resources. But you also need to choose your social support wisely. In addition to making sure you share enough information with others so that they understand you, you need to understand them. Adversity can change people, and family and friends might not respond positively to such a change.

Family and friends might well want the best for us, but change can upset the dynamics of relationships. Jane, for example, left her husband six years ago because his heavy drinking had become a problem in their relationship. One of her close friends at work, Simon, was a source of support. Simon and his wife, Jeannette, would invite Jane to dinner every so often. Jane would tell them about any dates she had been on. But when Jane met Robert, things were different. This relationship seemed to be going somewhere. At last Jane felt she had met someone with whom she could share her life. Jane arrived for dinner, arm in arm with Robert and looking forward to a great evening. Expecting Simon to be welcoming, Jane was shaken by Simon's hostility toward Robert. Although the evening started well, after a few glasses of wine Simon started to make jokes at Robert's expense. The fact was, Simon had been comfortable in his role as Jane's intimate confidante and now was threatened by the possibility of change. Afterward, Simon was as surprised as anyone at how he had behaved, but he hadn't thought through what the change meant for him and the situation unexpectedly triggered deep feelings in him. Sometimes the nature of what people have experienced means that those around don't understand and don't have the resources or the knowledge to be helpful.

Because of these difficulties, people often find it useful to meet up with others who have had similar experiences. Survivor groups can be helpful, whether they are set up by survivors themselves or run by health professionals. When run well, such groups can offer a real source of support, belonging, connection, and the opportunity to be with people who have had similar experiences—people who can learn from each other and who are all working together toward change.

Tuning in to your emotions. It is helpful to be able to talk about how we are feeling if there are people who are willing and able to listen and offer support. But some people have more difficulty than others expressing themselves emotionally. It can be useful to practice putting our feelings into words.

Sometimes, people will try to express how they feel by saying something like "I just feel terrible." Therapists, as well as family and friends, can help them to "unpack" their feelings with further skillful questioning:

"What do you mean by *terrible?*"
"I don't know, just terrible."
"Okay, let's pick that apart. By *terrible*, do you mean anxious, and tense in your body?"
"Yes, that's what I mean."
"Does that cover it? Or is there anything else?"
"I guess I feel angry, too."
"Anything else?"
"I don't want to worry my family."

"So, when you say you feel terrible, it's a mix of feeling anxious,
    angry, and not wanting to worry your family. Anything else?"
"I feel lonely as well."

And so forth.

(For those offering support: Listening well and helping people unpack how they are feeling requires being very attentive to what they are
saying. Simply try to understand, without offering advice.)

Another way to help tune in to yourself is by listening to your body.
The mind and body are interconnected. Ask yourself, "How do I feel in
my body?" Anger is frequently expressed in muscle tension; hence people
sometimes refer to things that anger them as causing them a pain in the
neck. If people feel sad they might feel a lump in their throat. They say
things like "I feel choked up." If people are frightened they might have a
racing heart, or they might talk about having butterflies in the stomach.
Take a few minutes to make yourself comfortable, close your eyes, rest
your hands palms down gently on your stomach, and let yourself get in
touch with what you are feeling within your body. Use your body to find
clues to how you might be feeling.

Think about how your emotions influence you. Strong emotions can be
powerful drivers. Sometimes people get locked into emotional states that
do not actually do them any good. Anger is a good example. It's important to know, for example, when to be angry and how to express it ap-
propriately, but it's also important to know when to let go of anger.
When we are driven by anger, we do things we would not otherwise do,
and often we regret our actions later. Feelings of shame lead us to hide
away from others when what we might really need is to seek the company
of others. Be aware of how your emotions are causing you to act.

Some emotions are hard to let go of. Anyone whose car has ever been
stuck in a snowdrift knows that pressing the accelerator harder makes the
wheels spin furiously but only gets us more and more stuck. When we panic
we are inclined to accelerate even more. To get free we need to apply pressure to the accelerator gently, let the car rock back and forth, and build up
a rhythm. Eventually, the car breaks free. What we need to do in the after-

math of adversity is not so different. We need to accept the reality of our situation. As one woman said: "Thinking back to times when it all seemed just too much to bear and you want to run away from it all . . . there comes another layer of learning and growth to accept things we cannot change."[5]

Consider the case of actor Michael J. Fox, who developed Parkinson's disease at the young age of thirty. In his memoir, *Always Looking Up*, he describes how he was inspired by the courage of cyclist Lance Armstrong in the face of his cancer.[6] Reflecting on his life before Parkinson's, and on how the disease proved to be a turning point, Fox wrote:

> It really is a course correction—at that point in my life, when I got Parkinson's, I had to look at the way I was living: the drinking. It wasn't like a little warning sign at the side of the road. It was a big caution in flashing lights. I don't know that I would have the family that I have now, the life I have, the sense of purpose, if none of this had happened. . . . The one choice I don't have is whether or not I have it. But beyond that my choices are infinite. How I approach it is up to me. It has a lot to do with—and this is hard for people to understand—accepting it. And that doesn't mean being resigned or not looking for a cure. But if you're trying to get away from it or change it, you're going to wear yourself out.[7]

Focus on what you can do and build on that. One woman found it too frightening to even walk down the street. Patricia told me: "I started shaking as soon as I set foot outside the door, but I realized that, okay, I can't walk down the street but I can go into my garden. I know it sounds simple, but it took me a long time to realize that I needed to stop focusing on what I couldn't do and begin to focus on what I could do. Just to be able to go into the garden, walk around, look at the flowers, sit outside and have my coffee in the morning. I even started doing a bit of gardening. I planted some lovely flowering climbers. It made a difference. Instead of hiding inside I was doing something for myself. It was like while I was tending the garden I was also tending myself. The more I started doing the things I could, the more I built my confidence. Then I was able to go out the front door, walk to the end of the street, and well, here I am now. It seems so obvious now, to focus on what I can do, not what I can't." Rather than focusing on what she couldn't do, she realized that she was holding herself back and that she needed to focus on what she *could* do.

Laughter and smiling. You might not feel like it, or you may think it will seem inappropriate to others, but laughter helps. First of all, if you are laughing and smiling, it gives you a breather from your worries. Second, good-natured behaviors like these will bring social benefits. Third, positive emotions are important because they begin to undo the knots of negative emotions. Positive emotions open our minds and our hearts and build our resources. So, watch movies that make you laugh. Read humorous books. Listen to comedians. Whenever opportunities arise that may bring a smile to your face, think about giving them a go—even if you don't feel like it.

Learning from the past. We have all dealt with difficult situations in the past. Think about past situations and how you coped with them. You can ask yourself: "What helped me cope then?" They don't have to be trau-matic situations. Any situation that you coped with successfully in the past can potentially offer inspiration to you for how to cope now. Reflect on what coping strategies you used and what function they served for you.

All of the above pointers are useful and will help you keep on track. However, if three or more months have passed and you have been at-tending to these basics but still feel distressed and troubled and struggling to cope at home or work, then it may be wise to seek professional help. (See Appendix 3.)

Signpost 2: Harvesting Hope

In order to thrive, people need to be able to nurture hope within them-selves. Hope can be the spark for change. All psychotherapists know that, no matter what else is going on, if a client feels hopeless change will be difficult to come by. Research has shown that hopeful children, adoles-cents, and adults do better in school and athletics, are in better health, have better problem-solving skills, and are better adjusted psychologi-cally. As you take control of your thinking habits, you will be switching your approach from brooding to reflective.

Yet trauma can often leave people feeling hopeless. It can be hard to get going in the mornings, to sustain energy throughout the day, and to think about the future in anything but pessimistic ways.

You might not be immediately able to reverse how you feel, but don't worry about that. What you *can* do now is decide that you would like to feel more hopeful. This will happen if you take some time to actively practice the exercises below.

Don't underestimate the power of hope. Hope is the secret ingredient of psychotherapy. If you possess hope that the future will bring new possibilities, you are already on the road to change. Hope is your motivator. After being diagnosed with a brain tumor in 2008 and told he was about to die, Edward Kennedy wrote:

> I am a realist, and I have heard bad news in my life. I don't expect or need to be treated with kid gloves. But I do believe in hope. And I believe that approaching adversity with a positive attitude at least gives you a chance for success. Approaching it with a defeatist attitude predestines the outcome: defeat.[8]

Remember: To be hopeful does not mean that you don't care. This is an important point for those who have lost a loved one. Be reassured that, although positive change is possible and the goal is to encourage you to find hope, this does not mean having to forget about what happened. Often a barrier to hope is the belief that to be hopeful for oneself is to diminish the memories of the past and of our loved ones. John, who lost his teenage daughter, Lara, says that he would never want to forget about her and the emotional pain he feels is meaningful to him. In that sense, it's important to him to feel as he does—but he also realizes that Lara would want him to get on with his life. Being hopeful does not mean that you don't care about what has happened, or love those you have lost any less. If you have lost someone close, it can indeed be hard to be hopeful about the future; the pain is understandable. But you can broaden your focus by exploring the deeper meanings of your loss.

It might be helpful to write a letter to the person you have lost. Here is an example:

Dear Lara, it is a year now since we said good-bye and it will soon be Christmas and I will miss you more than words can say. It is hard for me to look into the future and imagine life. When I do I think of you and all the things that were to happen in your life. I imagine us together for the first time visiting New York and all the shops you so wanted to see, your graduation, all the birthdays and Christmases yet to come. I feel empty without you but I feel you will always be around. I want you to know I love you and I always will. I have felt so ashamed of myself when I forget even for a second, or when I smile at something on the television, I know you would not want me to feel this way and as I write this I can hear your voice saying to me, dad, I want you to live your life. . . . Dad

Be inspired: Look for stories of personal growth. As we saw in Chapter 6, Michael Paterson found Douglas Baader's life story inspirational and helpful to him in finding the strength to overcome the loss of his arms. Look for stories that inspire you, perhaps among the following list of titles.

- Michael J. Fox, *Always Looking Up*
- Edward M. Kennedy, *True Compass: A Memoir*
- Nelson Mandela, *Long Walk to Freedom*
- Thomas Buergenthal, *A Lucky Child: A Memoir of Surviving Auschwitz as a Young Boy*
- Terry Waite, *Taken on Trust*
- Viktor Frankl, *Man's Search for Meaning*
- Elisabeth Kubler-Ross and David Kessler, *Life Lessons: How Our Mortality Can Teach Us About Life and Living*
- Lance Armstrong, *It's Not About the Bike: My Journey Back to Life*

Indeed, being hopeful will allow you to summon enough mental energy to set your sights on a more optimistic future and identify pathways to achieve your goals.

Hope is fueled by three ways of thinking: goal setting, agency thinking, and pathways thinking.

1. *Goal setting.* Trauma survivors need to have goals to aim for. There are significant goals such as obtaining one's college degree, getting promoted at work, opening a new business, becoming a writer, and so on. And there are mundane goals such as taking the car to the workshop for a yearly service or picking up the dry cleaning. Both kinds of goals fuel hope.
2. *Agency thinking.* Trauma survivors need to have a sense of personal agency that gives them the motivation to move toward their goals. In short, they need to be able to both initiate and sustain the motivation.
3. *Pathways thinking.* Trauma survivors need to know what pathways to take to get to their goals—the routes to take, what obstacles will be in the way, and how to get around these obstacles. They also need to develop specific strategies to reach their goals.[9]

Begin to practice hope. To practice hope you need to learn to break your long-range goals into steps or subgoals. As the saying goes, "Every journey begins with a single step." But of course not everything can be changed in one step. Thus it's important to concentrate on the first subgoal. Patricia, for example, was too frightened to leave her house. It was too big a step for her. Then she realized that an initial smaller step was just going out into the garden. As she built her confidence, she was able to begin thinking about a day trip to the city. She mentally rehearsed this in advance: walking to the train station, buying the ticket, sitting on the train, planning what galleries she would visit when she got there. She also made a plan for what she would do if she ran into difficulties. Specifically, a friend who lived in the city offered, if necessary, to jump in a taxi and be with her in fifteen minutes. What helped Patricia was realizing that she couldn't reach her big goals all at once.

Patricia developed a sense of agency by learning to talk to herself in a positive way (e.g., "I can do this"). In much the same way that children use self-talk when they are learning new skills, we can benefit by deliberately talking to ourselves. For example, when learning to drive, many of us say to ourselves: "Look into the rear-view mirror, put the car into gear, check the mirror again," and so on. By practicing self-talk, you can actually develop new skills.[10]

To explore your capacity for hope, think about a time in your past when you set yourself a goal. Take ten minutes to write in your notebook about how you pursued your goal, exploring the pathways and agency involved. Ask yourself questions. "How did I get motivated?" "How did I keep my motivation going?" "What were the strategies I used to get there?" "How did I know I was making progress?" You may find it helpful to repeat this exercise a few times.

As you review your stories you will realize that you already possess the resources necessary to cope with obstacles. Adversity often awakens strengths and abilities that were not recognized before. But most importantly, you are learning to use the language of hope by identifying your goals, your pathways, and your sources of personal agency. Don't expect to immediately find answers to all of your questions. Remember: You are learning the new skill of thinking hopefully, and this skill takes time.

Use the miracle question. Sometimes people find it difficult to focus on what their goals actually are. One exercise that therapists sometimes use is called the *miracle question*: Imagine that when you go to sleep tonight, a miracle happens and you wake up tomorrow morning and things are different in a good way. But since you are asleep, you don't know that the miracle has happened until you wake up tomorrow. Next, imagine that you look back on today. "What will have changed, and how will you feel that is different from the way you feel today?"

Spending some time thinking through your answers will help you clarify your goals. Having done that, you can then think more clearly about what you might do to reach those goals—a matter of figuring out the pathways and agency you need to get you there.[11]

Use your social support. Relationships can foster hope. Indeed, developing hope almost always occurs within the context of social relationships. And hope begets more hope. Hopeful family relationships and friendships serve as hope-enhancing agents. You can benefit from evaluating which relationships help you to feel hopeful and which ones drain this energy from you. Associate with individuals who are supportive of your goal pursuits, who challenge you to pursue your goals, and who encourage you to overcome barriers.

Look to the future. As a prisoner in the Nazi death camps, Viktor Frankl fell to the ground one day, weak and ill from hunger. A guard shouted at him to rise, but he was unable to do so. The guard began to beat him. While lying there, Frankl found himself imagining it was several years later. He was standing at a lectern in postwar Vienna giving a talk on the psychology of death camps. It was a brilliant talk, one in which he imagined describing himself lying on the ground being beaten, struggling to find the strength to get up—and as he described this to his imaginary future audience, he also imagined standing up and beginning to walk. Then, in real life, he stood up and walked away from the guard. Even in the darkest moments it is possible to find hope, and it is hope that allows us to begin to connect in our minds our present situation with a future in which we have overcome adversity. What gave Frankl the strength to go on was not just that he could visualize himself giving the lecture but also this was something worth living for.

Do you have a vision for your future? What do you imagine you'll be doing in one year? Five years? You might struggle to answer these questions, thinking that all you want is the current situation to end, but it is still useful to visualize what you want your future to look like. Begin to make it concrete. Visualize what you enjoy doing, what makes your heart lift, how you could contribute in some way to others, what would give you a sense of purpose. In the process, you might find yourself wrestling with the big questions of life and seeking out understandings of a more spiritual nature.

Signpost 3: Re-authoring

David Kessler is a leader in the field of hospice care. One night while he was working on the cancer ward, he began talking to a nurse who was emotionally devastated, having just lost a patient—her sixth that week. The nurse said to him that she felt she couldn't take it anymore. David asked her to follow him and, grabbing her hand, he led her to another wing of the hospital. He walked her up to a glass partition, behind which were the newborn babies in the maternity ward. "Doing what you do," he said, "you need to come here often to remind yourself that life is not only about loss."[12] He had helped her re-author her understanding of her job.

Re-authoring begins with how we think of ourselves in relation to trauma. Language is important. There is a big difference between describing ourselves as victims and describing ourselves as survivors or thrivers. The term *victim* implies passivity, defeat, helplessness whereas the term *survivor* implies recovery—a recognition that the person has gotten through adversity and taken back control of his or her life. But the term *thriver* goes even further. It implies activity, mastery, and hope. Thrivers have not only gotten through adversity but have moved beyond the trauma and found meaning and purpose. What other words would you associate with being a thriver? Take a few minutes to think about what words you associate with each of these terms: *victim, survivor*, and *thriver*. Which of these words describes you? Re-authoring involves moving from thinking of ourselves as victims to thinking of ourselves as survivors, and then as thrivers. How do we turn ourselves into thrivers?

Keep in mind that victims, survivors, and thrivers are not fixed personality types. Rather, they represent different mindsets. All of us can cultivate the thriver mindset if we choose to do so.

Cultivate the growth mindset. Thrivers are those who are able to re-author their experiences and tell themselves new stories. Thrivers possess a *growth mindset*. This is the view that change is possible. Those with a growth mindset see change as an opportunity to grow. By being flexible in their stories about who they are, what happened, who is responsible, such people are able to look at things from different angles, ask themselves awkward questions, and consider new perspectives.

Re-authoring involves telling a new story about who you are, about the role of the trauma in your life, and about how what happened was part of your life journey. It is a story of how the event fits in your life. Life is complex. Often there are different ways of looking at things. And, indeed, those people who are flexible enough to consider alternatives tend to do better. Making sense of ourselves is a lifelong process, and our life story is a work in progress. And the meaning of life is not fixed but, rather, varies from person to person, day to day, and hour to hour. What's important in re-authoring, then, is the ability to build connections between the past, the present, and the future—the ability to look at the past through a different lens.

The following example illustrates the difficulty of developing a new way of thinking once an old way has been established.

> Question: What do you call the tree that grows from acorns?
>   Answer: An oak.
> Question: What do you call a funny story?
>   Answer: A joke.
> Question: The sound made by a frog?
>   Answer: A croak.
> Question: The white of an egg?
>   Answer:_____ [13]

Use Metaphors. We need to choose our metaphors wisely because the wrong ones can limit the ways in which we cope. People think metaphorically all the time. Whether we are aware of it or not, this is what people do. If you want to change, you need to pay attention to the words you use. Sometimes people trap themselves in their stories. Traumatized people often say things like

> "I feel like a bird who has been put in a cage."
> "I feel like I'm in a fog."
> "It's like all the doors in the house have been bolted."
> "It's like I'm lost in a dark forest."
> "It's like I'm swimming against the tide."
> "It's like I'm standing on the edge of a cliff."
> "It's like I'm in a boat with no paddles being taken by the tide."
> "It's like I'm on a roller coaster."

Metaphors serve as guides to our actions. Do any of the above seem to fit you? Do you have any of your own? Take a few minutes to think about the metaphors you have used to describe yourself and how they have become part of your life story.

To free yourself of trauma, you need to use your images, stories, analogies, and metaphors creatively. After all, cages have doors that open, fogs eventually lift, bolts can be undone, if it's dark out we can wait until daylight, and if caught up in the tide we can point ourselves toward shore. The stories we use to describe our lives can trap us. But they can also *free* us if we think imaginatively.

After her husband left, Lynne wasn't coping well. She wasn't dealing effectively with the pressures at work, and she was frightened of losing her job. Suffering from anxiety, panic attacks, and depression, she went to see her general practitioner, who listened to her story, thought for a bit, and said to her that it sounded as if she were a pot about to boil over. In a state of desperation, Lynne eagerly latched onto this metaphor. It seemed to make sense to her. She started taking an antidepressant because the doctor told her that it would help turn the heat down a bit. At the time this seemed to make sense to Lynne. Several months later, I spoke to her. "I do feel better," she said, "but the problems at work are still there. I think the medication helped me feel better, but I think it did this by shutting me down to what was going on around me and what I needed to do. I didn't deal with the situation. I'm still not sure about my job but I just don't seem to be as worried. In fact, I feel I should be more worried but I'm not."

I talked to Lynne about how people choose their metaphors and how these metaphors shape the actions that people take. She nodded. "I hadn't thought of it like that," she said. "But I don't understand. Are you saying that it was wrong for the doctor to tell me I was like a pot starting to boil?" "No," I replied. "In this case, the doctor was using a metaphor that he believed would explain why he thought medication would be helpful to you. Someone else might have worded it differently. What about lifting the pot off the cooker? Or turning the gas off? That's what people would do if the pot was boiling, so what would that look like in your life?"

Lynne thought for a bit. Then she said, "I need a holiday actually, just to get away for a couple of weeks. I'm entitled to take a holiday. I don't know why I didn't think of doing that before. I think I need a good rest and some time away to think things through. I need to take the pot off the cooker for a bit." We talked some more and I asked her to think about different metaphors for her situation. She soon got the hang of it. She imagined herself on a raft floating down the river, when suddenly it hit the rapids. "What would you do then?" I asked. "There's not much you can do but hang on in that situation," she said. "Okay, what would that look like?" We explored this further, and some of my suggestions included making better use of her social support systems and teaching herself calming and relaxation exercises. We also explored other metaphors. "You are walking through a forest but the path disappears and you don't know what direction to go in." Lynne thought about this for a little longer. "Before Michael left, it was like I knew what my path was, but now I have to find my own way, and decide where I want to go. I have to make my own path."

Many therapists suggest metaphors to help people make sense of their experiences, and this can be helpful—but it can also be harmful. What's important is to know that metaphors are only tools for reflection about what's happening in your life—tools that can potentially allow you to see things from a new perspective and thereby seek new solutions. The lesson to be learned from this is that it's important to choose your metaphors consciously. Explore how you use them to make sense of your experiences and to guide your actions.

Play around with different metaphors. Many people use images of trees, saplings, thickets, and forests, whether dense, stunted, fruitful, dark, leafy, or sparse. Take a few minutes to use one of these images to describe yourself as you are now. Now think about how you can change this image. A sparse tree grows back its leaves in the summertime. And a dense thicket eventually clears if you keep walking.

Expressive writing. Re-authoring can sometimes take a very literal form. On a blank sheet of paper, write about what's bothering you. Write for ten solid minutes, and then stop. Do the same thing every day for the next week. Make it a ritual. Find a comfortable place to write, a place where you feel you have stepped outside of your everyday life. Vary the style in which you write. Try writing from someone else's perspective.

Or try writing a letter that you won't send. Try writing a fairy tale. At the top of the page begin with "Once upon a time . . . " and keep writing for ten minutes; don't let your pen leave the paper. When you come back to what you have written, ask yourself: Who are the main characters? A princess and a prince? A wicked witch and warlock? Consider who these characters might represent.

What is the story really about? Fighting evil? Trying to escape? How do the characters cope? What strategies do they use? What resources do they mobilize? What gives them strength to rise to the challenges they face? How does the story end? Asking yourself such questions can foster your sense of agency and bolster resilience through identifying new ways of coping.

Keep this process going for the next seven days, and let your imagination help you to see things differently. Remember, just put the pen to the paper and write. Don't stop. Just write whatever comes to mind. And after ten minutes, stop. Do this regularly, reflecting on what you have written. It can help you see things from new perspectives, make new connections, and find new insights.

Signpost 4: Identifying Change

It is common for positive changes to arise in the aftermath of adversity, even if only in small ways. Imagine that the trauma is a thick, prickly hedge. It seems impenetrable and blocks out all light. Yet if you look closely, you'll see the beautiful wildflowers that have been able to take root in its shelter. Personal transformation is like this: It takes root in adversity but is easily overlooked and trampled upon. People need to nurture growth in themselves. It is important that you begin to actively look for opportunities for positive change. This can be accomplished through a series of reflective exercises, done regularly.

Keep a diary of what goes well. Set aside ten minutes at the end of each day to think back. Even small things that seem a bit inconsequential are important.

"I've noticed today that I heard my children laughing, and I felt good about that. I don't think I would have noticed that before in the same way. I would have taken it for granted."

"The woman in the shop smiled at me when I bought my newspaper today, and I smiled back. I don't think I ever really looked at her before."

"At the meeting today, even when it got heated, I didn't get angry the way I used to. I've noticed that I'm calmer now."

"Little things didn't seem to bother me so much today. It's like I could see the big picture."

"I went to visit my brother in the hospital. I felt really sad but it's brought us closer."

"I found it difficult today to get going, but I did—and even though I was nervous I managed to make it to the meeting and I think I added something useful to the discussion."

"My partner told me she loved me today and it's good to know that I'm loveable."

"Just getting to the shops today felt like a real achievement; I'm proud that I did that."

You might also consider keeping a diary of those moments when you feel at your best. Identify the conditions that enabled such moments to happen and the coping resources that were most helpful to you. By taking note of your own growth, you'll find that it will deepen.

If you are feeling depressed or anxious, it's important to seek out positive experiences and nurture a positive view of yourself. At such times, positive thoughts and memories can be fleeting, easily dismissed, or forgotten. So, my advice is to keep a daily record and practice nurturing yourself. At first it might be hard to come up with positive thoughts, but write them down daily and let your list build up over several weeks. As Marie told me:

When I started keeping a diary, at first I thought this is no good. If I had anything positive to say, I wouldn't be asking for your help in the first place, but what amazed me was that after a week I had pages in my diary

full of things, and just reading it back over each night reminded me that
I was okay, and that I was on the road to recovery.

You can track your own growth by completing the Psychological Well-
Being Post-Traumatic Changes Questionnaire (see Appendix 2). The
PWB-PTCQ was designed to assess change in six areas of your life: self-
acceptance, autonomy, purpose in life, relationships, sense of mastery,
and personal growth. Add up your scores to the eighteen items. The lowest you can score is 0; the highest is 90. Scores over 54 indicate the presence of posttraumatic growth. On each of the six subscales, the lowest
you can score is 3 and the highest is 15. Scores between 10 and 12 indicate some positive change. Scores between 13 and 15 indicate a lot of
positive change. In what areas of your life have you experienced the greatest positive change?

There may be some areas of your life in which you score lower than
10. If so, that's understandable. Different areas will develop at different
speeds. There is no one correct way to score on this questionnaire; its
purpose is to give you a sense of where you are right now so that you can
reflect about yourself in terms of these six areas and begin to be aware of
how you are changing. Record your answers to this questionnaire once
every two weeks.

Signpost 5: Valuing Change

Much like seedlings taking root that need water and sunlight to thrive,
you need to nurture the changes in yourself that you have identified.

What are the lessons that life has taught you? How much do you live
out these lessons in your everyday life? Could you do more? Those who
can honestly say that they couldn't live more fully are few and far between. Most of us, if we are honest with ourselves, know that we don't
live life as wisely, responsibly, compassionately, and maturely as we could.
Take a moment to think about what makes your life meaningful, what
your values are, and what your goals are. Some of these may have arisen
because of past experience of trauma and adversity and ones that you
previously identified. Others may hark back many years to your up-
bringing. Are there some values, goals, meanings, that you would not be

willing to let go of? Are there others that may have outlived their useful-ness? Personal transformation is difficult because it means we have to change. It's not about feeling better but about creating new meanings, finding new values, and changing how you think about yourself and your goals in life.

Imagine suddenly waking up on a desert island, knowing that you will have to live the rest of your life there. Take a few minutes to reflect on the people you would miss the most. Then reflect on the places and the activities that you would miss. On a sheet of paper list all of these people, places, and activities.

Now think about how much time you spend with the people on your list, visiting those places, and doing those activities. Make a note of how much time you spend on them each week. Calculate how much time you wish you could spend on them. Looking at this list, you will likely see a big difference between how much time you spend and how much time you would like to spend on each of the items you've listed. Now choose one person, one place, and one activity and make a commitment to your-self to pay greater attention to these parts of your life. Write a contract to yourself promising to do this.

Those who have experienced losses may feel that it is inappropriate to focus on their own well-being. It may seem disrespectful in some way. This is understandable, particularly following bereavement, but by ap-preciating what you have right now does not mean that you appreciate who or what you have lost any less. Think about it. If you love someone and you were to die, would you not want that person to live life fully? As noted by John Harvey, who has studied bereavement, growth is encour-aged when we reflect on what we have gained from loved ones and find a way to use what we have learned from them to give to others.[14]

Often the seeds of growth are in small, everyday things. One man, for example, told me that he now appreciates time with his children in a way that he did not before:

> Jenny is six years old now. On Saturday, she asked me to help her make
> a birthday card for her Nan. I was busy and reluctantly agreed. But then
> I realized: This was one of the moments that I will look back on. Having

made the decision to value the opportunity, within minutes I was en-
grossed as she instructed me to cut pieces of paper, lick sticky stars, and
dab blobs of paint. An hour later we had created the most magnificent
card, which was overflowing with love. It didn't look like much compared to a shop-bought card, but, boy, it was special. On Sunday, Jenny
proudly presented it to her Nan. I felt lucky to have been part of this
special moment. I reflected on how easy it would have been for me to
have said I was too busy at that moment to help make the card and what
I would have missed as a result.

People can find special moments like this one every day. They are all
around us, but unless we know to value them they can slip by all too
easily.

Appreciative people behave differently from unappreciative ones.
Their coping strategies tend to be more adaptive, and they are more likely
to seek social support and to use positive reinterpretation strategies.[15] In
turn, their adaptive coping strategies help such people deal with stress.

Gratitude exercise. Take five minutes at the end of each day over the next
month to track your gratitude. Write down three things that make you
feel grateful. Think about the day and the things that have happened,
from the small things (perhaps a colleague offered to make you a cup of
tea at work) to the bigger things (such as an offer from a friend to help
you redecorate a room). Reflect on how much appreciation you feel.
Make gratitude a daily habit.

Imagining loss. Imagining loss that has *not* actually happened can be
equally useful. This is not a pleasant thing to do. It requires effort, as few
people are inclined to tabulate the things that they *haven't* lost. But by
imagining loss you can learn to value what you have. So while it can be
an uncomfortable exercise, it is one of the most powerful things you can
do to recognize what it is you deeply value.

In *A Christmas Carol*, Charles Dickens tells us the story of Ebenezer
Scrooge, a miserly man whose life has been devoted to accruing wealth.
Scrooge is compelled by the ghost of "Christmas yet to come" to stare

into the faces of lost loved ones, to contemplate future losses, and to ac-knowledge his own mortality. As a lonely corpse, he watches strangers paw through his belongings and listens to people talking about him with-out love in their voices. He is taken by the ghost to visit his own grave—and, running his fingers over the letters of his name engraved on the tombstone, he is transformed. Awakening on Christmas morning, Scrooge is now appreciative of his relationship with his nephew. He ex-periences compassion for others and decides to give his employee a huge raise in salary. He buys a turkey for his employee's family and, for the first time, embraces life with pleasure.

An exercise inspired by Scrooge's story is to imagine what your own headstone will say. This, too, will help you focus on what you most value in yourself. Put this book down for a few minutes and think about what your headstone would say if you were to die tomorrow. What words would appear on it? Are these the words you would like to see on your headstone? If not, write down the words you *would* like to read on it. Take a few minutes to really think about this. You might want to take the exercise a step further and write your own obituary as you would like it to read.

Signpost 6: Expressing Change in Action

It's not enough to intellectually reframe our experiences in positive terms. We must also express our growth in new behaviors. In short, we have to put growth into action.

Go back over your answers to the PWB-PTCQ (see Appendix 2) and think about examples of things you actually did that show that you ac-cepted yourself, acted autonomously, exhibited purpose in life, improved your relationships, achieved a sense of mastery, and found your way to personal growth. Also think about the ways in which you already ex-press how you have grown. It might be in the little things that you begin to see change:

"I spoke up at the meeting at work yesterday even though I knew oth-ers would disagree with me, because I believe in the issue. I wouldn't have done that before."

"When I got home last week to find the water heater leaking, I didn't panic but dealt with the situation very efficiently. I surprised myself that I was able to do that."

"I cooked a special dinner for my husband on Sunday to show him how much I love him."

"I won some money on the lottery and I gave half of it to the woman collecting for cancer."

"I was nervous about it, but I took a chance and enrolled in an evening class to learn how to paint."

"I took part in the charity run to raise money for the children's heart appeal."

Thinking in terms of concrete actions can help make your growth *real*, rather than something that just exists in your mind. Observe the little things and use them to learn about yourself—your strengths, abilities, and talents. It's useful once a week to take time out to reflect on the past week and find examples of how you succeeded in translating your growth into action—examples similar to those listed above. This exercise will also allow you to think about the week coming up.

What things have you done this past week, no matter how trivial they seem, that demonstrate that you are becoming more self-accepting, autonomous, purposeful in your life, focused on deepening your relationships, masterful over your situation, and open to personal growth?

And what things will you do next week that demonstrate these strengths? In this connection, you might find it helpful to think about expressing yourself in new and creative ways through activism, advocacy, and other forms of commitment to personal or social action. Are there things you can do that use your experiences for the better of others—your family, your friends, or your community as a whole?

By focusing on these six signposts—taking stock of where you are on your journey, finding hope within yourself, actively re-authoring the stories you tell yourself, identifying your changes, valuing your changes, and, finally, actively expressing these changes in your community—you will find that your posttraumatic growth is beginning to take root.

APPENDIX 1

Common Problems Associated with Posttraumatic Stress

This section provides information on posttraumatic stress that will be helpful in comparing your own reactions to the problems commonly reported by people with posttraumatic stress.[1] There are no "right" or "wrong" ways to react to adversity. Different people exposed to the same type of trauma may respond in quite different ways. Everyone's reactions will be individual. And not everybody will have all of the problems described below or experience them to the same degree.

- *Intrusive memories:* Intrusive thoughts, images, and feelings can seem to "come out of the blue." Often they will be about what happened during the trauma. These may be very unsettling and disturbing.
- *Vivid dreams, nightmares:* Traumatized people may have dreams that are upsetting and disturbing. Often these, too, will be about what happened. Consider this description by Adrian Tempany, one of the people caught up in a crush at a football game in which ninety-six people were trampled to death: "I was struggling with a recurring nightmare—of watching people having the life squeezed out of them, of the screaming, the crying, and the sound of bones breaking."[2]
- *Flashbacks:* Traumatized people sometimes experience "flashbacks," which cause them to feel as though the event is happening again. Consider this description by Anthony Browne, a writer and illustrator of

children's books, whose mother came into the house one day and found his father, who had been in World War II, "in a frenzy, wrestling on the floor with a vacuum cleaner: When he came to, he said he'd thought it was a German."[3]

- *Hypervigilance:* Trauma survivors may find themselves on edge and alert to danger. This reaction makes sense in the midst of trauma, as it helps to keep humans safe. But once switched on, it can take a while to switch off again—and thus survivors find themselves constantly on the lookout for signs of danger. They may even see threat in things that appeared innocent before the trauma occurred.

- *Increased startle response:* Survivors of trauma may find themselves becoming "jumpy" and easily startled by sudden noises or movements such as a car backfiring, a door slamming, or the phone ringing.

- *Mental avoidance:* Trauma survivors often try to push negative thoughts away and not think about what happened.

- *Behavioral avoidance:* Reminders of trauma may cause survivors to feel shaken up, distressed, on edge, and jumpy. Thus many survivors try to avoid reminders such as thoughts, feelings, and conversations associated with the trauma, as well as people, activities, or places that bring back memories of the event.

- *Emotional numbness:* Following a trauma, it is common to feel detached and withdrawn and to have difficulty experiencing emotions. Survivors may also shut down mentally and emotionally and have trouble remembering what happened, feel cut off from others, and be unable to have or express loving feelings.

- *Social withdrawal:* Trauma survivors commonly retreat into themselves, avoiding the company of others. Some may feel that other people do not really understand them. As we saw previously, trauma can strengthen relationships, but it can also place strains on them. Family and friends need to be aware of how trauma affects people, and to realize that traumatized individuals may be acting out of character.

- *Anxiety:* It is common for traumatized people to feel fearful and nervous; some may even be panicky—especially when faced with reminders. Many also have difficulty concentrating.

- *Sleep disturbance:* Many traumatized people have difficulty falling or staying asleep.
- *Shame:* After trauma, many people feel shame. This emotion may be related to their sense of themselves as "not good enough" in some way. Shame causes some survivors to want to go into hiding.
- *Guilt:* Many trauma survivors have feelings of guilt—about not having acted as they would have wished or about letting themselves or someone else down. In particular, they may feel guilty for having survived. This is known as *survivor guilt.*
- *Sadness:* Trauma survivors may have feelings of sadness and be excessively tearful.
- *Grief:* Feelings of grief may be overwhelming. Consider this description from Donna-Maria Barker, whose twelve-year-old son died in the bombing of the Irish town of Omagh: "It is with me morning, noon, and night. . . . It is like a cloak, a big, black cloak, smothering me."[4]
- *Irritability:* Trauma survivors may feel increasingly irritable and be prone to snap at other people.
- *Anger:* Survivors are often angry about the traumatic event, especially if they believe that some sort of injustice occurred.
- *Physical problems:* Trauma survivors may experience bodily sensations such as shakiness and trembling, tension and muscular aches (especially in the head and neck), fatigue, palpitations, shallow rapid breathing, dizziness, menstrual disturbances, loss of interest in sex, and gastrointestinal symptoms such as nausea, vomiting, or diarrhea.

APPENDIX 2

Psychological Well-Being Post-Traumatic Changes Questionnaire (PWB-PTCQ)

Think about how you feel about yourself at the present time. Please read each of the following statements and rate how you have changed as a result of the trauma.

5 = Much more so now
4 = A bit more so now
3 = I feel the same about this as before
2 = A bit less so now
1 = Much less so now

_____1. I like myself.
_____2. I have confidence in my opinions.
_____3. I have a sense of purpose in life.
_____4. I have strong and close relationships in my life.
_____5. I feel I am in control of my life.
_____6. I am open to new experiences that challenge me.
_____7. I accept who I am, with both my strengths and limitations.
_____8. I don't worry what other people think of me.
_____9. My life has meaning.
_____10. I am a compassionate and giving person.
_____11. I handle my responsibilities in life well.
_____12. I am always seeking to learn about myself.
_____13. I respect myself.

_____14. I know what is important to me and will stand my ground, even if others disagree.

_____15. I feel that my life is worthwhile and that I play a valuable role in things.

_____16. I am grateful to have people in my life who care for me.

_____17. I am able to cope with what life throws at me.

_____18. I am hopeful about my future and look forward to new possibilities.

SCORING

Add up your scores to all 18 statements.

The higher your score, the more positive change you have experienced. Scores greater than 54 on the PWB-PTCQ indicate the presence of positive change. Scores greater than 72 indicate a high level of positive change.[1]

To examine how you have changed on different domains of psychological well-being, you can look at your scores on each of the six groupings:

- Self-acceptance (statements 1, 7, and 13)
- Autonomy (statements 2, 8, and 14)
- Purpose in life (statements 3, 9, and 15)
- Relationships (statements 4, 10, and 16)
- Sense of mastery (statements 5, 11, and 17)
- Personal growth (statements 6, 12, and 18)

APPENDIX 3

Some Advice on Seeking Professional Help

This appendix is intended to provide some general advice about how to seek professional help, who to seek help from, and what to be on the lookout for. It will be useful to people seeking help for themselves, but also to family and friends who want to know more about the subject.

WHEN TO SEEK PROFESSIONAL HELP

Feelings of distress, confusion, and disorientation are common in the immediate aftermath of a traumatic event. If, however, your problems are particularly intense and upsetting and/or they have lasted for more than six to eight weeks, it might be appropriate to seek professional help.

The following is a checklist of various problems associated with the aftermath of trauma.[1] In the blank line next to each item, write "yes" if you agree with the statement and "no" if you do not agree.

_____ I feel overwhelmed and that I cannot handle my feelings and bodily sensations.

_____ I have no one to share my feelings with but I would like to talk to someone.

_____ I feel numb and empty.

_____ I always feel tense, confused, and exhausted.

_____ I have unpleasant sensations in my body.

_____ I keep busy to stop me from focusing on how I am feeling.

_____ I want to avoid thoughts, places, activities and people who remind me of what happened.

___ I have frequent distressing thoughts and recollections of what
happened.
___ I have nightmares.
___ I sleep badly.
___ My relationships seem to be suffering badly.
___ I have sexual difficulties that I didn't before.
___ I am drinking too much.
___ My performance at work has suffered.
___ I find it hard to concentrate.

If you answered "yes" to more than one or two of these items, and the
problem is causing you to struggle with everyday concerns at home or
work, you might consider seeking advice from a professional.

WHO TO SEEK HELP FROM

psychotherapist
psychologist
psychiatrist
clinical social worker
counselor
psychiatric nurse
clinical mental health counselor
certified pastoral counselor
marriage and family therapist

WHAT TO LOOK OUT FOR

Some of the above-listed professionals may not be experienced with
working with traumatized people, so check out the following:

1. Talk with the professionals about their training and experience,
   their approach to therapy,[2] what the therapy entails, and how
   long the therapy is likely to last. Different therapists will offer
   different techniques, but never be scared to ask them about what

they are doing. Some of the techniques might seem strange to you. Good therapists will be pleased to explain why they are doing what they are doing.

2. Make sure you feel comfortable with the professionals and confident in their ability to help you.
3. Find out whether they will be available to you in between sessions, in case you need their help then.

Good therapists will also answer all of your questions and put you at ease. They won't expect you to do anything you don't want to do or talk about anything you don't feel comfortable talking about. They will understand that the therapy needs to proceed at your speed and will let you set the pace. One thing that might help you is to confront your traumatic memories: Experienced therapists will not push you on this but, rather, will help you to do so when you are ready, in your own time, and at your own pace.

AND REMEMBER!

Therapists have probably seen other individuals with problems similar to yours. Many people are afraid of exposing themselves emotionally, letting someone else see their shame, guilt, disgust, or humiliation. They think that they are the only ones who feel this way. But the truth is, quite a few of us have these negative feelings—and thus therapists will not be shocked or surprised by anything you tell them. Traumatized people often have secrets—things that they don't want to talk to others about. Experienced therapists know this, too. Even so, remember that you need only share with your therapist what you feel comfortable with. They shouldn't pressure you to talk about anything that you don't want to discuss. At the same time, however, try to be as open as you can with your therapist about how you are feeling, particularly if you feel that you are losing touch with reality or going out of control, if you are becoming panicky, if you are experiencing extreme physical sensations or if you are having thoughts of hurting yourself or others.

Medication

If you are experiencing such symptoms as sadness, anxiety, or panic attacks, your therapist may recommend that you be supported with medications as well as talking therapy. The most common medications used to treat PTSD as an adjunct to psychological therapy are the antidepressants known as selective serotonin reuptake inhibitors (SSRIs). Some PTSD sufferers find these medications helpful; others do not. Also bear in mind that SSRIs can have harmful side effects, such as nausea, diarrhea, abdominal discomfort, and sexual dysfunction. If you are considering taking such medications, it is important that you discuss them thoroughly with both your therapist and your general practitioner. Generally, SSRIs should be discontinued after about four weeks, although some people will require a longer period.

The use of medication is controversial,[3] but some people do report that it helps them. In most cases of PTSD, psychological help is all that is needed for recovery from trauma. However, medication can always be considered at any point in therapy if additional support becomes necessary.

Professional Organizations

International Society for Traumatic Stress Studies
www.istss.org
European Society for Traumatic Stress Studies
www.estss.org
National Center for PTSD
www.ncptsd.va.gov
American Psychiatric Association
www.psych.org
American Psychological Association
www.apa.org
Australasian Trauma Society
http://www.traumasociety.com.au/
Australian Psychological Society
http://www.psychology.org.au/
British Psychological Society
www.bps.org.uk
British Association for Counselling and Psychotherapy
http://www.bacp.co.uk

ACKNOWLEDGMENTS

We know a huge amount about the effects of trauma and how to help sufferers due to the work of many brilliant academics and clinicians. Scientific research and scholarship is a communal endeavor, and there are many sources for the ideas expressed in this book (as indicated in the notes at the end of each chapter). But I am particularly grateful for the work of Professors Lawrence Calhoun, Viktor Frankl, Mardi Horowitz, Ronnie Janoff-Bulman, Carl Rogers, and Richard Tedeschi, whose writings and research on the topic of trauma, psychotherapy, and positive psychological change have been influential and paved the way for the ideas in this book.

There are a number of people who have helped this work through their direct support and it is a pleasure to recognize their contribution. First of all, very special thanks go to my friends Kevin Dutton and Elaine Fox; without their encouragement, inspiration, and assistance, this book would never have happened.

Thanks to my agents, Peter Tallack and Zoë Pagnamenta; my editors: Lara Heimert, at Basic Books, who kept me focused on the science of post-traumatic growth; and Anne Lawrance, at Little Brown, for her encouragement to develop the practical exercises. Behind the scenes, my thanks go to Brandon Proia for his skillful line-editing, and Christine Arden and Nancy King for their thoughtful and thorough copyediting; they helped smooth my awkward turns of phrase and improved the readability of the book. And thanks to Melissa Veronesi, my project editor at Perseus Books, for her guidance and support through the final stages of production, and to Katy O'Donnell for her editorial support.

Most of all I want to thank the people who shared their experiences with me, especially Michael Paterson and Terry Waite, and the many others whose stories I have told in this book but who remain anonymous, and the hundreds of people who have taken part in the research studies I have conducted over the years.

Writing a book is a lonely task, so my thanks go to the friends and colleagues who read earlier drafts of chapters and allowed me to bounce ideas around, especially John Durkin, Lynn Hendrickson, Vanessa Markey, Lynne McCormack, David Murphy, Eleanor Pardess, Steve Regel, and Claire Stone.

Of the many former students who have worked with me on trauma-related research projects, many are cited in the book. My thanks to them, but thanks especially to Alex Linley, and Hannah Stockton, whose collaborations with me have particularly enriched this volume.

My thanks to all of those who attended the trauma studies programme at the University of Nottingham over the last few years—they are too numerous to list individually, but for all the lively discussions, my thanks.

Thanks also to the friends and colleagues with whom I have collaborated on various trauma-related projects, many of which are cited in this book. Again, they are far too many to include every name here, but I wish to call out two I have worked with in the past few years: John Maltby and Alex Wood.

One writes a book in the midst of one's other activities and responsibilities, including teaching, research, and clinical practice. And so my thanks go to past and present friends and colleagues at the Centre for Trauma, Resilience, and Growth, with a special thanks to Liz Edwards who keeps the show on the road. And to my friends and colleagues at the University of Nottingham—again space prevents me from mentioning more than a few—Saul Becker, Belinda Harris, Nigel Hunt, and Hugh Middleton.

It is now over twenty years since I was awarded my PhD, but I remain grateful to Bill Yule and Ruth Williams, who offered me my first opportunities to work in this field and who supervised my thesis.

Positive psychology shows us the importance of gratitude. I find the more I reflect on the influence of others, the more I realize there is for me to be grateful for, and so my thanks again to all those above, and to the many other friends, colleagues, and students not mentioned by name.

NOTES

Nietzsche's Dictum

1. See "Leon Greenman, Englishman who survived Auschwitz and dedicated the rest of his life to a campaign against the resurgence of fascism," his obituary in the *Times* online, March 10, 2008: http://www.timesonline.co.uk/tol/comment/obituaries/article3524503.ece. See also "The only Englishman at Auschwitz," Greenman's autobiography (2001), which is part of the Library of Holocaust Testimonies.

2. See Brugha, Bebbington, Tennant, and Hurry (1985), who developed a checklist of the twelve most common life-events. The more life-events one reports in the previous few months, the greater the person's vulnerability to mental distress. This study is only one of many on life-events, to say nothing of the vast literature on the harmful effects of traumatic events.

3. Nietzsche was an existential philosopher. Among his ideas was the notion that a full life involved living passionately and always pushing oneself to the edges. "What doesn't kill me makes me stronger" is one of the most famous quotes from his book *Twilight of the Idols*. Of course, one can debate the merits of the quote and find cases that prove to be exceptions in one way or another. Nevertheless, it seems to capture an essential truth: that when we are pushed to our limits we can emerge stronger in some respects.

4. Armstrong (2000, p. 4).

5. Kushner (1981, pp. 133–134).

6. See also McHugh and Treisman (2007).

7. See, for example, Bonanno (2004, 2005) as well as Bonanno, Rennick, and Dekel (2005) and Bonanno, Galea, Bucciarelli, and Vlahov (2006). After studying various trajectories of adjustment following trauma, these researchers concluded that most people seem to be fairly resilient to the effects of trauma.

8. See Joseph, Maltby, Wood, Stockton, Hunt, and Regel (forthcoming).

Chapter 1

1. PTSD is the term used by the American Psychiatric Association (2000) to describe the problems often experienced by survivors of trauma. It consists of: problems of persistent re-experiencing of the event in intrusive thoughts, memories, and dreams; persistent avoidance of reminders and emotional numbness; and persistent symptoms of increased arousal such as difficulty sleeping, concentrating, or being easily startled by reminders. Chapter 2 will describe PTSD in more detail.

2. Forty-five survivors—9 percent of the surviving population—attended the Institute of Psychiatry within the first year for assessment related to compensation claims. See, Dalgleish, Joseph, and Yule (2000) for a summary.

3. Joseph, Brewin, Yule, and Williams (1991); see also Joseph, Brewin, Yule, and Williams (1993). In these two studies, the 1991 study involving adult survivors of the *Herald* disaster and the 1993 study involving adolescent survivors of the *Jupiter* cruise ship disaster, we investigated how causal attributions related to psychological functioning and posttraumatic stress. Specifically, we used the Leeds Attribution Coding System to analyze transcripts of the survivors' descriptions of what they had experienced during the disaster. What we found was that those who described their experiences in guilt- or shame-provoking terms were more likely to experience posttraumatic stress and poorer functioning several months later. See also Joseph, Williams, and Yule (1997).

4. The three-year survey was with a sample of 73 survivors—18 percent of the surviving population. Results were reported in Yule, Hodgkinson, Joseph, Murray-Parkes, and Williams (1990). See Dalgleish, Joseph, and Yule (2000) for a summary of our research studies with survivors of the *Herald*. On average, levels of distress seemed to decrease over this time, but a substantial minority remained highly distressed.

5. See Joseph, Yule, Williams, and Hodgkinson (1994).

6. See Brewin, Andrews, and Valentine (2000), Bonanno, Brewin, Kaniasty, and La Greca (2010), and Kaniasty (2008), which provide summaries of the trauma literature showing that social support is one of the key factors in recovery.

7. See Joseph, Hodgkinson, Yule, and Williams (1993).

8. See Joseph, Yule, Williams, and Hodgkinson (1993).

9. The first study utilizing the Changes in Outlook Questionnaire was written up by Joseph, Williams, and Yule (1993) in the *Journal of Traumatic Stress*. Since then, the CiOQ has been used in many other studies and has thus been extensively tested. Typically, people score between 39 and 46 on the positive scale and between 26 and 33 on the negative scale. People who score high on the negative scale tend to be at risk for psychological problems and PTSD, as more fully discussed in Joseph, Linley, Andrews, Harris, Howle, Woodward, and Shevlin (2005).

10. Occasional mentions of positive change in survivors appear in the psychological literature from the late 1970s onward; see, for example, Taylor (1977), Hamera and Shontz (1978), Miles and Crandall (1983), Veronen and Kilpatrick (1983), Taylor, Wood, and Lichtman (1983), Lehman, Wortman, and Williams (1987), Calhoun and Tedeschi (1989–1990), and Collins, Taylor, and Skokan (1990). However, this topic went largely unnoticed by mainstream clinical psychology (with its emphasis on psychopathology) until the mid-1990s, when it began to attract greater interest; for example, Abraido-Lanza, Guier, and Colón (1998), Fromm, Andrykowski, and Hunt (1996), O'Leary and Ickovics (1995), and Park, Cohen, and Murch (1996). See Joseph and Butler (2010) for an overview.

11. See Maddux, Snyder, and Lopez (2004), Maddux, Gosselin, and Winstead (2005), and Maddux (2008), which discuss how the origins of psychology were influenced by the medical profession of psychiatry.

12. Frankl ([1946] 1985, p. 88). See also Frankl (2000).

13. Maslow (1955).

14. Yalom (1980).

15. See Seligman (1999, 2002, 2011), who is credited with coining the term positive psychology and providing the impetus for this new area of research. See also Seligman and Csikszentmihalyi (2000). Positive psychology is the science of what makes life worth living. It is not to be confused with the power of positive thinking and other untested self-help techniques promoted by self-appointed gurus that offer simple-minded, one-size-fits-all advice to bring wealth, success, and happiness.

16. For discussions of the research and practice of positive psychology, see major texts by Linley and Joseph (2004a), Csikszentmihalyi and Csikszentmihalyi (2006), Lopez and Snyder (2009), and Sheldon, Kashdan, and Steger (2011). See Joseph and Wood (2010), Seligman, Steen, Park, and Peterson (2005), and Tedeschi and Kilmer (2005) for examples of how positive psychology research has become a focus for clinical psychology research and practice. Also see Fredrickson (2001, 2009), who has demonstrated the importance of positive emotions in well-being.

17. See, for example, Weiss and Berger (2010).

18. See Tedeschi and Calhoun (1996), who coined the term *posttraumatic growth*, developed the Posttraumatic Growth Inventory (PTGI)—a self-report questionnaire designed to measure people's perceptions of how much they have grown—and with their colleague Crystal Park edited the first major scholarly book on the topic, see Tedeschi, Park, and Calhoun (1998). Posttraumatic growth has since become the most widely used term to describe this field of study, but, as noted, it is one among several others that have been used interchangeably: benefit-finding, growth following adversity, personal transformation, positive changes, stress-related growth, and thriving. Throughout I have drawn on this wider literature, but I have generally used the term posttraumatic growth as it is the most widely known of all of the terms. More recent texts on the topic include Calhoun and Tedeschi (2006), Joseph and Linley (2008), and Weiss and Berger (2010).

19. See Keyes, Shmotkin, and Ryff (2002), McGregor and Little (1998), Ryan and Deci (2001), and Ryan, Huta, and Deci (2008) whose studies have helped to show the distinction between hedonic well-being and eudaimonic well-being.

20. See Kasser (2004) for an overview.

21. See, for example, Kasser and Ryan (1993), who reported this finding in the United States, and Chan and Joseph (2000), who reported it in the U.K.

22. See Ryff (1989) and Ryff and Singer (1996), who defined *psychological well-being* as consisting of six aspects: 1. self-acceptance (the extent to which people possess a positive attitude toward themselves, are satisfied with themselves, and feel positive about their life); 2. positive relations with others (the extent to which people have satisfying relationships, are capable of empathy, warmth, and intimacy, and understand the give and take of relationships); 3. autonomy (the extent to which people are able to resist social pressures, think for themselves, and take responsibility); 4. a sense of mastery (the extent to which people have a sense of competence, are able to manage everyday affairs, and are able to pursue their goals); 5. purpose in life (the extent to which people have a sense of meaning in life, goals, and a sense of direction); and 6. personal growth (the extent to which people see themselves as continually developing, are open to new experiences, and are curious about life).

23. Both groups of people are described in the positive psychology literature as "off-diagonal."

24. Ruini, Ottolini, Rafanelli, Tossani, Ryff, and Fava (2003). Wood and Joseph (2010).

25. Frankl ([1946] 1985, p. 162).

Chapter 2

1. This estimate is reported in Breslau and Kessler (2001).

2. Kessler, Sonnega, Bromet, Hughes, and Nelson (1995); Elliot and Briere (1995).

3. Freud ([1920] 1955).

4. American Psychiatric Association (1980).

5. As quoted by Ford (2009); available online at www.ancienttexts.org/library/mesopotamian/gilgamesh/.

6. Shay (1995).

7. Quoted in Regel and Joseph (2010).

8. Hunt (2010).

9. See Daly (1983).

10. Quoted in Trimble (1981, p. 28).

11. Page (1883, pp. 171–173).

12. Breuer and Freud ([1893] 1957). Although a turning point in the history of psychological medicine, the case of Anna O remains controversial, with some modern commentators claiming it was likely that in fact she suffered from a form of epilepsy and that she was misdiagnosed by Breuer and Freud.

13. Freud ([1896] 1959, p. 198).

14. Sándor Ferenczi (1873–1933) was one who maintained that childhood experiences of sexual abuse were traumatic, see Van Der Hart (2008).

15. Herman (1992).

16. As reported in Holden (1998).

17. Quoted in Regel and Joseph (2010, p. 3).

18. As reported in Holden (1998). The effects of trench warfare on soldiers and the medical treatment they received are graphically described in Pat Barker's 1991 book *Regeneration*. See also Piers (1996) and Hunt (2010) for descriptions of how war trauma was managed by the psychiatric establishment of the time.

19. Freud ([1920] 1955); see also Freud, Ferenczi, Abraham, Simmel, and Jones (1921).

20. Janet ([1911] 1983). Janet's work was largely forgotten until the 1970s, when interest was revived through the publication of Ellenberger's 1970 book, *The Discovery of the Unconscious*.

21. See Gersons and Carlier (1992) for a review of these historical terms.

22. Adler (1943).

23. See Figley (1978).

24. American Psychiatric Association (1980). The *Diagnostic and Statistical Manual of Mental Disorders* is the handbook used by psychiatrists. First published in 1952, it has since been revised and updated six times. The most recent edition was published in 2000.

25. See Lifton (1967, 1973, 1986).

26. The exceptions are organic brain syndromes, substance abuse disorders, and puerperal psychosis.

27. Quoted in Summerfield (2001).

28. See Herman (1992).

29. Humphreys and Joseph (2004).

30. See Marsella and Wilson (2008) for a discussion of the relation between culture and trauma. See also Horwitz (2002) and Summerfield (2004) for a discussion of the topic of medicalization, and the social construction of mental illness, respectively. PTSD is criticized as a concept that wrongly medicalizes normal psychological distress and has been inappropriately exported to other non-Western cultures.

31. While accepting that there are core reactions to trauma consisting of intrusions and avoidance which may be hardwired in us, the argument in this book is that the concept of posttraumatic growth gives us a new non-medical way of understanding the adaptive significance of these phenomena. In light of the cultural criticisms of PTSD, however, we might ask about the cultural applicability of posttraumatic growth. See Weiss and Berger (2010) for evidence of the universality of posttraumatic growth across cultures, ranging from survivors of earthquakes in Turkey and Japan to Israelis and Palestinians exposed to political conflict, immigrants to the United States and Australia, and people across Europe exposed to a variety of stressors. And see Splevins, Cohen, Bowley, and Joseph (2010), who also discuss the

cultural applicability of the concept of posttraumatic growth and make the point that the idea of growth via suffering is a notion within the world's major religions of Christianity, Buddhism, Hinduism, Islam, and Judaism.

32. American Psychiatric Association (2000).

33. Case reported in Joseph, Williams and Yule (1997, p. 122).

34. See the case of Mac in Murphy (2009).

35. Quoted in McCormack (2010, p. 158).

36. This case is described in Regel and Joseph (2010, p. 73).

37. Andrews, Joseph, Shevlin, and Troop (2006), for example, report data showing that four clusters might be a better way to represent the experiences of posttraumatic stress. In their scheme, avoidance and emotional numbing are seen as separate clusters rather than as two parts of a single cluster. At the time of writing, PTSD is defined by the three clusters of symptoms: re-experiencing, avoidance and numbing, and arousal. But this is not set in stone, and the next edition of the DSM will likely change the number of clusters and reorganize which symptoms belong in each in light of research that has been carried out since the last edition was published in 2000, e.g., Armour, McBride, Shevlin, and Adamson (2011).

38. In this book I take a dimensional approach that is not concerned with classifying people but views posttraumatic stress as a continuum of response ranging from low levels to high levels. See Joseph, Williams, and Yule (1997). I use the term *PTSD* when referring to research that has used a categorical approach, but it is controversial whether there really is any distinction between so-called normal and abnormal states of mind. This is an issue I will return to in the next chapter when the biological basis of posttraumatic stress reactions will be considered. The challenge is made to those who adopt a categorical approach to define PTSD clearly in relation to dysfunction of a mental mechanism.

39. As specified in American Psychiatric Association (2000), these symptoms have to be present for at least a month after the event in order for a diagnosis of PTSD to be made.

40. American Psychiatric Association (1980), as quoted in Weathers and Keane (2008, p. 658), who discuss the definition of trauma and the difficulties in defining it. See also Joseph, Williams, and Yule (1997) for a discussion on normal and abnormal reactions to trauma. Debate continues to this day about how trauma should be defined within the DSM criteria for PTSD, with some arguing for reformulations in the existing definition—see, for example, Kilpatrick, Resnick, and Acierno (2009)—and others arguing that the event criterion be abolished altogether—see, for example, Brewin, Lanius, Novac, Schnyder, and Galea (2009).

41. See Bailham and Joseph (2003) and Ayers, Joseph, McKenzie-McHarg, Slade, and Wijma (2008) for a discussion on posttraumatic stress following childbirth.

42. Koffka (1936). A real-life example is cited by Kilpatrick et al. (1989) regarding a rape victim who developed PTSD only when it came to her attention, months after the event, that her attacker had killed another rape victim.

43. See Joseph and Masterson (1999) for a discussion of traumatic brain injury and how PTSD may arise in survivors of accidents who have no memory of their trauma.

44. American Psychiatric Association (1994). As quoted in Joseph, Williams, and Yule (1997, p. 13). This two-part definition was maintained in the subsequent edition of the DSM (American Psychiatric Association, 2000, pp. 467–468).

45. Breslau and Kessler (2001). See also Joseph, Williams, and Yule (1997) and Weathers and Keane (2008).

46. Regarding conceptual bracket creep, McNally (2004, 2010) cites a study by De Jongh, Olff, Van Hoolwerff, et al. (2008) on PTSD following wisdom-tooth extraction as well as a study by Banyard and Shevlin (2001) on PTSD following defeat of a football team.

Studies of 9/11 include Schlenger et al. (2002) and Silver et al. (2002), who point out that 17 percent of the U.S. population outside the New York area reported symptoms of PTSD two months after the attacks, even though only 2 percent of that sample knew someone who was directly affected. In addition, Schuster et al. (2001), who conducted a telephone survey of 560 adults across the United States on the weekend after 9/11, found that 44 percent had substantial trauma-related symptoms. And Park, Aldwin, Fenster, and Snyder (2008), who found in a nationally representative sample of 1,004 U.S. adults that greater television watching of the events of 9/11 was associated with higher rates of reported symptoms of PTSD. The question being raised here is whether normal reactions to upsetting but common events and events that are not directly experienced are being pathologized by the broader definition of what constitutes trauma.

Chapter 3

1. Walter Cannon first identified the fight-or-flight response. See Cannon (1914, 1932) as well as Selye ([1956] 1976).

2. Mayes (2000).

3. Quoted in Regel and Joseph (2010).

4. See Konner (2008).

5. Yule, Hodgkinson, Joseph, Murray-Parkes, and Williams (1990). Percentages reported on sample of 73 survivors.

6. Heidt, Marx, and Forsyth (2005).

7. For a discussion of the amygdala, see LeDoux (2000). Also see Bremner, Vermetten, Schmahl, Vaccarino, Vythilingam, Afzal, et al. (2005), who conducted a study of eight women with childhood sexual abuse–related PTSD and eleven women without abuse or PTSD. All underwent a positron emission tomography (PET) scan, during which a mild but annoying electric shock was administered to the arm paired with exposure to a blue square. Results showed that through association the blue square could elicit amygdala activation. The PTSD patients had increased amygdala activation with fear acquisition relative to the control group.

8. Turnbull (2010). Also see Bremner, Narayan, et al. (1999), who showed that people with PTSD exhibit reduced hippocampal activation.

9. See Bagot, Parent, Bredy, Zhang, Gratton, and Meaney (2008) as well as Konner (2008).

10. This expression was coined by Nesse (2001).

11. *Situationally accessible memory* is a term used by Brewin, Dalgleish, and Joseph (1996), who distinguish such memories from those that are stored at a conscious level called *verbally accessible memories* (VAMs). Unlike SAMs, VAMs can be deliberately accessed.

12. This exposure to feared stimuli usually takes place in gradual steps. For example, patients generate a list of the situations that cause them anxiety. Then, with the help of a therapist, they place themselves in the least anxiety-provoking situation and, as they learn to manage that situation, they move on to the next least anxiety-provoking situation, gradually working up to the situation that causes the most distress. Sometimes this is done in real-life situations and sometimes the patient uses his or her imagination to conjure the particular situation.

13. Foa and Kozak (1986).

14. Barad and Cain (2008); Bouton and Waddell (2008).

15. For a discussion of the extinction process as a function of the inhibitory effect exerted by the hippocampus on the amygdala, see Benoit et al. (1999). For details on research suggesting that chronic and intense trauma leads to changes in certain regions of the brain, see

Bremner, Randall, Scott, Bronen, Seibyl, Southwick, Delaney, McCarthy, Charney, and Innis (1995), who found that the volume of the hippocampus is reduced in combat veterans; Stein, Koverola, Hanna, Torchia, and McClarty (1997), who found that the volume of the hippocampus is reduced in survivors of childhood abuse; and Teicher (2000), who found that the corpus callosum is reduced in children who have been subjected to sexual and emotional abuse. Shin and Handwerger (2009) suggest that PTSD is a circuitry disorder. Nevertheless, while there is little doubt that the experience of posttraumatic stress is reflected in brain mechanisms, we have to be careful not to assume that PTSD automatically leads to neuropsychological complications or that neuropsychological complications lead to PTSD. As Richard Bentall (2004) writes: "Psychological changes are always accompanied by changes in the brain. Each new skill, or piece of information that we learn, is accompanied by the creation of new neural circuits that make new patterns of behaviour possible. These changes reflect the endless interaction between ourselves and the physical and social environment in which we live. Put crudely, our brains are constantly being rewired in response to our experiences. . . . Plainly, these findings do not imply that post-traumatic stress can be adequately understood as a disorder of the brain. It is better thought of as a psychological reaction to adverse events that manifests itself, at the biological level, as changes in brain structure" (p. 160). See also McNally (2006).

16. The term *disorder* implies a dysfunction of a mental mechanism to perform a natural function for which it was "designed" by evolution, see Wakefield (1992). It is not clear that the current definition of PTSD accurately identifies those for whom this definition fits. Some of those diagnosed with PTSD may have a neuropsychological dysfunction that prevents them from cognitively processing memories of trauma, but the argument here is that in general, PTSD does not represent the dysfunction of a mental mechanism but rather the function of normal and natural cognitive processes of adaptation. The challenge for those who adopt the categorical approach is to define PTSD in relation to the biological dysfunction of a mental mechanism failing to perform a natural function for which it was designed by evolution.

17. Studies have shown that, among Vietnam veterans, around 15 percent of males and 9 percent of females had PTSD, with higher rates reported for those with high war-zone exposure (36 percent and 18 percent, respectively). See, for example, Kulka, Schlenger, Fairbank, et al. (1990). As Bullman and Kang (1994) note, Vietnam veterans of both sexes also exhibit an increased risk of suicide.

18. See Kessler, Sonnega, Bromet, Hughes, and Nelson (1995) as well as Breslau and Kessler (2001). The incidence of PTSD in those who experience a traumatic event has been estimated at around 8 percent, but it is important to note that this figure varies depending on the type of events in question—some of which are intrinsically more traumatic than others (insofar as people will almost invariably experience them as frightening, uncontrollable, and horrific, and as life-threatening). Nevertheless, as Bonanno, Brewin, Kaniasty, and La Greca (2010) have documented, the prevalence of PTSD rarely exceeds a ceiling of 30 percent, even at the highest levels of trauma exposure.

19. Bradley, Greene, Russ, Dutra, and Western (2005).

20. Bonanno, Galea, Bucciarelli, and Vlahov (2006).

Chapter 4

1. The idea of bouncing back from adversity is discussed by Smith, Dalen, Wiggins, Tooley, Christopher, and Bernard (2008), who developed a questionnaire with which to assess people's ability to bounce back. The questionnaire consists of six statements—"I tend to

bounce back quickly after hard times," "I have a hard time making it through stressful events," "It does not take me long to recover from a stressful event," "It is hard for me to snap back when something bad happens," "I usually come through difficult times with little trouble," and "I tend to take a long time to get over setbacks in my life"—and respondents are asked to indicate the extent to which they agree with them on a 5-point scale ranging from "strongly disagree" to "strongly agree." (Each of the positively worded statements is scored as strongly disagree = 1, disagree = 2, neutral = 3, agree = 4, and strongly agree = 5, and each of the negatively worded statements is scored as strongly disagree = 5, disagree = 4, neutral = 3, agree= 2, and strongly agree = 1.) The researchers found that most respondents scored between 18 and 24 and that those who scored higher were more optimistic, more purposeful, had more social support, used more active coping, were less stressed, and exhibited lower levels of depression and anxiety.

2. See Lepore and Revenson (2006), who describe resistance, recovery, and reconfiguration and how it is the process of reconfiguration that posttraumatic growth refers to. Confusingly the term *recovery* has recently been used by psychiatrists to refer to the establishment of a more meaningful and fulfilling life (see Schrank and Slade, 2007), but here I use the term specifically to refer to when people return to their pre-trauma levels of functioning as opposed to posttraumatic growth, which implies going beyond one's pre-trauma level of functioning.

3. Joseph, Linley, and Harris (2005) asked 176 people who had experienced a range of life-events to complete several measures of positive change. Based on a statistical procedure called factor analysis, their results suggested that there are three main categories of positive change: (a) personal changes such as increased self-efficacy, personal strength, a positive attitude, and increased patience; (b) increased relationship strengths such as community closeness, compassion, more faith in people, appreciation of family and friends; and (c) philosophical and spiritual changes.

4. Smith, Joseph, and Nair (2011).

5. Quoted in McCormack (2010).

6. Defined in this way, posttraumatic growth should be distinguished from other benefits that people may report in the aftermath of adversity but which don't have this deep-seated transformational nature. See also Davis and Nolen-Hoeksema (2009), who use the term benefit-finding in a distinct way to posttraumatic growth. A further point of distinction is that benefits can be found following a range of life-events which are not necessarily traumatic, but here I use the term posttraumatic growth specifically in the context of events which have led the person to experience some degree of posttraumatic stress (although not necessarily to such an extent that they would fulfill the diagnostic criteria for PTSD).

7. See Lehman, Davis, Delongis, et al. (1993). This was one of the earliest studies to document positive changes following adversity. Ninety-four people who had lost a spouse or a child in a motor vehicle accident four to seven years previously were interviewed. They were asked questions about what their life was like, whether they now did things differently, and whether the death had affected their life goals or philosophy of life. A total of 203 life changes were cited, 140 of which were positive and 63 negative. Most of the respondents (74 percent) mentioned at least 1 positive change: 29 percent mentioned 1 positive change; 26 percent, 2 positive changes; 14 percent, 3 positive changes; 4 percent, 4 positive changes; and 2 percent, 5 positive changes. Only 44 percent mentioned at least 1 negative change: 28 percent mentioned 1 negative change; 10 percent, 2 negative changes; 5 percent, 3 negative changes; and 1 percent, 4 negative changes. In terms of specific categories of positive change, 35 percent mentioned increased self-confidence; 26 percent, a focus on enjoying the present; 23

percent, an increased acceptance of mortality; 23 percent, a greater appreciation of life; 19 percent, an increased emphasis on family; 15 percent, increased religiosity; and 7 percent, increased openness and concern for others. In terms of specific categories of negative changes, 26 percent mentioned shattered life goals; 15 percent, an increased awareness of fragility; 15 percent, social isolation; 6 percent, struggling to get through each day; and 5 percent, decreased religiosity.

8. Several studies were conducted following 9/11; see, for example, those by Morland, Butler, and Leskin (2008); Park, Aldwin, Fenster, and Snyder (2008); Schuster et al. (2001); and Butler et al. (2005).

9. Poulin et al. (2009). Higher levels of growth seem to be reported in this study than in the study by Butler et al. (2005), although the two studies are not directly comparable because of the varying ways in which they measured growth; for instance, a higher number of reports of growth might reflect a more representative sample or different ways of eliciting people's reports of growth. Also see Ai et al. (2005), who report changes in political views, and Vollhardt (2009), who discusses how people can become more altruistic and helpful towards each other than they were beforehand.

10. Vázquez, Hervás, and Pérez-Sales (2006) surveyed 502 people a few weeks after these attacks in Madrid and found that 31 percent of the respondents reported perceived positive consequences; 61 percent, learning; 80 percent, feeling closer to others; 79 percent, increased social cohesion; 31 percent, feeling more prepared for future similar situations; 85 percent, increased solidarity; and 82 percent, feeling that they were part of a community. See also Vázquez, Pérez-Sales, and Hervás (2008).

11. Medical problems [see, Kennedy, Tellegen, et al. (1976), and Martin, Tolosa, and Joseph (2004), whose studies focused on cancer patients; Fromm et al. (1996) and Widows et al. (2005), bone marrow transplant patients; Morrill, Brewer, O'Neill, Lillie, Dees, Carey, and Rimer (2008), Weiss (2002), and Zenmore et al. (1989), women with breast cancer; Rieker, Edbril, and Garnick (1985), testicular cancer patients; Dirik and Karanci (2008), rheumatoid arthritis patients; Affleck et al. (1987), male cardiac patients; Sheikh (2004), people with a history of heart disease; Cohen Konrad (2006), mothers whose children had acquired permanent physical disabilities]. Loss and bereavement [see, Edmonds and Hooker (1992), adults who were bereaved; Engelkemeyer and Marwit (2008), bereaved parents; Abbott (2009), Israeli and Palestinian families following the violent death of a family member; Al Qaisy (2010), Iraqi families]. Adverse interpersonal experiences [see Burt and Katz (1987), rape survivors; Woodward and Joseph (2003), adults who had been abused as children; Cobb et al. (2006), partner violence; Peltzer (2000), community violence]. Accidents and disasters [see Lindgaard, Iglebaek, and Jensen (2009), parents who were on vacation in Thailand or Sri Lanka when the tsunami hit the coast of Southeast Asia in 2004; Cieslak, Benight, Schmidt, Luszczynska, Curtin, Clark, and Kissinger (2009), Hurricane Katrina survivors living with HIV; Tang (2006), survivors of the Southeast Asian earthquake-tsunami].

12. See Feder, Southwick, Goetz, Wang, Alonso, Smith, Buchholz, Waldeck, Ameli, Moore, Hain, Charney, and Vythilingam (2008), who studied Vietnam veterans and Lev-Weisel and Amor, who studied Holocaust child survivors. Also see Carmil and Breznitz (1991), who interviewed a nationwide sample of 533 Israelis. The sample included 125 Holocaust survivors. The aim was to see how the experience of the Holocaust had affected these people in terms of their political attitudes, religious identity, and orientation to the future. Toward this end, the authors asked a series of questions on topics such as the respondents' voting intentions, whether they regarded themselves as religious, and whether they believed the future would be better. Similar questions were asked of 128 people who

immigrated to Israel before 1939. Would the Holocaust survivors give different answers? According to the results, the Holocaust survivors were more likely to hold moderate political opinions (90 percent versus 71 percent of the comparison group), to be religious (14 percent versus 7 percent), and to be optimistic about the future (42 percent believed in a better future compared to 23 percent).

13. Mosher, Danoff-Burg, and Brunker (2006) studied daughters of women with breast cancer; Weiss (2004), husbands of breast cancer survivors; Dekel (2007), wives of former prisoners of war; Linley and Joseph (2005a), disaster workers; Linley and Joseph (2005b), funeral directors; Linley and Joseph (2007), psychotherapists; and Arnold, Calhoun, Tedeschi, and Cann (2005), trauma therapists.

14. See Milam, Ritt-Olsen, and Unger (2004); Ickovics, Meade, Kershaw, Milan, Lewis, and Ethier (2006); and Salter and Stallard (2004).

15. Harvey (2008). For reviews of research with younger people, see also Clay, Knibbs, and Joseph (2009), and Joseph, Knibbs, and Hobbs (2007).

16. Most other studies on this topic corroborate this range of 30 to 70 percent. For general reviews of the literature, see Linley and Joseph (2004b), and Helgeson et al. (2006).

17. Miller and C'deBaca (2001).

18. See Tedeschi and Calhoun (1996). The PTGI can be completed online at http://cust-cf.apa.org/ptgi/index.cfm.

19. For further details on this study, see Manne et al. (2004). A related example is Powell et al. (2007), who contacted 51 patients who had previously attended a head injury clinic, most of whom were classified as having at least mild to moderate disability as a result: 25 had experienced injury one to three years previously and 27 had experienced injury nine to twelve years previously. The researchers found that those in the "later" group scored higher on a measure of posttraumatic growth than those in the "earlier" group. Another example is Feigelman, Jordan, and Gorman (2009), who found their sample of subjects through newsletters and organizations concerned with suicide survivors. A total of 462 parents who had lost a child through suicide participated in the survey. Nine percent had sustained their loss within the past year; 40 percent, between 1 and 4 years earlier; 30 percent, between 4 and 10 years earlier; and 21 percent, more than 10 years previously. Parents completed several questionnaires including the Hogan Grief Reaction Checklist (HGRC), a specially designed tool for use with bereaved people that asks people to rate statements such as "I have learned to cope better with life," "I have more compassion for others." The authors used this questionnaire to measure growth. What they found was that the greater the amount of time since the loss, the greater the growth, although there was a drop in personal growth in the first year. And by year five, nearly two-thirds scored above average. Bear in mind that, as this study asked people to take part through suicide-related newsletters, the incidence of growthful responses may be overestimated. In other words, those who found benefits might simply be the ones who were most likely to reply. The authors themselves caution that because of their sampling procedure they cannot be sure that their sample was representative of parents who had experienced such loss.

20. Shakespeare-Finch and Enders (2008).

21. Nakonezny, Reddick, and Rodgers (2004).

22. Peterson and Seligman (2003).

23. Frazier, Tennen, Gavian, Park, Tomich, and Tashiro (2009). It was also found that perceived growth was associated with increased distress from pre- to posttrauma, whereas actual growth was related to decreased distress, a pattern suggesting that perceived and actual growth reflect different processes.

24. Ransom, Sheldon, and Jacobsen (2008), who found perceived growth to be related to actual changes in goal orientation in cancer patients. See also Joseph, Maltby, Wood, Stockton, Hunt, and Regel (forthcoming).

25. Gunty, Frazier, Tennen, Tomich, Tashiro, and Park (2011).

26. McFarland and Alvaro (2000).

27. Smith, Joseph, and Nair (2011).

28. Smith, Joseph, and Nair (2011).

29. Coyne and Tennen (2010) discuss other research in personality psychology showing that people are poor judges of personal change. And see Zoellner and Maercker (2006), who also discuss how reports of growth might reflect self-deceptive coping in some people and genuine change in others.

30. Taylor, Lichtman, and Wood (1984).

31. Taylor and Brown (1994); Taylor and Armor (1996). Also see Engelkemeyer and Marwit (2008), who, in a study of bereaved parents, found that those with more growth reported greater self-esteem. They raise the possibility that it is the need to protect self-esteem that can sometimes lead to reports of growth.

32. Frazier and Burnett (1994). Responses were categorized into nine groups: "more cautious," "appreciate life more," "change relationships," "reevaluate goals," "take care of self better," "be more assertive," "realize strengths," "choose different types of men," and "closer to God."

33. Frazier, Conlon, and Glaser (2001).

34. The best evidence for this comes from Helgeson, Reynolds, and Tomich (2006). This is a review of 77 articles that concludes that benefit-finding following adversity is related to more intrusive and avoidant posttraumatic experiences. As intrusion and avoidance are generally seen as symptoms of PTSD, at first glance this result would seem to suggest that benefit-finding is indicative of poor mental health, but what Helgeson et al. suggest is that these constructs reflect cognitive processing: "Experiencing intrusive thoughts about a stressor may be a signal that people are working through the implications of the stressor for their lives, and these implications could lead to growth. In fact, some might argue that a period of contemplation and consideration of the stressor is necessary for growth to occur" (p. 810).

35. Butler, Blasey, Garlan, McCaslin, Azarow, Chen, Desjardins, DiMiceli, Seagraves, Hastings, Kraemer, and Spiegel (2005). The inverted U-shape relationship between posttraumatic stress and posttraumatic growth has been reported in several studies. For example, McCaslin, de Zoysa, Butler, Hart, Marmar, Metzler, and Koopman (2009) found a curvilinear relationship between posttraumatic stress and posttraumatic growth among 93 Sri Lankan university students who experienced a traumatic event; Colville and Cream (2009) reported a curvilinear relationship among 50 parents of children admitted to a pediatric intensive care unit; Kleim and Ehlers (2009) found a curvilinear relationship in two samples of 180 and 70 assault survivors, respectively; and Kunst (2010) found a curvilinear relationship among 678 victims of violence. At the lower end of the curve, see Levine, Laufer, Stein, Hamama-Raz, and Solomon (2009), who studied 2,908 adolescents exposed to terror as well as 588 adults and army personnel following the second Lebanon war and found that those subjects who exhibited the most resilience (fewest PTSD symptoms) had the lowest growth scores.

36. Stump and Smith (2008).

37. This is not say that positive changes cannot come about through other means, but here I use the term posttraumatic growth to refer to the specific process of how growth arises in relation to posttraumatic stress.

38. McMillen, Fisher, and Smith (1997), in their study of 195 survivors of disaster, found that those who reported benefits within four to six weeks were less likely to be diagnosed with PTSD three years later. Butler, Blasey, Garlan, McCaslin, Azarow, Chen, Desjardins, DiMiceli, Seagraves, Hastings, Kraemer, and Spiegel (2005) found that following 9/11, those who reported growth in the initial few days and weeks experienced lower posttraumatic stress six months later. Davis, Nolen-Hoeksema, and Larson (1998) found that those who reported posttraumatic growth following the loss of a loved one exhibited lower distress over a year later. Also see Linley, Joseph, and Goodfellow (2008). Bearing in mind the distinction made earlier between perceived and actual growth, what this research tells us is that perceptions of growth generally seem to play a valuable role in later adjustment.

39. Frazier, Tashiro, Berman, Steger, and Long (2004).

40. Morrill et al. (2008).

41. A meta-analysis of studies concluded that growth was related to decreased depression and greater positivity; see Helgeson, Reynolds, and Tomich (2006). For examples of specific studies mentioned, see Luszczynska, Sarkar, and Knoll (2007), who found that growth was associated with better adherence to antiretroviral medication in HIV patients; Frazier, Conlon, and Glaser (2001), who studied growth following sexual assault; Davis et al. (1998), who studied growth following bereavement of a close family member; Feigelman, Jordan, and Gorman (2009), who studied 462 parents who lost a child through suicide finding that higher scores on personal-growth measures were associated with fewer mental health problems; and McMillen, Fisher, and Smith (1997), who studied growth following various disasters— a tornado in Florida, a mass killing in Texas, and a plane crash in Indiana; Kessler, Galea, Jones, and Parker (2006), who found that growth was associated with less suicidality in survivors of Hurricane Katrina; and Butler et al. (2005), who studied growth following 9/11 finding that people who reported religious benefits two months after the attacks were the ones who were most well-adjusted thirty-six months later.

42. Wood and Joseph (2010). In this study, a large cohort of 5,630 people completed survey measures at two time points: Time 1 at ages fifty-five to fifty-six and Time 2 at ages sixty-five to sixty-six. To measure eudaimonic well-being, the Scales of Psychological Well-Being (PWB) were used. These provided a taxonomy of positive functioning, comprising self-acceptance, autonomy, purpose in life, positive relationships with others, environmental mastery, and personal growth. Depression was measured via the Centre for Epidemiological Studies Depression Scale (CES-D). The researchers found that people with low PWB were 7.2 times more likely to be depressed ten years later. After personality, negative functioning, prior depression, and demographic, economic, and physical health variables were controlled for, people with low PWB were still found to be more than twice as likely to be depressed. Although this study was not concerned with trauma survivors, I mention it to underscore the role of PWB in creating positive mental health because insofar as posttraumatic growth implies an increase in eudaimonic well-being, we expect it to improve mental health. But one caveat: Imagine two people who have encountered adversity. One person grows a little, but this person was already showing a high level of PWB; the other person grows a great deal but initially exhibited a low level of PWB. So, despite the greater growth of the second person, his overall level of PWB is lower than that of the first person. Ultimately, then, it's not just the growth in PWB that's important but also the gross amount of PWB.

43. For example, in a study that surveyed fifty-six women who had been diagnosed with breast cancer, Holland and Holahan (2003) found that those who exhibited higher levels of psychological well-being were the ones who had greater perceived social support and who engaged in more approach-oriented coping and less avoidant coping.

44. Peterson et al. (2008). This was an Internet study that used the Values in Action (VIA) survey developed by Christopher Peterson and Martin Seligman to assess the range of human strengths.

45. Affleck, Tennen, Croog, and Levine (1987).

46. Danoff-Burg and Revenson (2005).

47. Bower, Kemeny, Taylor, and Fahey (1998). In this study, benefit-finding was found to be related to a slower decline in CD4-T cells over a two- to three-year follow-up. CD4-T cells are part of the immune system, and their loss is related to disease progression. Similar results were reported by Ickovics, Milan, Boland, Schoenbaum, Schuman, and Vlahov (2006), who found that benefit-finding was related to positive changes in neuroendocrine function, including decreased production of cortisol (the stress hormone), and by Carrico, Ironson, Antoni, Lechner, Duran, Kumar, and Schneiderman (2006), who found slower loss of CD4-T cells and lower AIDS-related mortality among those who reported benefits.

48. Brewin, Andrews, and Valentine (2000). A meta-analysis of the literature on factors related to PTSD concludes that one of the most important protective factors is social support. Meta-analysis is a statistical method that allows one to examine the results of many studies and reach a general conclusion.

49. Joseph, Williams, and Yule (1995, 1997) describe the interaction of appraisal processes, emotional states, ways of coping, and how they can lead to a downward spiral in functioning. Also, recent research shows that traumatic events, particularly those involving early abuse and sexual molestation, may be related to psychotic experiences later in life, possibly caused by dissociative forms of coping. See Bentall (2004), Shevlin, Dorahy, and Adamson (2007).

50. Joseph, Williams, and Yule (1992). Also see Joseph, Yule, Williams, and Andrews (1993) as well as Dalgleish, Joseph, Thrasher, Tranah, and Yule (1996).

51. This is described by Morland, Butler, and Leskin (2008).

Chapter 5

1. Horowitz (1976).

2. As quoted in McCormack, Hagger, and Joseph (2010, p. 281).

3. Hart (1962).

4. Wegner (1994).

5. From O'Hanlon and Bertolino (1998).

6. Quoted in Crown (2009, pp. 12–13).

7. See Janoff-Bulman (1992), who developed the theory of shattered assumptions to explain posttraumatic stress.

8. Becker (1997, p. 87).

9. Weinstein and Klein (1996).

10. Epstein (1991). And see Janoff-Bulman (1992).

11. Quoted in McCormack (2010, p. 139).

12. Gluhoski and Wortman (1990). In this study, 3,617 people with an average age of fifty-three years were interviewed about their worldviews at two points in time separated by three years. The researchers found that perceptions of vulnerability and self-view were altered among those respondents who had experienced traumatic events, including job loss, life-threatening illness, physical assault, and the death of a spouse, parent, or child. Specifically, they were more likely after trauma than before to agree with statements like "I worry that something bad will happen to me."

13. Becker (1997, p. 133).

14. According to De Silva (2006), who explored the Buddhist response to the 2004 tsunami in Sri Lanka, there will be no PTSD when the event is not perceived as traumatic.

15. Trauma researchers generally tend to regard intrusive ruminations as symptoms of PTSD, but they can also be viewed as an index of adaptive cognitive processing. See Park (2010), Janoff-Bulman (1992), Creamer, Burgess, and Pattison (1992), Joseph, Williams, and Yule (1995). Whether intrusive thoughts are adaptive or not seems to depend on a number of factors, such as their timing and content. See Greenberg (1995) and Joseph, Dalgleish, Thrasher, Yule, Williams, and Hodgkinson (1996). More recently, Park, Chmielewski, and Blank (2009), who, in a study of 167 survivors of cancer, found that intrusive thoughts were related to poorer quality of life—except among those who scored high on a measure of posttraumatic growth, in which case their intrusive thoughts were related to better quality of life.

16. See Joseph and Linley (2005, 2006a, 2008) for a detailed description of this new theory of posttraumatic growth. See also Ransom, Sheldon, and Jacobsen (2008).

17. Quotation, Rogers (1963, pp. 1–2). Tedeschi and Calhoun (1996) compared people who had experienced a traumatic event in the past year with people who had not, but who were asked to think about the changes they had experienced in the previous year. What the researchers found was that those who had experienced trauma exhibited higher levels of posttraumatic growth than those who had not, but also that those who had not experienced trauma reported a certain amount of growth. Over a period of a year, many people—whether traumatized or not—will experience some degree of personal growth.

18. This theory is based on the idea that posttraumatic growth arises through rebuilding of the assumptive world (Janoff-Bulman, 1992), but as noted in the previous chapter, there is a distinction to be made between posttraumatic growth, which arises through this process, and other positive benefits that people report that may arise through other means. See also Janoff-Bulman (2004), who discusses how growth can arise through other means such as self-understanding. An example of this is a study of 1,287 Vietnam veterans, many of whom said that they had experienced positive outcomes of service—such as learning to cope with adversity, self-discipline, and having a broader perspective. If they could cope with the war, soldiers said, they could cope with anything; see Aldwin, Levenson, and Spiro III (1994). Through coping with trauma, people learn about themselves. Their capabilities are put to the test. As a result, their boundaries of self-knowledge are expanded and their hidden strengths are revealed. As one woman put it in another study, "I guess it taught me that you don't know how strong you are until you confront each thing as it happens, and you take it one piece at a time—you call a lot on your own reserves and you've got to be strong so that you don't collapse in a heap—you've got to think, 'I've got to get through this' and it's amazing how you do." As quoted in McCormack, Hagger, and Joseph (2010, p. 285). Such learning about oneself may be better thought of as benefit-finding. Shattered vase theory refers to the mechanism through which posttraumatic growth arises via the rebuilding of assumptions, but it is important to note that there may be other routes by which people find benefits.

19. Joseph and Williams (2005) and Joseph, Williams, and Yule (1995, 1997) emphasize the role of appraisal processes and rumination. See also Calhoun, Cann, and Tedeschi (2011).

20. See Stockton, Hunt, and Joseph (2011). This article presents two studies exploring two differing conceptualizations of cognitive processing following trauma. The results indicate that adaptive forms of cognitive processing—namely, deliberate rumination and reflective pondering—are significantly positively associated with posttraumatic growth. For similar studies, see Taku, Cann, Tedeschi, and Calhoun (2009) and Gangstad, Norman, and Barton (2009).

21. This is particularly true with regard to the inevitability of death. Jonas, Schimel, Greenberg, and Pyszczynski (2002) suggest that when people are reminded of this inevitability, their worldview defense strengthens and they seek to conform to the accepted beliefs and behaviors of their culture. For example, people interviewed close to a funeral home were more likely to give to charity when later asked. The authors called this the "scrooge effect." See also Calhoun and Tedeschi (1991) who note that beliefs that are less easily disconfirmed, such as religious beliefs, may be more likely subject to assimilation.

22. Ortega (1957, pp. 156–157).

23. Joseph (1999).

24. King (2001).

25. See Resick and Schnicke (1993). Joseph and Linley (2005) also refer to positive and negative accommodation in the context of changes in worldview. I would argue that human beings are intrinsically motivated to increase their psychological well-being—becoming autonomous, self-accepting, and masterful and developing their relationships as well as their potential for further growth. So, even change that seems negative to an outside observer is ultimately directed by the same growthful urge toward the expression of psychological well-being. In short, individuals grow as best they can in a hostile environment—in much the same sense that a tree deprived of sunlight develops in stunted or thwarted ways.

26. Ryan and Deci (2000). See also Patterson and Joseph (2007) who discuss self-determination theory in relation to Carl Rogers' theory.

27. Joseph and Linley (2005).

28. Woodward and Joseph (2003).

29. Scrignaro, Barni, and Magrin (2010).

30. This view is not rose-tinted, however, inasmuch as it recognizes that the expression of the drive toward psychological well-being can manifest itself in destructive and harmful ways. See Joseph and Worsley (2005).

31. Joseph and Linley (2006b).

32. Dalai Lama ([1995] 2001).

33. Davis, Wortman, Lehman, and Silver (2000) explored the issue of meaning making and found in their study of people bereaved through the loss of a child or spouse, that even when meaning is found, people do not set aside the search for meaning, rather it is ongoing. The search for answers is ongoing—the point is that posttraumatic growth is best seen as a process, not simply as an outcome.

Chapter 6

1. See, for example, Billings and Moos (1981); Joseph, Williams, and Yule (1992); Ferguson and Cox (1997); and Folkman and Lazarus (1985).

2. See, for example, Littleton, Horsley, John, and Nelson (2007).

3. Kubler-Ross and Kessler (2001, p. 87). See also Butler, Blasey, Garlan, McCaslin, Azarow, Chen, Desjardins, DiMiceli, Seagraves, Hastings, Kraemer, and Spiegel (2005), who found that denial in the weeks following 9/11 seemed to be adaptive; and Aldwin (1993), who provides a review of studies that focus on coping with traumatic stress.

4. Carver, Scheier, and Weintraub (1989).

5. Folkman and Lazarus (1985).

6. Stiles (1987).

7. Scrignaro et al. (2010). For further evidence of the role of social support, see Schroevers, Helgeson, Sanderman, and Ranchor (2010), who conducted a study of 206 long-term cancer survivors. What they found was a statistically significant correlation between receipt

of emotional support at three months after diagnosis and positive medical outcome at eight years after diagnosis. This association remained significant after the researchers controlled for concurrent levels of emotional support at eight years after diagnosis. Because of the longitudinal time frame of this study, it provides reliable evidence for the role of social support in recovery. See also Siegel, Schrimshaw, and Pretter (2005), who found perceived emotional support to be associated with growth among 138 women living with HIV/AIDS.

8. Pakenham, Dadds, and Terry (1994).

9. Cieslak, Benight, Schmidt, Luszczynska, Curtin, Clark, and Kissinger (2009).

10. Wood, Joseph, and Linley (2007).

11. Butler, Blasey, Garlan, McCaslin, Azarow, Chen, Desjardins, DiMiceli, Seagraves, Hastings, Kraemer, and Spiegel (2005). An increase in religious practice can be experienced as growthful. Indeed, religion is included in the widely used Posttraumatic Growth Inventory. But in my view, it is misleading to include religion in the definition of growth because for some it is actually the loss of their religion that is experienced as growthful. More useful is to understand religion as a coping strategy and how it is related to growth.

12. Feigelman, Jordan, and Gorman (2009) studied 462 parents who lost a child through suicide finding that those who participated in weekly religious services were more likely to report growth than those attending services less often—but it is unclear whether this finding reflects meaning provided by religious participation or benefits that accrue from the social support that comes with attendance. See also Thombre et al. (2010), who found that religious coping fostered meaning among family caregivers of cancer patients; Askay and Magyar-Russell (2009), who found that religious beliefs facilitated growth among burn patients; Cadell, Regehr, and Hemsworth (2003), who found that spirituality was associated with growth among 174 bereaved HIV/AIDS caregivers; and Shaw, Joseph, and Linley (2005), who provide a review of research findings on the relation between religion and posttraumatic growth.

13. Mayer and Salovey (1997, p. 5).

14. Linley et al. (2011) investigated the relationship between emotional intelligence and growth. They used the emotional intelligence questionnaire developed by Schutte et al. (1998), which consists of thirty-three items (e.g., "I am aware of my emotions as I experience them," "I know what other people are feeling just by looking at them") rated on the basis of a 5-point scale (1 = strongly disagree, 5 = strongly agree). The researchers found that emotion-focused coping (i.e., seeking support and venting emotions) was related to posttraumatic growth in those participants with higher emotional intelligence.

15. Numerous studies show that problem-focused and emotion-focused coping strategies are related to growth. See, for example, Park, Aldwin, Fenster, and Snyder (2008); Stump and Smith (2008); Pakenham, Chiv, Bursnall, and Cannon (2009); Mosher, Danoff-Burg, and Brunker (2006); Hall, Hobfoll, Canetti, Johnson, Palmieri, and Galea (2010); Schultz and Mohamed (2004); Bussell and Naus (2010); Schroevers and Teo (2008); Morris, Shakespeare-Finch, and Scott (2007); Thornton and Perez (2006); Widows, Jacobsen, Booth-Jones, and Fields (2005); Karanci and Erkham (2007); Kinsinger, Penedo, Antoni, Dahn, Lechner, and Schneiderman (2006); Dirik and Karanci (2008); Luszczynska, Sarkar, and Knoll (2007); Frazier, Tashiro, Berman, Steger, and Long (2004); and Cieslak, Benight, Schmidt, Luszczynska, Curtin, Clark, and Kissinger (2009). For a summary of research on coping methods, see Prati and Pietrantoni (2009), who conducted a meta-analysis of 103 studies showing that optimism, social support, spirituality, acceptance coping, reappraisal coping, religious coping, and seeking social support were associated with posttraumatic growth.

16. Antoni, Wimberly, Lechner, Kazi, Sifre, Urcuyo, et al. (2006).

17. Kissane, Bloch, Smith, et al. (2003).

18. Hefferon, Grealy, and Mutrie (2008).

19. Lazarus and Folkman (1984); Folkman and Lazarus (1985); Bonanno, Pat-Horenczyk, and Noll (2011).

20. See Carver (1997) and Carver, Scheier, and Weintraub (1989).

21. The Functional Dimensions of Coping Scale was developed by Professors Eamonn Ferguson and Tom Cox (1997).

22. Joseph, Dalgleish, Williams, Thrasher, Yule, and Hodgkinson (1997).

23. Frankl (1985, p. 157).

24. Neimeyer (2006).

25. From Churchill's speech at a Civil Defence Services' luncheon, July 14, 1941.

26. From Kennedy's inaugural address, January 20, 1961.

27. See Weiss and Berger (2010). See also Pals and McAdams (2004).

28. For example, see Tuval-Mashiach, Freedman, Bargai, Boker, Hadar, and Shalev (2004), who examined narratives of five men who were exposed to a life-threatening terror attack showing that when their narratives were well-built, coherent, and possessing significance, levels of posttraumatic stress were lower.

29. Research has investigated the relation between personality factors and posttraumatic growth, finding that people who exhibit optimism, hopefulness, locus of control, self-efficacy, hardiness, and a sense of coherence, for example, are more likely to report posttraumatic growth than those who do not exhibit such traits. For example, in a study of thirty former prisoners of war, Feder et al. (2008) found that optimism was related to greater growth. Also see Linley and Joseph (2004b) for a review of the factors that are related to posttraumatic growth. The reason why personality is related to growth is thought to be because of how personality influences coping. Shakespeare-Finch, Gow, and Smith (2005), for example, found that personality traits—specifically, extraversion, openness, agreeableness, and conscientiousness—were associated with growth in 526 emergency service personnel, and that these associations were mediated by coping. Sheikh (2004), in a study of 110 people with a history of heart disease, investigated the relationship between posttraumatic growth and the Big Five personality dimensions—extraversion, neuroticism, agreeableness, openness, and conscientiousness—and found that extraversion was the chief predictor of growth and that this relationship was partly mediated by problem-focused coping. And Schultz and Mohamed (2004) found that coping mediated the relationship between self-efficacy and growth in 105 cancer patients.

30. See Meichenbaum (2006), who explains how stories are the pathway through which coping exerts its influence; in turn, as posttraumatic growth develops, it is also likely that people become more effective copers. Littlewood, Vanable, Carey, and Blair (2008), who, in a survey of 221 HIV patients, found that benefit-finding led to increased social support; and Mohr, Dick, Russo, et al. (1999), who, in a study of 94 multiple sclerosis patients, found that benefit-finding was related to adaptive coping strategies such as seeking social support and positive reappraisal.

31. McAdams (2001). See also Haidt (2006), who discusses how posttraumatic growth may require coherence between these three levels of personality.

32. See Wood, Linley, Maltby, Baliousis, and Joseph (2008), who discuss authenticity.

Chapter 7

1. Joseph and Linley (2005); Joseph (2004). See also Joseph and Patterson (2008).

2. Brewin, Dalgleish, and Joseph (1996).

3. The rewind technique was developed following a two-year follow-up of nineteen policemen showing that their initial improvement in symptoms was maintained following treatment with the technique. It has since become a widely known technique for the alleviation of PTSD; see Muss (1991a, 1991b, 2002).

4. See Shapiro (1995) for a description of EMDR and how it was developed; Foa, Keane, Friedman, and Cohen (2008) for a review of effective therapies for PTSD. EMDR seems to be helpful, but it is controversial because research has not conclusively demonstrated that it is helpful because of the role of eye movements or whether it is helpful because it is really just a version of exposure therapy.

5. The road to resilience. See: http://www.apa.org/helpcenter/resilience-road.pdf.

6. See also Calhoun and Tedeschi (1999), who have pioneered an approach to therapy in which the therapist is referred to as an expert companion. This seems broadly similar to the humanistic approach on which the views presented here are based.

7. See Worsley and Joseph (2007). See also Joseph and Worsley (2005) for recent research and theory on the applications of person-centered therapy with a variety of conditions.

8. See, Murphy, Joseph, and Durkin (2010) for an overview of literature on psychotherapy factors.

9. See also Stanton, Bower, and Low (2006), who are among a number of authors who urge caution by therapists in "prescribing" growth.

10. Joseph, Maltby, Wood, Stockton, Hunt, and Regel (forthcoming).

11. Impact of Event Scale, see Horowitz, Wilner, and Alvarez (1979); Joseph (2000).

12. See, for example, Calhoun and Tedeschi (1999), and discussions by Cordova (2008) on facilitating posttraumatic growth following cancer, and Lyons (2008) on working with traumatized veterans.

13. Gilbert and Proctor (2006) and Gilbert (2010).

14. Feigelman, Jordan, and Gorman (2009). See also Murphy, Johnson, and Lohan (2003), who found parents who attended a bereavement support group following the loss of a child were four times more likely to find a sense of meaning five years after their loss.

15. The road to resilience. See: http://www.apa.org/helpcenter/resilience-road.pdf.

16. Quote from Woodward and Joseph (2003, p. 276).

17. As described by Pennebaker at a workshop of his I attended in the summer of 2009 at the University of Central Lancashire, England. For a summary of this work, see also Pennebaker (1997).

18. Pennebaker (2009). For some practical advice on writing, see Pennebaker's home page at the University of Texas: http://homepage.psy.utexas.edu/homepage/Faculty/Pennebaker/Home2000/WritingandHealth.html.

19. Frisina, Borod, and Lepore (2004), who conducted a meta-analysis to examine the effects of written emotional disclosure on health outcomes of people with physical or psychiatric disorders. Nine studies were meta-analyzed. Results showed that expressive writing significantly improved health. See also Frattaroli (2006), who reported results from a meta-analysis of 146 studies on experimental disclosure and concluded that such disclosure is beneficial to health. Since Frattaroli's study, there has been other specific research showing that expressive writing is related to posttraumatic growth; see, for example, Smyth, Hockemeyer, and Tulloch (2008).

20. See Stanton, Danoff-Burg, Sworowski, Collins, Branstetter, Rodriguez-Hanley, Kirk, and Austenfeld (2002). For a comprehensive overview of the research on writing and talking about emotional experience, see Niederhoffer and Pennebaker (2009).

21. Fredrickson (2009).

22. Tedeschi and Kilmer (2005).

23. Danieli (1981); Danieli (1984).
24. Danieli (2009).

Chapter 8

1. Frankl (1985, p. 87).
2. See Weiss and Berger (2010).
3. For example, Ehrenreich (2010) has criticized positive psychology for unrealistically emphasizing the role of positivity and overplaying the science behind it—and, in doing so, she provides useful corrective balance. However, her sharpest criticisms are targeted at the positive thinking industry, which promotes the bright side of cancer. This is not the same as the posttraumatic growth literature, which does not adopt an ideological stance to welcome misfortune. See also Held (2004).
4. Buergenthal (2010, p. 210).
5. Buergenthal (2010, p. xxiii).
6. Mandela (1995, pp. 614–615).

Postscript

1. For evidence that survivors become more impulsive and apt to take risks, see Joseph, Dalgleish, Thrasher, and Yule (1997).
2. See Gilbert and Proctor (2006) and Gilbert (2010).
3. Quoted in Frager and Fadiman (1998, p. 73).
4. Muss (2002).
5. McCormack, Hagger, and Joseph (2010, p. 282).
6. Fox (2010).
7. Interview with Michael J. Fox in Brockes (2009, pp. 20–22).
8. Kennedy (2009).
9. Snyder (1994, 2000).
10. See Meichenbaum (1977) for an account of self-instructional training (SIT).
11. De Shazer (1988, p. 78).
12. Quoted in Kubler-Ross and Kessler (2001, p. 94).
13. Kimble and Perlmuter (1970).
14. Harvey (2008).
15. Wood, Joseph, and Linley (2007).

Appendix 1

1. Adapted from Regel and Joseph (2010).
2. Tempany (2009, p. 24).
3. See Crown (2009, p. 12).
4. Mullin (2009, pp. 30–31).

Appendix 2

1. Details on scale development are available in Joseph, Maltby, Wood, Stockton, Hunt, and Regel (forthcoming). Across three samples, evidence is provided for high internal consistency, six-month stability, incremental validity over and above existing measures of posttraumatic growth as a predictor of subjective well-being, convergent validity with existing

measures of posttraumatic growth, concurrent validity with personality and coping measures, predictive validity of change in well-being over time, discriminant validity with social desirability, and prediction of clinical caseness.

Appendix 3

1. Adapted from Regel and Joseph (2010).

2. There are several different approaches to psychological therapy, usually grouped into three main types: psychodynamic, humanistic, and cognitive-behavioral. For an overview, see Joseph (2010). For the treatment of PTSD, cognitive-behavioral approaches are typically recommended, but sometimes other therapies may be beneficial, too. For posttraumatic growth, humanistic therapies may be valuable—particularly client-centered therapy, which is a relationship-based approach; see also Calhoun and Tedeschi (1999), who describe a related expert companion approach.

3. See Moncrieff (2009) for an overview of psychiatric drugs and the issues surrounding their use.

REFERENCES

Abbott, D. A. (2009). Violent death: A qualitative study of Israeli and Palestinian families. *Journal of Loss and Trauma, 14,* 117–128.

Abraido-Lanza, A. F., Guier, C., and Colón, R. M. (1998). Psychological thriving among Latinas with chronic illness. *Journal of Social Issues, 54,* 405–424.

Adler, A. (1943). Neuropsychiatric complications in victims of Boston's Cocoanut Grove disaster. *Journal of the American Medical Association, 123,* 1098–1101.

Affleck, G., Tennen, H., Croog, S., and Levine, S. (1987). Causal attributions, perceived benefits, and morbidity after a heart attack: An 8-year study. *Journal of Consulting and Clinical Psychology, 55,* 29–35.

Ai, A. L., Cascio, T., Santangelo, L. K., and Evans-Campbell, T. (2005). Hope, meaning, and growth following the September 11, 2001, terrorist attacks. *Journal of Interpersonal Violence, 20,* 523–548.

Aldwin, C. M. (1993). Coping with traumatic stress. *The National Center for Post-Traumatic Stress Disorder: PTSD Research Quarterly* (summer).

Aldwin, C. M., Levenson, M. R., and Spiro III, A. (1994). Vulnerability and resilience to combat exposure: Can stress have lifelong effects? *Psychology and Aging, 9,* 34–44.

Al Qaisy, A. (2010). Posttraumatic growth in Iraqi women who have lost close relatives. Paper presented at a research seminar titled "Responses to Distressful Events," University of Nottingham, June 24.

American Psychiatric Association. (1980). *Diagnostic and statistical manual of mental disorders,* 3rd ed. Washington, DC: American Psychiatric Association.

American Psychiatric Association. (1994). *Diagnostic and statistical manual of mental disorders,* 4th ed. Washington, DC: American Psychiatric Association.

American Psychiatric Association. (2000). *Diagnostic and statistical manual of mental disorders,* 4th ed., text revision. Washington, DC: American Psychiatric Association.

Andrews, L., Joseph, S., Shevlin, M., and Troop, N. (2006). Confirmatory factor analysis of posttraumatic stress symptoms in emergency personnel: An examination of seven alternative models. *Personality and Individual Differences, 41,* 213–224.

Antoni, M. H., Wimberly, S. R., Lechner, S. C., Kazi, A., Sifre, T., and Urcuyo, K. R., et al. (2006). Reduction of cancer-specific thought intrusions and anxiety symptoms with a stress management intervention among women undergoing treatment for breast cancer. *American Journal of Psychiatry, 163,* 1791–1797.

Armour, C., McBride, O., Shevlin, M., and Adamson, G. (2011). Testing the robustness of the dysphoria factor of the Simms et al. (2002) model of posttraumatic stress disorder. *Psychological Trauma: Theory, Research, Practice, and Policy, 3,* 139–147.

Armstrong, L. (2000). *It's not about the bike: My journey back to life.* New York: Berkley Publishing Group.

Arnold, D., Calhoun, L. G., Tedeschi, R. G., and Cann, A. (2005). Vicarious posttraumatic growth in psychotherapy. *Journal of Humanistic Psychology, 45*, 239–263.

Askay, S. W, and Magyar-Russell, G. (2009), "Post-traumatic growth and spirituality in burn recovery," *International Review of Psychiatry*, 21, 570–79.

Ayers, S., Joseph, S., McKenzie-McHarg, K., Slade, P., and Wijma, K. (2008). Post-traumatic stress following childbirth: Current issues and recommendations for future research. *Journal of Psychosomatic Obstetrics and Gynaecology, 29*, 240–250.

Bagot, R., Parent, C., Bredy, T. W., Zhang, T., Gratton, A., and Meaney, M. J. (2008). Developmental origins of neurobiological vulnerability for PTSD. In L. K. Kirmayer, R. Lemelson, and M. Barad (Eds.), *Understanding trauma: Integrating biological, clinical, and cultural perspectives*, 98–117. Cambridge: Cambridge University Press.

Bailham, D., and Joseph, S. (2003). Post-traumatic stress following childbirth: A review of the emerging literature and directions for research and practice. *Psychology, Health, and Medicine, 8*, 159–168.

Banyard, P., and Shevlin, M. (2001). Responses of football fans to relegation of their team from the English Premier League: PTS? *Irish Journal of Psychological Medicine, 18*, 66–67.

Barad, M., and Cain, C. K. (2008). Mechanisms of fear extinction: Toward improved treatment for anxiety. In L. K. Kirmayer, R. Lemelson, and M. Barad (Eds.), *Understanding trauma: Integrating biological, clinical, and cultural perspectives*, 78–97. Cambridge: Cambridge University Press.

Barker, P. (1991). *Regeneration*. London: Viking.

Becker, E. (1997). *The denial of death*. New York: Free Press.

Benoit, S. C., Davidson, T. L., Chan, K. H., Trigilio, T., and Jarrard, L. E. (1999). Pavlovian conditioning and extinction of context cues and punctate CSs in rats with ibotenate lesions of the hippocampus. *Psychobiology, 27*, 26–39.

Bentall, R. P. (2004). *Madness explained: Psychosis and human nature*. London: Penguin Books.

Bettelheim, B. (1952). *Surviving and other essays*. New York: Random House.

Billings, A. G., and Moos, R. H. (1981). The role of coping resources and social resources in attenuating the stress of life events. *Journal of Behavioural Medicine, 4*, 139–157.

Bonanno, G. A. (2004). Loss, trauma, and human resilience: Have we underestimated the human capacity to thrive after extremely aversive events? *American Psychologist, 59*, 20–28.

Bonanno, G. A. (2005). Clarifying and extending the concept of adult resilience. *American Psychologist, 60*, 265–267.

Bonanno, G. A., Brewin, C. R., Kaniasty, K., and La Greca, A. M. (2010). Weighing the costs of disaster: Consequences, risks, and resilience in individuals, families, and communities. *Psychological Science in the Public Interest, 11*, 1–49.

Bonanno, G. A., Galea, S., Bucciarelli, A., and Vlahov, D. (2006). Psychological resilience after disaster: New York City in the aftermath of the September 11th terrorist attack. *Psychological Science, 17*, 181–186.

Bonanno, G. A., Pat-Horenczyk, R., and Noll, J. (2011). Coping flexibility and trauma: The perceived ability to cope with trauma (PACT) scale. *Psychological Trauma: Theory, Research, Practice, and Policy, 3*, 117–129.

Bonanno, G. A., Rennick, C., and Dekel, S. (2005). Self-enhancement among high-exposure survivors of the September 11th terrorist attack: Resilience or social maladjustment? *Journal of Personality and Social Psychology, 88*, 984–998.

Bouton, M. E., and Waddell, J. (2008). Some biobehavioral insights into persistent effects of emotional trauma. In L. K. Kirmayer, R. Lemelson, and M. Barad (Eds.), *Understanding trauma: Integrating biological, clinical, and cultural perspectives*, 41–59. Cambridge: Cambridge University Press.

Bower, J. E., Kemeny, M. E., Taylor, S. E., and Fahey, J. L. (1998). Cognitive processing, discovery of meaning, CD4 decline, and AIDS-related mortality among bereaved HIV-seropositive men. *Journal of Consulting and Clinical Psychology, 66,* 979–986.

Bradley, R., Greene, J., Russ, E., Dutra, L., and Western, D. (2005). A multi-dimensional meta-analysis of psychotherapy for PTSD. *American Journal of Psychiatry, 162,* 214–227.

Bremner, J. D., Narayan, M., Staib, L. H., Southwick, S. M., Soufer, R., and Charney, D. S. (1999). Neural correlates of memories of childhood sexual abuse in women with and without posttraumatic stress disorder. *American Journal of Psychiatry, 156,* 1787–1795.

Bremner, J. D., Randall, P., Scott, T. M., Bronen, R. A., Seibyl, J. P., Southwick, S. M., Delaney, R. C., McCarthy, G., Charney, D. S., and Innis, R. D. (1995). MRI-based measurement of hippocampal volume in patients with combat-related posttraumatic stress disorder. *American Journal of Psychiatry, 152,* 973–981.

Bremner, J. D., Vermetten, E., Schmahl, C., Vaccarino, V., Vythilingam, M., and Afzal, N., et al. (2005). Positron emission tomographic imaging of neural correlates of a fear acquisition and extinction paradigm in women with childhood sexual-abuse-related post-traumatic stress disorder. *Psychological Medicine, 35,* 791–806.

Breslau, N., and Kessler, R. C. (2001). The stressor criterion in DSM-IV posttraumatic stress disorder: An empirical investigation. *Biological Psychiatry, 50,* 699–704.

Breuer, J., and Freud, S. (1957). On the psychical mechanism of hysterical phenomena: Preliminary communication. In J. Breuer and S. Freud, *Studies on hysteria,* 3–17. New York: Basic Books. Originally published in 1893.

Brewin, C. R., Andrews, B., and Valentine, J. D. (2000). Meta-analysis of risk factors for posttraumatic stress disorder in trauma-exposed adults. *Journal of Consulting and Clinical Psychology, 68,* 748–766.

Brewin, C. R., Dalgleish, T., and Joseph, S. (1996). A dual representation theory of post-traumatic stress disorder. *Psychological Review, 23,* 339–376.

Brewin, C. R., Lanius, R. A., Novac, A., Schnyder, U., and Galea, S. (2009). Reformulating PTSD for DSM-V: Life after criterion A. *Journal of Traumatic Stress, 22,* 366–373.

Brockes, E. (2009). Interview with Michael J. Fox. *Guardian Weekend Magazine,* April 11.

Brugha, T., Bebbington, P., Tennant, C., and Hurry, J. (1985). The list of threatening experiences: A subset of 12 life-event categories with considerable long-term contextual threat. *Psychological Medicine, 15,* 189–194.

Buergenthal, T. (2010). *A lucky child: A memoir of surviving Auschwitz as a young boy.* Profile Books: London.

Bullman, T. A., and Kang, H. K. (1994). Posttraumatic stress disorder and the risk of traumatic deaths among Vietnam veterans. *Journal of Nervous and Mental Disease, 182,* 604–610.

Burt, M. R., and Katz, B. L. (1987). Dimensions of recovery from rape: Focus on growth outcomes. *Journal of Interpersonal Violence, 2,* 57–81.

Bussell, V. A., and Naus, M. J. (2010). A longitudinal investigation of coping and posttraumatic growth in breast cancer survivors. *Journal of Psychosocial Oncology, 28,* 61–78.

Butler, L. (2010). Personal e-mail communication, May 20, 2010.

Butler, L. D., Blasey, C. M., Garlan, R. W., McCaslin, S. E., Azarow, J., Chen, X., Desjardins, J. C., DiMiceli, S., Seagraves, D. A., Hastings, T. A., Kraemer, H. C., and Spiegel, D. (2005). Posttraumatic growth following the terrorist attacks of September 11th, 2001: Cognitive coping and trauma symptom predictors in an Internet convenience sample. *Traumatology, 11,* 247–267.

Cadell, S., Regehr, C. D., and Hemsworth, D. (2003). Factors contributing to posttraumatic growth: A proposed structural equation model. *American Journal of Orthopsychiatry, 73,* 279–287.

Calhoun, L. G., Cann, A., and Tedeschi, R. G. (2011). The posttraumatic growth model: Sociocultural considerations. In T. Weiss and R. Berger (Eds.), *Posttraumatic growth and culturally competent practice: Lessons learned from around the globe*, 1–14. Hoboken, NJ: Wiley.

Calhoun, L. G., and Tedeschi, R. G. (1989–1990). Positive aspects of critical life problems: Recollections of grief. *Omega, 20*, 265–272.

Calhoun, L. G., and Tedeschi, R. G. (1991). Perceiving benefits in traumatic events: Some issues for practicing psychologists. *The Journal of Training and Practice in Professional Psychology, 5*, 45–52.

Calhoun, L. G., and Tedeschi, R. G. (1999). Facilitating posttraumatic growth: A clinician's guide. Mahwah, NJ: Lawrence Erlbaum Associates.

Calhoun, L. G., and Tedeschi, R. G. (Eds.). (2006). *Handbook of posttraumatic growth: Research and practice*. Mahwah, NJ: Lawrence Erlbaum.

Cannon, W. B. (1914). Emergency function of adrenal medulla in pain and major emotions. *American Journal of Physiology, 3*, 356–372.

Cannon, W. B. (1932). *The wisdom of the body*. New York: Norton.

Cantor, C. (2005). *Evolution and posttraumatic stress: Disorders of vigilance and defence*. London: Routledge.

Carmil, D., and Breznitz, S. (1991). Personal trauma and world view: Are extremely stressful experiences related to political attitudes, religious beliefs, and future orientation? *Journal of Traumatic Stress, 4*, 393–405.

Carrico, A. W., Ironson, G., Antoni, M. H., Lechner, S. C., Duran, R. E., Kumar, M., and Schneiderman, N. (2006). A path model of the effects of spirituality on depressive symptoms and 24-h urinary-free cortisol in HIV-positive persons. *Journal of Psychosomatic Research, 61*, 51–58.

Carver, C. S. (1997). You want to measure coping but your protocol's too long: Consider the brief COPE. *International Journal of Behavioural Medicine, 4*, 92–100.

Carver, C. S., Scheier, M. F., and Weintraub, J. K. (1989). Assessing coping strategies: A theoretically based approach. *Journal of Personality and Social Psychology, 56*, 267–283.

Chan, R., and Joseph, S. (2000). Dimensions of personality, domains of aspiration, and subjective well-being. *Personality and Individual Differences, 28*, 347–354.

Cieslak, R., Benight, C. S., Schmidt, N., Luszczynska, A., Curtin, E., Clark, R. A., and Kissinger, P. (2009). Predicting posttraumatic growth among Hurricane Katrina survivors living with HIV: The role of self-efficacy, social support, and PTSD. *Anxiety, Stress, and Coping, 22*, 449–463.

Clay, R., Knibbs, J., and Joseph, S. (2009). Measurement of posttraumatic growth in young people: A review. *Clinical Child Psychology and Psychiatry, 14*, 411–422.

Cobb, A. R., Tedeschi, R. G., Calhoun, L. G., and Cann, A. (2006). Correlates of posttraumatic growth in survivors of intimate partner violence. *Journal of Traumatic Stress, 19*, 895–903.

Cohen Konrad, S. (2006). Posttraumatic growth in mothers of children with acquired disabilities. *Journal of Loss and Trauma, 11*, 101–113.

Collins, R. L., Taylor, S. E., and Skokan, L. A. (1990). A better world or a shattered vision? Changes in perspectives following victimization. *Social Cognition, 8*, 263–285.

Colville, G. A., and Cream, P. (2009). Posttraumatic growth in parents after a child's admission to intensive care: Maybe Nietzsche was right? *Intensive Care Medicine, 35*, 919–923.

Cordova, M. J. (2008). Facilitating posttraumatic growth following cancer. In S. Joseph and P. A. Linley (Eds.), *Trauma, recovery, and growth: Positive psychological perspectives on posttraumatic stress*, 185–205. Hoboken, NJ: Wiley.

Coyne, J. C., and Tennen, H. (2010). Positive psychology in cancer care: Bad science, exaggerated claims, and unproven medicine. *Annals of Behavioral Medicine, 39,* 16–26.

Creamer, M., Burgess, P., and Pattison, P. (1992). Reaction to trauma: A cognitive processing model. *Journal of Abnormal Psychology, 101,* 452–459.

Crown, S. (2009). Interview with Anthony Browne. *The Guardian,* July 4.

Csikszentmihalyi, M., and Csikszentmihalyi, I. S. (Eds.). (2006). *A life worth living: Contributions to positive psychology.* New York: Oxford University Press.

Dalai Lama. (2001). *The art of living: A guide to contentment, joy, and fulfilment.* Translated by G. T. Jinpa. London: Thorsons. Originally published in 1995.

Dalgleish, T., Joseph, S., Thrasher, S., Tranah, T., and Yule, W. (1996). Crisis support following the Herald of Free Enterprise disaster: A longitudinal perspective. *Journal of Traumatic Stress, 9,* 833–846.

Dalgleish, T., Joseph, S., and Yule, W. (2000). The *Herald of Free Enterprise* disaster: Lessons from the first 6 years. *Behavior Modification, 24,* 673–699.

Daly, R. J. (1983). Samuel Pepys and post-traumatic stress disorder. *British Journal of Psychiatry, 143,* 64–68.

Danieli, Y. (1981). On the achievement of integration in ageing survivors of the Nazi Holocaust. *Journal of Geriatric Psychiatry, 14,* 191–210.

Danieli, Y. (1984). Psychotherapists' participation in the conspiracy of silence about the Holocaust. *Psychoanalytic Psychology, 1,* 23–42.

Danieli, Y. (2009). Massive trauma and the healing role of reparative justice. *Journal of Traumatic Stress, 22,* 351–357.

Danoff-Burg, S., and Revenson, T. A. (2005). Benefit-finding among patients with rheumatoid arthritis: Positive effects on interpersonal relationships. *Journal of Behavioural Medicine, 28,* 91–102.

Davis, C. G., and Nolen-Hoeksema, S. (2009). Making sense of loss, perceiving benefits, and posttraumatic growth. In S. J. Lopez and C. R. Snyder (Eds.), *Oxford handbook of positive psychology,* 2nd ed., 641–649. New York: Oxford University Press.

Davis, C. G., Nolen-Hoeksema, S., and Larson, J. (1998). Making sense of loss and benefiting from the experience: Two construals of meaning. *Journal of Personality and Social Psychology, 75,* 561–574.

Davis, C. G., Wortman, C. B., Lehman, D. R., and Silver, R. C. (2000). Searching for meaning in loss: Are clinical assumptions correct? *Death Studies, 24,* 497–540.

De Jongh, A., Olff, M., Van Hoolwerff, H., et al. (2008). Anxiety and post-traumatic stress symptoms following wisdom tooth removal. *Behaviour Research and Therapy, 46,* 1305–1310.

Dekel, R. (2007). Posttraumatic distress and growth among wives of prisoners of war: The contribution of husbands' posttraumatic stress disorder and wives' own attachments. *American Journal of Orthopsychiatry, 77,* 419–426.

Dekel, S. (2009). Changes in trauma-memory over time and their association with posttraumatic stress: The case of the September 11th terrorism attacks. Conference paper presented at The Psycho-Social Aftermaths of Terror Attacks—Theoretical and Therapeutic Perspectives, New School of Psychology at the Interdisciplinary Center Herzliya, Israel, September 13–15.

De Shazer, S. (1988). *Clues: Investigating solutions in brief therapy.* New York. Norton.

De Silva, P. (2006). The "tsunami" and its aftermath: Explorations of a Buddhist perspective. *International Review of Psychiatry, 18,* 281–287.

Dirik, G., and Karanci, A. N. (2008). Variables related to posttraumatic growth in Turkish rheumatoid arthritis patients. *Journal of Clinical Psychology in Medical Settings, 15,* 193–203.

Edmonds, S., and Hooker, K. (1992). Perceived changes in life meaning following bereavement. *Omega: Journal of Death and Dying, 25,* 307–318.

Ehrenreich, B. (2010). *Smile or die: How positive thinking fooled America and the world.* London: Granta.

Ellenberger, H. F. (1970). Pierre Janet and psychological analysis. In H. F. Ellenberger (Ed.), *The discovery of the unconscious,* 331–417. New York: Basic Books.

Elliot, D. M., and Briere, J. (1995). Posttraumatic stress associated with delayed recall of sexual abuse: A general population study. *Journal of Traumatic Stress, 8,* 629–648.

Engelkemeyer, S. M., and Marwit, S. J. (2008). Posttraumatic growth in bereaved parents. *Journal of Traumatic Stress, 21,* 344–346.

Epstein, S. (1991). The self-concept, the traumatic neurosis, and the structure of personality. In D. Ozer, J. M. Healy Jr., and A. J. Stewart (Eds.), *Perspectives in personality: Self and emotion,* Vol. 3 (Part A), 63–90. London: Jessica Kingsley.

Feder, A., Southwick, S. M., Goetz, R. R., Wang, Y., Alonso, A., Smith, B. W., Buchholz, K. R., Waldeck, T., Ameli, R., Moore, J. L., Hain, R., Charney, D. S., and Vythilingam, M. (2008). Posttraumatic growth in former Vietnam prisoners of war. *Psychiatry, 71,* 359–370.

Feigelman, W., Jordan, J. R., and Gorman, B. S. (2009). Personal growth after a suicide loss: Cross-sectional findings suggest growth after loss may be associated with better mental health among survivors. *Omega, 59,* 181–202.

Ferguson, E., and Cox, T. (1997). The functional dimensions of coping scale: Theory, reliability, and validity. *British Journal of Health Psychology, 2,* 109–129.

Figley, C. R. (Ed.). (1978). *Stress disorders among Vietnam veterans.* New York: Brunner/Mazel.

Foa, E. B., Keane, T. M., Friedman, M. J., and Cohen, J. A. (Eds.). (2008). *Effective treatments for PTSD: Practice guidelines from the International Society for Traumatic Stress Studies* (Second edition). New York: Guilford Press.

Foa, E. B., and Kozak, M. J. (1986). Emotional processing of fear: Exposure to corrective information. *Psychological Bulletin, 99,* 20–35.

Folkman, S., and Lazarus, R. S. (1985). If it changes it must be a process: A study of emotion and coping during three stages of a college examination. *Journal of Personality and Social Psychology, 48,* 150–170.

Ford, J. D. (2009). History of psychological trauma. In G. Reyes., J. D. Elhai, and J. D. Ford (Eds.), *The encyclopedia of psychological trauma,* 315–319. Hoboken, NJ: Wiley.

Fox, M. J. (2010). *Always looking up: The adventures of an incurable optimist.* London: Ebury Press.

Frager, R., and Fadiman, J. (1998). *Personality and personal growth,* 4th ed. New York: Longman.

Frankl, V. E. (1985). *Man's search for meaning.* New York: Washington Square Press. Originally published in 1946.

Frankl, V. E. (2000). *Man's search for ultimate meaning: A psychological exploration of the religious quest.* New York: Perseus.

Frattaroli, J. (2006). Experimental disclosure and its moderators: A meta-analysis. *Psychological Bulletin, 132,* 823–865.

Frazier, P., and Burnett, J. (1994). Immediate coping strategies among rape victims. *Journal of Counseling and Development, 72,* 633–639.

Frazier, P., Conlon, A., and Glaser, T. (2001). Positive and negative life changes following sexual assault. *Journal of Consulting and Clinical Psychology, 69,* 1048–1055.

Frazier, P., Tashiro, T., Berman, M., Steger, M., and Long, J. (2004). Correlates of levels and patterns of positive life changes following sexual assault. *Journal of Consulting and Clinical Psychology, 72,* 19–30.

Frazier, P., Tennen, H., Gavian, M., Park, C., Tomich, P., and Tashiro, T. (2009). Does self-reported posttraumatic growth reflect genuine positive change? *Psychological Science: Research, Theory, and Application in Psychology and Related Sciences, 20,* 912–919.

Fredrickson, B. (2009). *Positivity: Groundbreaking research to release your inner optimist and thrive.* Oxford: One World.

Fredrickson, B. L. (2001). The role of positive emotions in positive psychology: The broaden-and-build theory of positive emotions. *American Psychologist, 56,* 218–226.

Freud, S. (1955). Beyond the pleasure principle. In J. Strachey (Ed.), *Complete Psychological Works,* Standard Edition (Vol. 18). London: Hogarth Press. Originally published in 1920.

Freud, S. (1959). The aetiology of hysteria. In J. Strachey (Ed.), *Complete Psychological Works,* Standard Edition (Vol. 3). London: Hogarth Press. Originally published in 1896.

Freud, S., Ferenczi, S., Abraham, K., Simmel, E., and Jones, E. (1921). *Psychoanalysis and the war neurosis.* New York: International Psychoanalysis Press.

Frisina, P. G., Borod, J. C., and Lepore, S. J. (2004). A meta-analysis of the effects of written emotional disclosure on the health outcomes of clinical populations. *Journal of Nervous and Mental Disease, 192,* 629–634.

Fromm, K., Andrykowski, M. A., and Hunt, J. (1996). Positive and negative psychological sequelae of bone marrow transplantations: Implications for quality of life assessments. *Journal of Behavioural Medicine, 19,* 221–240.

Gangstad, B., Norman, P., and Barton, J. (2009). Cognitive processing and posttraumatic growth after stroke. *Rehabilitation Psychology, 54,* 69–75.

Gersons, P. R., and Carlier, I. V. E. (1992). Post-traumatic stress disorder: The history of a recent concept. *British Journal of Psychiatry, 161,* 742–748.

Gilbert, P. (2010). *The compassionate mind.* London: Constable.

Gilbert, P., and Proctor, S. (2006). Compassionate mind training for people with high shame and self-criticism: Overview and pilot study of a group therapy approach. *Clinical Psychology and Psychotherapy, 13,* 353–379.

Gluhoski, V. L., and Wortman, C. B. (1996). The impact of trauma on world views. *Journal of Social and Clinical Psychology, 15,* 417–429.

Greenberg, M. A. (1995). Cognitive processing of traumas: The role of intrusive thoughts and reappraisals. *Journal of Applied Social Psychology, 25,* 1262–1296.

Greenman, L. (2001). *An Englishman in Auschwitz.* London: Vallentine Mitchell.

Gunty, A. L., Frazier, P. A., Tennen, H., Tomich, P., Tashiro, T., and Park, C. (2011). Moderators of the relation between perceived and actual posttraumatic growth. *Psychological Trauma: Theory, Research, Practice, and Policy, 3,* 61–66.

Haidt, J. (2006). *The happiness hypothesis: Putting ancient wisdom to the test of modern science.* London: William Heinemann.

Hall, B. J., and Hobfoll, S. E. (2006). Posttraumatic growth actions work, posttraumatic growth cognitions fail: Results from the Intifada and Gaza Disengagement. *The European Health Psychologist, 3,* 3–6.

Hall, B. J., Hobfoll, S. E., Canetti, D., Johnson, R. J., Palmieri, P. A., and Galea, S. (2010). Exploring the association between posttraumatic growth and PTSD: A national study of Jews and Arabs following the 2006 Israel-Hezbollah war. *Journal of Nervous and Mental Disease, 198,* 180–186.

Hamera, E. K., and Shontz, F. C. (1978). Perceived positive and negative effects of life-threatening illness. *Psychosomatic Medicine, 22,* 419–424.

Hart, K. (1962). *I am alive.* London: Abelard Schuman.

Harvey, J. (2008). Growth through loss and adversity in close relationships. In S. Joseph and P. A. Linley (Eds.), *Trauma, recovery, and growth: Positive psychological perspectives on post-traumatic stress*, 125–143. Hoboken, NJ: Wiley.

Hefferon, K., Grealy, M., and Mutrie, N. (2008). The perceived influence of an exercise class intervention on the process and outcomes of post-traumatic growth. *Journal of Mental Health and Physical Activity*, *1*, 32–39.

Heidt, J. M., Marx, B. P., and Forsyth, J. P. (2005). Tonic immobility and childhood sexual abuse: A preliminary report evaluating the sequela of rape-induced paralysis. *Behaviour Research and Therapy*, *43*, 1157–1171.

Held, B. S. (2004). The negative side of positive psychology. *Journal of Humanistic Psychology*, *44*, 9–46.

Helgeson, V. S., Reynolds, K. A., and Tomich, P. L. (2006). A meta-analytic review of benefit finding and growth. *Journal of Consulting and Clinical Psychology*, *74*, 797–816.

Herman, J. L. (1992). *Trauma and recovery*. New York: Basic Books.

Hickling, E. J., Blanchard, E. B., Mundy, E., and Galovski, T. E. (2002). Detection of malingered MVA related posttraumatic stress disorder: An investigation of the ability to detect professional actors by experienced clinicians, psychological tests and psychophysiological assessment. *Journal of Forensic Psychology Practice*, *2*, 33–54.

Hobfoll, S. E., Hall, B., Canetti-Nisim, D., Galea, S., Johnson, R. J., and Palmieri, P. A. (2007). Refining our understanding of traumatic growth in the face of terrorism: Moving from meaning cognitions to doing what is meaningful. *Applied Psychology: An International Review*, *56*, 345–366.

Holden, W. (1998). *Shell shock*. Basingstoke: Channel 4 Books.

Holland, K. D., and Holahan, C. K. (2003). The relation of social support and coping to positive adaptation to breast cancer. *Psychology and Health*, *18*, 15–29.

Horowitz, M. (1976). *Stress response syndromes*. New York: Jason Aronson.

Horowitz, M. J., Wilner, N., and Alvarez, M. A. (1979). Impact of Event Scale: A measure of subjective distress. *Psychosomatic Medicine*, *41*, 209–218.

Horwitz, A. V. (2002). *Creating mental illness*. Chicago: University of Chicago Press.

Humphreys, C., and Joseph, S. (2004). Domestic violence and the politics of trauma. *Women's Studies International Forum*, *27*, 559–570.

Hunt, N. (2010). *Memory, war and trauma*. Cambridge: Cambridge University Press.

Ickovics, J. R., Meade, C. S., Kershaw, T. S., Milan, S., Lewis, J. B., and Ethier, K. A. (2006). Urban teens: Trauma, posttraumatic growth, and emotional distress among female adolescents. *Journal of Consulting and Clinical Psychology*, *74*, 841–850.

Ickovics, J. R., Milan, S., Boland, R., Schoenbaum, E., Schuman, P., and Vlahov, D. (2006). Psychological resources protect health: 5-year survival and immune functioning among HIV-infected women from four US cities. *AIDS*, *20*, 1851–1860.

Janet, P. (1973). *L'automatisme psychologique: Essai de psychologie expérimentale sur les formes inférieures de l'activité humaine*. Paris: Société Pierre Janet/Payot. Originally published in 1889.

Janet, P. (1983). *L'état mental des hystériques*, 2nd ed. Marseille: Lafitte Reprints. Originally published in 1911.

Janoff-Bulman, R. (1992). *Shattered assumptions: Towards a new psychology of trauma*. New York: Free Press.

Janoff-Bulman, R. (2004). Posttraumatic growth: Three explanatory models. *Psychological Inquiry*, *15*, 30–34.

Jonas, E., Schimel, J., Greenberg, J., and Pyszczynski, T. (2002). The scrooge effect: Evidence that mortality salience increases prosocial attitudes and behavior. *Personality and Social Psychology Bulletin*, *28*, 1342–1353.

Joseph, S. (1999). Attributional processes, coping, and post-traumatic stress disorders. In W. Yule (Ed.), *Post-traumatic stress disorders: Concepts and therapy*, 51–70. Chichester, UK: Wiley.

Joseph, S. (2000). Psychometric evaluation of Horowitz's Impact of Event Scale: A review. *Journal of Traumatic Stress*, *13*, 101–113.

Joseph, S. (2004). Client-centred therapy, post-traumatic stress disorder and post-traumatic growth: Theoretical perspectives and practical implications. *Psychology and Psychotherapy: Theory, Research and Practice*, *77*, 101–119.

Joseph, S. (2010). *Theories of counselling and psychotherapy: An introduction to the different approaches*. Basingstoke, UK: Palgrave Macmillan.

Joseph, S., Brewin, C. R., Yule, W., and Williams, R. (1991). Causal attributions and psychiatric symptoms in survivors of the *Herald of Free Enterprise* disaster. *British Journal of Psychiatry*, *159*, 542–546.

Joseph, S., Brewin, C. R., Yule, W., and Williams, R. (1993). Causal attributions and post-traumatic stress in adolescents. *Journal of Child Psychology and Psychiatry*, *34*, 247–253.

Joseph, S., and Butler, L. D. (2010). Positive changes following trauma. *National Centre for PTSD Research Quarterly* (summer). Available online for free download: http://www.ptsd .va.gov/professional/newsletters/research-quarterly/v21n3.pdf.

Joseph, S., Dalgleish, T., Thrasher, S., and Yule, W. (1997). Impulsivity and post-traumatic stress. *Personality and Individual Differences*, *22*, 279–281.

Joseph, S., Dalgleish, T., Thrasher, S., Yule, W., Williams, R., and Hodgkinson, P. (1996). Chronic emotional processing in survivors of the *Herald of Free Enterprise* disaster: The relationship of intrusion and avoidance at 3 years to distress at 5 years. *Behaviour Research and Therapy*, *34*, 357–360.

Joseph, S., Dalgleish, T., Williams, R., Thrasher, S., Yule, W., and Hodgkinson, P. (1997). Attitudes towards emotional expression and post-traumatic stress in survivors of the *Herald of Free Enterprise* disaster. *British Journal of Clinical Psychology*, *36*, 133–138.

Joseph, S., Hodgkinson, P., Yule, W., and Williams, R. (1993). Guilt and distress 30 months after the capsize of the *Herald of Free Enterprise*. *Personality and Individual Differences*, *14*, 271–273.

Joseph, S., Knibbs, J., and Hobbs, J. (2007). Trauma, resilience and growth in children and adolescents. In A. A. Hosin (Ed.), *Responses to traumatized children*, 148–161. Houndmills, UK: Palgrave Macmillan.

Joseph, S., and Linley, P. A. (2005). Positive adjustment to threatening events: An organismic valuing theory of growth through adversity. *Review of General Psychology*, *9*, 262–280.

Joseph, S., and Linley, P. A. (2006a). Growth following adversity: Theoretical perspectives and implications for clinical practice. *Clinical Psychology Review*, *26*, 1041–1053.

Joseph, S., and Linley, P. A. (2006b). *Positive therapy: A meta-theoretical approach to positive psychological practice*. London: Routledge.

Joseph, S., and Linley, P. A (Eds.). (2008). *Trauma, recovery, and growth: Positive psychological perspectives on posttraumatic stress*. Hoboken, NJ: Wiley.

Joseph, S., Linley, P. A., Andrews, L., Harris, G., Howle, B., Woodward, C., and Shevlin, M. (2005). Assessing positive and negative changes in the aftermath of adversity: Psychometric evaluation of the Changes in Outlook Questionnaire. *Psychological Assessment*, *17*, 70–80.

Joseph, S., Linley, P. A., and Harris, G. J. (2005). Understanding positive change following trauma and adversity: Structural clarification. *Journal of Loss and Trauma*, *10*, 83–96.

Joseph, S., Maltby, J., Wood, A. M., Stockton, H., Hunt, N., and Regel, S. (forthcoming). The Psychological Well-Being–Post-Traumatic Changes Questionnaire (PWB-PTCQ): Reliability and validity. *Psychological Trauma: Theory, Research, Practice and Policy.*

Joseph, S., and Masterson, J. (1999). Posttraumatic stress disorder and traumatic brain injury: Are they mutually exclusive? *Journal of Traumatic Stress, 12,* 437–453.

Joseph, S., and Patterson, T. G. (2008). The actualising tendency: A meta-theoretical perspective for positive psychology. In B. E. Levitt (Ed.), *Reflections on human potential: Bridging the person-centred approach and positive psychology.* Ross-on-Wye, UK: PCCS Books.

Joseph, S., and Williams, R. (2005). Understanding posttraumatic stress: Theory, reflections, context, and future. *Behavioural and Cognitive Psychotherapy, 33,* 423–441.

Joseph, S., Williams, R., and Yule, W. (1992). Crisis support, attributional style, coping style, and post-traumatic symptoms. *Personality and Individual Differences, 13,* 1249–1251.

Joseph, S, Williams, R., and Yule, W. (1993). Changes in outlook following disaster: The preliminary development of a measure to assess positive and negative responses. *Journal of Traumatic Stress, 6,* 271–279.

Joseph, S., Williams, R., and Yule, W. (1995). Psychosocial perspectives on post-traumatic stress. *Clinical Psychology Review, 15,* 515–544.

Joseph, S., Williams, R., and Yule, W. (1997). *Understanding post-traumatic stress: Psychosocial perspectives on PTSD and treatment.* Chichester, UK: Wiley.

Joseph, S, and Wood, A. (2010). Positive functioning and its measurement in clinical psychology research and practice. *Clinical Psychology Review, 30,* 830–838.

Joseph, S., and Worsley, R. (Eds.). (2005). *Person-centred psychopathology: A positive psychology of mental health.* Ross-on-Wye, UK: PCCS Books.

Joseph, S., Yule, W., Williams, R., and Andrews, B. (1993). Crisis support in the aftermath of disaster: A longitudinal perspective. *British Journal of Clinical Psychology, 32,* 177–185.

Joseph, S., Yule, W., Williams, R., and Hodgkinson, P. (1993). Increased substance use in survivors of the *Herald of Free Enterprise* disaster. *British Journal of Medical Psychology, 66,* 185–191.

Joseph, S., Yule, W., Williams, R., and Hodgkinson, P. (1994). Correlates of post-traumatic stress at 30 months: The *Herald of Free Enterprise* disaster. *Behaviour Research and Therapy, 32,* 521–524.

Kaniasty, K. (2008). Social support. In G. Reyes., J. D. Elhai, and J. D. Ford (Eds.), *The encyclopedia of psychological trauma,* 607–612. Hoboken, NJ: Wiley.

Karanci, A. N., and Erkham, A. (2007). Variables related to stress-related growth among Turkish breast cancer patients. *Stress and Health, 23,* 315–322.

Kasser, T. (2004). The good life or the goods life? Positive psychology and personal well-being in the culture of consumption. In P. A. Linley and S. Joseph (Eds.), *Positive psychology in practice,* 55–67. Hoboken, NJ: Wiley.

Kasser, T., and Ryan, R. M. (1993). A dark side of the American dream: Correlates of financial success as a central life aspiration. *Journal of Personality and Social Psychology, 65,* 410–422.

Kennedy, B. J., Tellegen, A., Kennedy, S., and Havernick, N. (1976). Psychological response of patients cured of advanced cancer. *Cancer, 38,* 2184–2191.

Kennedy, E. M. (2009). *True compass: A memoir.* New York: Twelve.

Kessler, R. C., Galea, S., Jones, R. T., and Parker, H. A. (2006). Mental illness and suicidality after Hurricane Katrina. *Bulletin of the World Health Organisation, 84,* 930–939.

Kessler, R. C., Sonnega, A., Bromet, E., Hughes, M., and Nelson, C. (1995). Posttraumatic stress disorder in the national comorbidity survey. *Archives of General Psychiatry, 52,* 1048–1060.

Keyes, C. L., Shmotkin, M., and Ryff, C. D. (2002). Optimizing well-being: The empirical encounter of two traditions. *Journal of Personality and Social Psychology, 82,* 1007–1022.

Kilpatrick, D. G., Resnick, H. S., and Acierno, R. (2009). Should PTSD criterion A be retained? *Journal of Traumatic Stress, 22,* 374–383.

Kilpatrick, D. G., Saunders, B. E., Amick-McMullan, A., Best, C. L., Veronen, L. J., and Resnick, H. S. (1989). Victim and crime factors associated with the development of crime-related post-traumatic stress disorder. *Behavior Therapy, 20,* 199–214.

Kimble, G. A., and Perlmuter, L. C. (1970). The problem of volition. *Psychological Record, 77,* 361–384.

King, L. A. (2001). The hard road to the good life: The happy, mature person. *Journal of Humanistic Psychology, 41,* 51–72.

Kinsinger, D. P., Penedo, F. J., Antoni, M. H., Dahn, J. R., Lechner, S., and Schneiderman, N. (2006). Psychosocial and sociodemographic correlates of benefit finding in men treated for localized prostate cancer. *Psycho-Oncology, 15,* 954–961.

Kissane, D. W., Bloch, S., Smith, G. C., Miach, P., Clarke, D. M., Ikin, J., et al. (2003). Cognitive-existential group psychotherapy for women with primary breast cancer: A randomised controlled trial. *Psycho-Oncology, 12,* 532–546.

Kleim, B., and Ehlers, A. (2009). Evidence for a curvilinear relationship between posttraumatic growth and posttrauma depression and PTSD in assault survivors. *Journal of Traumatic Stress, 22,* 45–52.

Koffka, K. (1936). *Principles of Gestalt psychology.* London: Routledge and Kegan Paul.

Konner, M. (2008). Trauma, adaptation, and resilience: A cross-cultural and evolutionary perspective. In L. K. Kirmayer, R. Lemelson, and M. Barad (Eds.), *Understanding trauma: Integrating biological, clinical, and cultural perspectives,* 300–338. Cambridge: Cambridge University Press.

Kubler-Ross, E., and Kessler, D. (2001). *Life lessons: How our mortality can teach us about life and living.* New York: Simon & Schuster.

Kulka, R. A., Schlenger, W. E., Fairbank, J. A., Hough, R. L., Jordan, B. K., Marmar, C. R., and Weiss, D. S. (1990). *Trauma and the Vietnam War generation: Report of findings from the National Vietnam Veterans Readjustment Study.* New York: Brunner/Mazel.

Kunst, M. J. J. (2010). Peritraumatic distress, posttraumatic stress disorder symptoms, and posttraumatic growth in victims of violence. *Journal of Traumatic Stress, 23,* 514–518.

Kushner, H. S. (1981). *When bad things happen to good people.* New York: Schocken Books.

Lazarus, R. S., and Folkman, S. (1984). *Stress, appraisal and coping.* New York: Springer.

LeDoux, J. E. (2000). Emotion circuits in the brain. *Annual Review of Neuroscience, 23,* 155–184.

Lehman, D. R., Davis, C. G., Delongis, A., Wortman, C. B., Bluck, S., Mandel, D. R., and Ellard, J. H. (1993). Positive and negative life changes following bereavement and their relations to adjustment. *Journal of Social and Clinical Psychology, 12,* 90–112.

Lehman, D. R., Wortman, C. B., and Williams, A. F. (1987). Long-term effects of losing a spouse in a motor vehicle accident. *Journal of Personality and Social Psychology, 52,* 218–231.

Lepore, S., and Revenson, T. A. (2006). Resilience and posttraumatic growth: Recovery, resistance, and reconfiguration. In L. G. Calhoun and R. G. Tedeschi (Eds.), *Handbook of posttraumatic growth: Research and practice,* 24–46. Mahwah, NJ: Lawrence Erlbaum.

Levine, S. Z., Laufer, A., Stein, E., Hamama-Raz, Y., and Solomon, Z. (2009). Examining the relationship between resilience and posttraumatic growth. *Journal of Traumatic Stress, 22,* 282–286.

Lev-Wiesel, R., and Amir, M. (2006). Growing out of the ashes: Posttraumatic growth among Holocaust child survivors—is it possible? In L. G. Calhoun and R. G. Tedeschi (Eds.), *Handbook of posttraumatic growth: Research and practice*, 248–263. Mahwah, NJ: Lawrence Erlbaum.

Lifton, R. J. (1967). *Death in life: Survivors of Hiroshima*. New York: Random House.

Lifton, R. J. (1973). *Home from the war: Vietnam veterans—neither victims nor executioners*. New York: Simon & Schuster.

Lifton, R. J. (1986). *The Nazi doctors: Medical killing and the psychology of genocide*. New York: Basic Books.

Lindgaard, C. V., Iglebaek, T., and Jensen, T. K. (2009). Changes in family functioning in the aftermath of a natural disaster: The 2004 tsunami in Southeast Asia. *Journal of Loss and Trauma, 14,* 101–116.

Linley, P. A., Felus, A., Gillett, R., and Joseph, S. (2011). Emotional expression and growth following adversity: Emotional expression mediates subjective distress and is moderated by emotional intelligence. *Journal of Loss and Trauma.* Online pre-publication. http://www.informaworld.com/smpp/content~content=a935845323~db=all~jump type=rss.

Linley, P. A., and Joseph, S. (Eds.). (2004a). *Positive psychology in practice*. Hoboken, NJ: Wiley.

Linley, P. A., and Joseph, S. (2004b). Positive change following trauma and adversity: A review. *Journal of Traumatic Stress, 17,* 11–21.

Linley, P. A., and Joseph, S. (2005a). The positive and negative effects of disaster work: A preliminary investigation. *Journal of Loss and Trauma, 11,* 229–245.

Linley, P. A., and Joseph, S. (2005b). Positive and negative changes following occupational death exposure. *Journal of Traumatic Stress, 18,* 751–758.

Linley, P. A., and Joseph, S. (2007). Therapy work and therapists' positive and negative well-being. *Journal of Social and Clinical Psychology, 26,* 385–403.

Linley, P. A., Joseph, S., and Goodfellow, B. (2008). Positive changes in outlook following trauma and their relationship to subsequent posttraumatic stress, depression, and anxiety. *Journal of Social and Clinical Psychology, 27,* 877–891.

Littleton, H., Horsley, S., John, S., and Nelson, D. (2007). Trauma coping strategies and psychological distress: A meta-analysis. *Journal of Traumatic Stress, 20,* 977–988.

Littlewood, R. A., Vanable, P. A., Carey, M. P., and Blair, D. C. (2008). The association of benefit finding to psychosocial and health behaviour adaptation among HIV+ men and women. *Journal of Behavioral Medicine, 31,* 145–155.

Lopez, S. J., and Snyder, C. R. (Eds.). (2009). *Oxford handbook of positive psychology*, 2nd ed. New York: Oxford University Press.

Luszczynska, A., Sarkar, Y., and Knoll, N. (2007). Received social support, self-efficacy, and finding benefits in disease as predictors of physical functioning and adherence to anti-retroviral therapy. *Patient Education and Counseling, 66,* 37–42.

Lyons, J. A. (2008). Using a life-span model to promote recovery and growth in traumatized veterans. In S. Joseph and P. A. Linley (Eds.), *Trauma, recovery, and growth: Positive psychological perspectives on posttraumatic stress*, 233–258. Hoboken, NJ: Wiley.

Maddux, J. (2008). Positive psychology and the illness ideology: Toward a positive clinical psychology. *Applied Psychology: An International Review, 57,* 54–70.

Maddux, J. E., Gosselin, J. T., and Winstead, B. A. (2005). Conceptions of psychopathology: A social constructionist perspective. In J. E. Maddux and B. A. Winstead (Eds.), *Psychopathology: Foundations for a contemporary understanding*, 3–18. Mahwah, NJ: Lawrence Erlbaum.

Maddux, J. E., Snyder, C. R., and Lopez, S. J. (2004). Toward a positive clinical psychology: Deconstructing the illness ideology and constructing an ideology of human strengths and potential. In P. A. Linley and S. Joseph (Eds.), *Positive psychology in practice*, 320–334. Hoboken, NJ: Wiley.

Mandela, N. (1995). *Long walk to freedom: The autobiography of Nelson Mandela.* London: Little, Brown and Co.

Manne, S., Ostroff, J., Winkel, G., Goldstein, L., Fox, K., and Grana, G. (2004). Posttraumatic growth after breast cancer: Patient, partner, and couple perspectives. *Psychosomatic Medicine, 66,* 442–452.

Marsella, A. J., and Wilson, J. P. (2008). Culture and trauma. In G. Reyes., J. D. Elhai, and J. D. Ford (Eds.), *The encyclopedia of psychological trauma*, 190–194. Hoboken, NJ: Wiley.

Martin, J., Tolosa, I., and Joseph, S. (2004). Adversarial growth following cancer and support from health professionals. *Health Psychology Update, 13,* 11–17.

Maslow, A. (1955). Deficiency motivation and growth motivation. In M. R. Jones (Ed.), *Nebraska Symposium on Motivation*, 1–30. Lincoln: University of Nebraska Press.

Mayer, J. D., and Salovey, P. (1997). What is emotional intelligence? In P. Salovey and D. J. Sluyter (Eds.), *Emotional development and emotional intelligence*, 3–31. New York: Basic Books.

Mayes, L. C. (2000). A developmental perspective on the regulation of arousal states. *Seminars in Perinatology, 24,* 267–279.

McAdams, D. P. (2001). The psychology of life stories. *Review of General Psychology, 5,* 100–122.

McCaslin, S. E., de Zoysa, P., Butler, L. D., Hart, S., Marmar, C. R., Metzler, T. J., and Koopman, C. (2009). The relationship of posttraumatic growth to peritraumatic reactions and posttraumatic stress symptoms among Sri Lankan university students. *Journal of Traumatic Stress, 22,* 334–339.

McCormack, L. (2010). Primary and vicarious posttraumatic growth following genocide, war and humanitarian emergencies. PhD thesis, University of Nottingham.

McCormack, L., Hagger, M. S., and Joseph, S. (2010). Vicarious growth in wives of Vietnam veterans: A phenomenological investigation into "decades" of lived experience. *Journal of Humanistic Psychology, 51,* 273–290.

McFarland, C., and Alvaro, C. (2000). The impact of motivation on temporal comparisons: Coping with traumatic events by perceiving personal growth. *Journal of Personality and Social Psychology, 79,* 327–343.

McGregor, I., and Little, B. R. (1998). Personal projects, happiness, and meaning: On doing well and being yourself. *Journal of Personality and Social Psychology, 74,* 494–512.

McHugh, P. R., and Treisman, G. (2007). PTSD: A problematic diagnostic category. *Journal of Anxiety Disorders, 21,* 211–222.

McMillen, J. C., and Fisher, R. H. (1998). The perceived benefit scales: Measuring perceived positive life changes after negative events. *Social Work Research, 22,* 173–187.

McMillen, J. C., Fisher, R. H., and Smith E. M. (1997). Perceived benefit and mental health after three types of disaster. *Journal of Consulting and Clinical Psychology, 65,* 733–739.

McNally, R. J. (2004). Conceptual problems with the DSM-IV criteria for posttraumatic stress disorder. In G. M. Rosen (Ed.), *Posttraumatic stress disorder: Issues and controversies*, 1–14. Chichester, UK: Wiley.

McNally, R. J. (2006). Cognitive abnormalities in posttraumatic stress disorder. *Trends in Cognitive Science, 10,* 271–277.

McNally, R. J. (2010). Can we salvage the concept of psychological trauma? *The Psychologist, 23,* 386–389.

Meichenbaum, D. H. (1977). *Cognitive-behavior modification*. New York: Plenum.

Meichenbaum, D. (2006). Resilience and posttraumatic growth: A constructive narrative perspective. In L. G. Calhoun and R. G. Tedeschi (Eds.), *Handbook of posttraumatic growth: Research and practice*, 355–368. Mahwah, NJ: Lawrence Erlbaum.

Milam, J. E., Ritt-Olsen, A., and Unger, J. B. (2004). Posttraumatic growth among adolescents. *Journal of Adolescent Research, 19*, 192–204.

Miles, M. S., and Crandall, E. K. B. (1983). The search for meaning and its potential for affecting growth in bereaved parents. *Health Values, 7*, 19–23.

Milgram, N. A. (1986). An attributional analysis of war-related stress: Modes of coping and help seeking. In N. A. Milgram (Ed.), *Stress and coping in time of war: Generalizations from the Israeli experience*, 255–267. New York: Brunner/Mazel.

Miller, W. R., and C'deBaca, J. (2001). *Quantum change: When epiphanies and sudden insights transform ordinary lives*. New York: Guilford.

Mohr, D. C., Dick, L. P., Russo, D., Pinn, J., Boudewyn, A. C., Likosky, W., and Goodkin, D. E. (1999). The psychosocial impact of multiple sclerosis: Exploring the patient's perspective. *Health Psychology, 18*, 376–382.

Moncrieff, J. (2009). *A straight talking introduction to psychiatric drugs*. Ross-on-Wye, UK: PCCS Books.

Morland, L. A., Butler, L. D., and Leskin, G. A. (2008). Resilience and thriving in a time of terrorism. In S. Joseph and P. A. Linley (Eds.), *Trauma, recovery, and growth: Positive psychological perspectives on posttraumatic stress*, 39–61. Hoboken, NJ: Wiley.

Morrill, E. F., Brewer, N. T., O'Neill, S. C., Lillie, S. E., Dees, E. C., Carey, L. A., and Rimer, B. K. (2007). The interaction of post-traumatic growth and post-traumatic stress symptoms in predicting depressive symptoms and quality of life. *Psycho-Oncology, 17*, 948–953.

Morris, B. A., Shakespeare-Finch, J. E., and Scott, J. L. (2007). Coping processes and dimensions of posttraumatic growth. *Australasian Journal of Disaster and Trauma Studies, 1*, 1–12.

Mosher, C. E., Danoff-Burg, S., and Brunker, B. (2006). Post-traumatic growth and psychosocial adjustment of daughters of breast cancer survivors. *Oncology Nursing Forum, 33*, 543–551.

Mullin, J. (2009). The interview. *The Independent*, Sunday, June 14.

Murphy, D. (2009). Client-centred therapy for severe childhood abuse: A case study. *Counselling and Psychotherapy Research, 9*, 3–10.

Murphy, D., Joseph, S., and Durkin, J. (2010). Growth in relationship: A post-medicalised vision for positive transformation. In N. Tehrani (Ed.), *Managing trauma in the workplace*. London: Routledge.

Murphy, S., Johnson, L. C., and Lohan, J. (2003). Finding meaning in a child's violent death: A five-year prospective analysis of parents' personal narratives and empirical data. *Death Studies, 27*, 381–404.

Muss, D. (1991a). A new technique for treating posttraumatic stress disorder. *British Journal of Clinical Psychology, 30*, 91–92.

Muss, D. (1991b). *The trauma trap*. London: Doubleday.

Muss, D. (2002). The rewind technique in the treatment of posttraumatic stress disorder. In C. R. Figley (Ed.), *Brief treatments for the traumatized: A project of the Green Cross Foundation*, 306–314. Westport, CT: Greenwood Press.

Nakonezny, P. A., Reddick, R., and Rodgers, J. L. (2004). Did divorces decline after the Oklahoma City bombing? *Journal of Marriage and the Family, 66*, 90–100.

Niederhoffer, K. G., and Pennebaker, J. W. (2009). Sharing one's story: On the benefits of writing or talking about emotional experience. In S. J. Lopez and C. R. Snyder (Eds.), *Oxford handbook of positive psychology*, 2nd ed., 621–632. New York: Oxford University Press.

Neimeyer, R. A. (2006). Re-storying loss: Fostering growth in the posttraumatic narrative. In L. G. Calhoun and R. G. Tedeschi (Eds.), *Handbook of posttraumatic growth: Theory and practice*, 68–80. Mahwah, NJ: Lawrence Erlbaum.

Nesse, R. M. (2001). The smoke detector principle: Natural selection and the regulation of defensive responses. *Annals of the New York Academy of Sciences, 935*, 75–85.

Nietzsche, F. (1997). *Twilight of the idols*. Translated by R. Polt. Indianapolis, IN: Hackett. Originally published in 1889.

O'Hanlon, B., and Bertolino, B. (1998). *Even from a broken web: Brief, respectful, solution-oriented therapy for sexual abuse and trauma*. New York: W. W. Norton.

O'Leary, V. E., and Ickovics, J. R. (1995). Resilience and thriving in response to challenge: An opportunity for a paradigm shift in women's health. *Women's Health: Research on Gender, Behaviour, and Policy, 1*, 121–142.

Ortega, J. (1957). *The revolt of the masses*. New York: Norton.

Page, H. W. (1883). *Injuries of the spine and spinal cord without apparent mechanical lesion, and nervous shock in their surgical and medico-legal aspects*. London: J. & A. Churchill.

Pakenham, K. I., Chiu, J., Bursnall, S., and Cannon, T. (2009). Relations between social support, appraisal and coping, and both positive and negative outcomes in young carers. *Journal of Health Psychology, 12*, 89–102.

Pakenham, K. I., Dadds, M. R., and Terry, D. J. (1994). Relationships between adjustment to HIV and both social support and coping. *Journal of Consulting and Clinical Psychology, 62*, 1194–1203.

Pals, J. L., and McAdams, D. P. (2004). The transformed self: A narrative understanding of posttraumatic growth. *Psychological Inquiry, 15*, 65–69.

Park, C. L. (2010). Making sense of the meaning literature: An integrative review of meaning making and its effects on adjustment to stressful life events. *Psychological Bulletin, 136*, 257–301.

Park, C. L., Aldwin, C. M., Fenster, J. R., and Snyder, L. B. (2008). Pathways to posttraumatic growth versus posttraumatic stress: Coping and emotional reactions following the September 11, 2001, terrorist attacks. *American Journal of Orthopsychiatry, 78*, 300–312.

Park, C. L., Chmielewski, J., and Blank, T. O. (2009). Post-traumatic growth: Finding positive meaning in cancer survivorship moderates the impact of intrusive thoughts on adjustment in younger adults. *Psycho-Oncology, 19*, 1137–1149.

Park, C. L., Cohen, L. H., and Murch, R. (1996). Assessment and prediction of stress-related growth. *Journal of Personality, 64*, 71–105.

Park, C. L., and Lechner, S. C. (2006). Measurement issues in assessing growth following stressful life experiences. In L. G. Calhoun and R. G. Tedeschi (Eds.), *Handbook of posttraumatic growth: Research and practice*, 47–67. Mahwah, NJ: Lawrence Erlbaum.

Patterson, T., and Joseph, S. (2007). Person-centered personality theory: Support from self-determination theory and positive psychology. *Journal of Humanistic Psychology, 47*, 117–139.

Peltzer, K. (2000). Trauma symptom correlates of criminal victimization in an urban community sample, South Africa. *Journal of Psychology in Africa, 10*, 49–62.

Pennebaker, J. W. (1997). *Opening up: The healing power of expressing emotions*, rev. ed. New York: Academic Press.

Pennebaker, J. W. (2009). Expressive writing: Research and practice. Workshop. University of Central Lancashire, Preston, June 30.

Peterson, C., Park, N., Pole, N., D'Andrea, W., and Seligman, M. E. P. (2008). Strengths of character and posttraumatic growth. *Journal of Traumatic Stress, 21*, 214–217.

Peterson, C., and Seligman, M. E. P. (2003). Character strengths before and after September 11th. *Psychological Science, 14*, 381–384.

Piers, C. (1996). A return to the source: Rereading Freud in the midst of contemporary trauma theory. *Psychotherapy, 33*, 539–548.

Poulin, M. J., Silver, R. C., Gil-Rivas, V., Holman, E. A., and McIntosh, D. N. (2009). Finding social benefits after a collective trauma: Perceiving societal changes and well-being following 9/11. *Journal of Traumatic Stress, 22*, 81–90.

Powell, T., Ekin-Wood, A., and Collin, C. (2007). Post-traumatic growth after head injury: A long-term follow-up. *Brain Injury, 21*, 31–38.

Prati, G., and Pietrantoni, L. (2009). Optimism, social support, and coping strategies as factors contributing to posttraumatic growth: A meta-analysis. *Journal of Loss and Trauma, 14*, 364–388.

Ransom, S., Sheldon, K. M., and Jacobsen, P. B. (2008). Actual change and inaccurate recall contribute to posttraumatic growth following radiotherapy. *Journal of Consulting and Clinical Psychology, 76*, 811–819.

Regel, S., and Joseph, S. (2010). *Post-traumatic stress: The facts*. Oxford: Oxford University Press.

Resick, P. A., and Miller, M. W. (2009). Posttraumatic stress disorder: Anxiety or traumatic stress disorder? *Journal of Traumatic Stress, 22*, 384–390.

Resick, P. A., and Schnicke, M. K. (1993). *Cognitive processing therapy for rape victims*. Newbury Park, CA: Sage.

Reznek, L. (1987). *The nature of a disease*. London: Routledge and Kegan Paul.

Rieker, P. P., Edbril, S. D., and Garnick, M. B. (1985). Curative testis cancer therapy: Psychosocial sequelae. *Journal of Clinical Oncology, 3*, 1117–1126.

Rogers, C. R. (1959). A theory of therapy, personality, and interpersonal relationships as developed in the client-centered framework. In S. Koch (Ed.), *Psychology: A study of a science*. Vol. 3, *Formulations of the person and the social context*, 184–256. New York: McGraw-Hill.

Rogers, C. R. (1961). *On becoming a person*. Boston: Houghton Mifflin.

Rogers, C. R. (1963). The actualizing tendency in relation to "motives" and to consciousness. In M. Jones (Ed.), *Nebraska symposium on motivation* (Vol. 11), 1–24. Lincoln: University of Nebraska Press.

Ruini, C., Ottolini, F., Rafanelli, C., Tossani, E., Ryff, C. D., and Fava, G. A. (2003). The relationship of psychological well-being to distress and personality. *Psychotherapy and Psychosomatics, 72*, 268–275.

Ryan, R. M., and Deci, E. L. (2000). Self-determination theory and the facilitation of intrinsic motivation, social development, and well-being. *American Psychologist, 55*, 68–78.

Ryan, R. M., and Deci, E. L. (2001). On happiness and human potentials: A review of research on hedonic and eudaimonic well-being. *Annual Review of Psychology, 52*, 141–166.

Ryan, R. M., Huta, V., and Deci, E. L. (2008). Living well: A self-determination theory perspective on eudaimonia. *Journal of Happiness Studies, 9*, 139–170.

Ryff, C. D. (1989). Happiness is everything, or is it? Explorations on the meaning of psychological well-being. *Journal of Personality and Social Psychology, 57*, 1069–1081.

Ryff, C. D., and Singer, B. (1996). Psychological well-being: Meaning, measurement, and implications for psychotherapy research. *Psychotherapy and Psychosomatics, 65*, 14–23.

Salter, E., and Stallard, P. (2004). Posttraumatic growth in child survivors of a road traffic accident. *Journal of Traumatic Stress, 17*, 335–340.

Schlenger, W. E., Caddell, J. M., Ebert, L., et al. (2002). Psychological reactions to terrorist attacks. *Journal of the American Medical Association, 288*, 581–588.

Schrank, B., and Slade, M. (2007). Editorial: Recovery in psychiatry. *The Psychiatrist, 31*, 321–325.

Schroevers, M. J., Helgeson, V. S., Sanderman, R., Ranchor, A. V. (2010). Type of social support matters for prediction of posttraumatic growth among cancer survivors. *Psycho-Oncology, 19*, 46–53.

Schroevers, M. J., and Teo, I. (2008). The report of posttraumatic growth in Malaysian cancer patients: Relationships with psychological distress and coping strategies. *Psycho-Oncology, 17*, 1239–1246.

Schultz, U., and Mohamed, N. E. (2004). Turning the tide: Benefit finding after cancer surgery. *Social Science and Medicine, 59*, 653–662.

Schuster, M. A., Stein, B. D., Jaycox, L. H., Collins, R. L., Marshall, G. N., Elliott, M. N. et al. (2001). A national survey of stress reactions after the September 11, 2001, terrorist attacks. *New England Journal of Medicine, 345*, 1507–1512.

Schutte, N. S., Malouff, J. M., Hall, L. E., Haggerty, D. J., Cooper, J. T., Golden, C. J., and Dornheim, L. (1998). Development and validation of a measure of emotional intelligence. *Personality and Individual Differences, 25*, 167–177.

Schwarzer, R., Luszcynska, A., Boehmer, S., Taubert, S., and Knoll, N. (2006). Changes in finding benefit after cancer surgery and the prediction of well-being one year later. *Social Science and Medicine, 63*, 1614–1624.

Scrignaro, M., Barni, S., and Magrin, M. E. (2010). The combined contribution of social support and coping strategies in predicting post-traumatic growth: A longitudinal study on cancer patients. *Psycho-Oncology.* Online first publication. http://onlinelibrary.wiley.com/doi/10.1002/pon.1782/abstract.

Sheldon, K. M., Kashdan, T. B., and Steger, M. F. (Eds.). (2011). *Designing positive psychology: Taking stock and moving forward.* New York: Oxford University Press.

Shevlin, M., Dorahy, M. J., and Adamson, G. (2007). Trauma and psychosis: An analysis of the National Comorbidity Survey. *American Journal of Psychiatry, 164*, 166–169.

Seligman, M. E. P. (1999). The president's address. *American Psychologist, 54*, 559–562.

Seligman, M. E. P. (2002). *Authentic happiness: Using the new positive psychology to realize your potential for lasting fulfillment.* New York: Free Press.

Seligman, M. E. P. (2011). *Flourish.* New York: Free Press.

Seligman, M. E. P., and Csikszentmihalyi, M. (2000). Positive psychology: An introduction. *American Psychologist, 55*, 5–14.

Seligman, M. E. P., Steen, T. A., Park, N., and Peterson, C. (2005). Positive psychology progress: Empirical validation of interventions. *American Psychologist, 60*, 410–421.

Selye, H. (1976). *The stress of life.* New York: McGraw-Hill. Originally published in 1956.

Shakespeare-Finch, J., and Enders, T. (2008). Corroborating evidence of posttraumatic growth. *Journal of Traumatic Stress, 21*, 421–424.

Shakespeare-Finch, J. E., Gow, K. M., and Smith, S. (2005). Personality, coping and posttraumatic growth in emergency ambulance personnel. *Traumatology, 11*, 325–334.

Shapiro, F. (1995). *Eye movement desensitization and reprocessing: Basic principles, protocols, and procedures.* New York: Guilford Press.

Shaw, A., Joseph, S., and Linley, P. A. (2005). Religion, spirituality, and posttraumatic growth: A review. *Mental Health, Religion, and Culture, 8*, 1–11.

Shay, J. (1995). *Achilles in Vietnam: Combat trauma and the undoing of character.* New York: Simon & Schuster.

Sheikh, A. I. (2004). Posttraumatic growth in the context of heart disease. *Journal of Clinical Psychology in Medical Settings, 11*, 265–273.

Shin, L. M., and Handwerger, K. (2009). Is posttraumatic stress disorder a stress-induced fear circuitry disorder? *Journal of Traumatic Stress, 22,* 409–415.

Siegel, K., Schrimshaw, E. W., and Pretter, S. (2005). Stress-related growth among women living with HIV/AIDS: Examination of an explanatory model. *Journal of Behavioral Medicine, 28,* 403–414.

Silver, R. C., Holman, E. A., McIntosh, D. N., Poulin, M., and Gilrivas, V. (2002). Nationwide longitudinal study of psychological responses to September 11. *Journal of the American Medical Association, 288,* 1235–1244.

Smith, A., Joseph, S., and Nair, R. D. (2011). An interpretative phenomenological analysis of post-traumatic growth in adults bereaved by suicide. *Journal of Loss and Trauma.* Online first publication. http://www.informaworld.com/smpp/content-db=all-content =a936083790-frm=abslink.

Smith, B. W., Dalen, J., Wiggins, K., Tooley, E., Christopher, P., and Bernard, J. (2008). The Brief Resilience Scale: Assessing the ability to bounce back. *International Journal of Behavioral Medicine, 15,* 194–200.

Smyth, J. M., Hockemeyer, J. R., and Tulloch, H. (2008). Expressive writing and posttraumatic stress disorder: Effects on trauma symptoms, mood states, and cortisol reactivity. *British Journal of Health Psychology, 13,* 85–93.

Snyder, C. R. (1994). *The psychology of hope: You can get there from here.* New York: Free Press.

Snyder, C. R. (Ed.). (2000). *Handbook of hope: Theory, measures, and applications.* San Diego: Academic Press.

Splevins, K., Cohen, K., Bowley, J., and Joseph, S. (2010). Theories of posttraumatic growth: Cross-cultural perspectives. *Journal of Loss and Trauma, 15,* 259–277.

Stanton, A. L., Bower, J. E., and Low, C. A. (2006). Posttraumatic growth after cancer. In L. G. Calhoun and R. G. Tedeschi (Eds.), *Handbook of posttraumatic growth: Research and practice,* 138–175. Mahwah, NJ: Lawrence Erlbaum Associates.

Stanton, A. L., Danoff-Burg, S., Sworowski, L. A., Collins, C. A., Branstetter, A. D., Rodriguez-Hanley, A., Kirk, S. B., and Austenfeld, J. L. (2002). Randomized, controlled trial of written emotional expression and benefit finding in breast cancer patients. *Journal of Clinical Oncology, 20,* 4160–4168.

Stein, M. B., Koverola, C., Hanna, C., Torchia, M. G., and McClarty, B. (1997). Hippocampal volume in women victimized by child sexual abuse. *Psychological Medicine, 27,* 951–959.

Stiles, W. B. (1987). "I have to talk to somebody": A fever model of disclosure. In V. J. Derlega and J. H. Berg (Eds.), *Self-disclosure: Theory, research, and therapy,* 257–282. New York: Plenum Press.

Stockton, H., Hunt, N., and Joseph, S. (2011). Cognitive processing, rumination, and posttraumatic growth. *Journal of Traumatic Stress, 24,* 85–92.

Stump, M. J., and Smith, J. E. (2008). The relationship between posttraumatic growth and substance use in homeless women with histories of traumatic experience. *American Journal on Addictions, 17,* 478–487.

Summerfield, D. (2001). The invention of post-traumatic stress disorder and the social usefulness of a psychiatric category. *British Medical Journal, 322,* 95–98.

Summerfield, D. (2004). Cross-cultural perspectives on the medicalization of human suffering. In G. M. Rosen (Ed.), *Posttraumatic stress disorder: Issues and controversies,* 233–246. Chichester, UK: Wiley.

Swickert, R., and Hittner, J. (2009). Social support coping mediates the relationship between gender and posttraumatic growth. *Journal of Health Psychology, 14,* 387–393.

Taku, K., Cann, A., Tedeschi, R. G., and Calhoun, L. G. (2009). Intrusive versus deliberate rumination in posttraumatic growth across US and Japanese samples. *Anxiety, Stress, and Coping, 22*, 129–136.

Tang, C. S. (2006). Positive and negative postdisaster psychological adjustment among adult survivors of the Southeast Asian earthquake-tsunami. *Journal of Psychosomatic Research, 61*, 699–705.

Taylor, S. E., and Armor, D. A. (1996). Positive illusions and coping with adversity. *Journal of Personality, 64*, 873–898.

Taylor, S. E., and Brown, J. (1994). Positive illusions and well-being revisited: Separating fact from fiction. *Psychological Bulletin, 116*, 21–27.

Taylor, S. E., Lichtman, R. R., and Wood, J. V. (1984). Attributions, beliefs about control, and adjustment to breast cancer. *Journal of Personality and Social Psychology, 46*, 489–502.

Taylor, S. E., Wood, J. V., and Lichtman, R. R. (1983). It could be worse: Selective evaluation as a response to victimization. *Journal of Social Issues, 39*, 19–40.

Taylor, V. (1977). Good news about disaster. *Psychology Today, 11* (October), 93–96.

Tedeschi, R. G., and Calhoun, L. G. (1996). Posttraumatic growth inventory: Measuring the positive legacy of trauma. *Journal of Traumatic Stress, 9*, 455–471.

Tedeschi, R. G., and Kilmer, R. P. (2005). Assessing strengths, resilience, and growth to guide clinical interventions. *Professional Psychology: Research and Practice, 36*, 230–237.

Tedeschi, R. G., Park, C. L., and Calhoun, L. G. (Eds.). (1998). *Posttraumatic growth: Positive changes in the aftermath of crisis.* Mahwah, NJ: Lawrence Erlbaum Associates.

Teicher, M. H. (2000). Brain abnormalities common in survivors of childhood abuse. *Cerebrum, 2*, 50–67.

Tempany, A. (2009). First person. *Observer*, April 12.

Thombre, A., Sherman, A. C., and Simonton, S. (2010). Religious coping and posttraumatic growth among family caregivers of cancer patients in India. *Journal of Psychosocial Oncology, 28*, 173–188.

Thornton, A. A., and Perez, M. A. (2006). Posttraumatic growth in prostate cancer survivors and their partners. *Psycho-Oncology, 15*, 285–296.

Tjaden, P., and Thoennes, N. (2000). *Full report of the prevalence, incidence, and consequences of violence against women.* Washington, DC: U.S. Department of Justice.

Trimble, M. (1981). *Post-traumatic neurosis: From railway spine to the whiplash.* Chichester, UK: Wiley.

Turnbull, G. (2010). PTSD: Friend or foe? Keynote paper presented at the Psychological Approaches to Trauma, Resilience, and Growth Conference, University of Nottingham, June 29 to July 1.

Tuval-Mashiach, R., Freedman, S., Bargai, N., Boker, R., Hadar, H., and Shalev, A. Y. (2004). Coping with trauma: Narrative and cognitive perspectives. *Psychiatry, 67*, 280–293.

Van Der Hart, O. (2008). Ferenczi, Sándor (1873–1933). In G. Reyes, J. D. Elhai, and J. D. Ford (Eds.), *The encyclopedia of psychological trauma*, 280–281. Hoboken, NJ: Wiley.

Vázquez, C., Hervás, G., and Pérez-Sales, P. (2006). The role of positive emotions on the psychological reactions following the Madrid March 11, 2004, terrorist attacks. Paper presented at the Third European Conference on Positive Psychology, Braga, Portugal, July.

Vázquez, C., Pérez-Sales, P., and Hervás, G. (2008). Positive effects of terrorism and posttraumatic growth: An individual and community perspective. In S. Joseph and P. A. Linley (Eds.), *Trauma, Recovery, and Growth: Positive psychological perspectives on posttraumatic stress*, 63–91. Hoboken: Wiley.

Veronen, L. J., and Kilpatrick, D. G. (1983). Rape: A precursor of change. In E. J. Callahan and K. A. McCluskey (Eds.), *Life-span developmental psychology: Non-normative life events*, 167–190. New York: Academic Press.

Vollhardt, J. R. (2009). Altruism born of suffering and prosocial behaviour following adverse life events: A review and conceptualization. *Social Justice Research, 22*, 53–97.

Waite, T. (1994). *Taken on trust.* London: Coronet.

Wakefield, J. C. (1992). The concept of mental disorder: On the boundary between biological facts and social values. *American Psychologist, 47*, 373–388.

Weathers, F. W., and Keane, T. M. (2008). Trauma, definition. In G. Reyes., J. D. Elhai, and J. D. Ford (Eds.), *The Encyclopedia of Psychological Trauma*, 657–660. Hoboken, NJ: Wiley.

Wegner, D. M. (1994). Ironic processes of mental control. *Psychological Review, 101*, 34–52.

Weinstein, N. D., and Klein, W. M. (1996). Unrealistic optimism: Present and future. *Journal of Social and Clinical Psychology, 15*, 1–8.

Weiss, T. (2002). Posttraumatic growth in women with breast cancer and their husbands: An intersubjective validation study. *Journal of Psychosocial Oncology, 20*, 65–80.

Weiss, T. (2004). Correlates of posttraumatic growth in husbands of breast cancer survivors. *Psycho-Oncology, 13*, 260–268.

Weiss, T., and Berger, R. (Eds.). (2010). *Posttraumatic growth and culturally competent practice: Lessons learned from around the globe.* Hoboken, NJ: Wiley.

Widows, M. R., Jacobsen, P. B., Booth-Jones, M., and Fields, K. K. (2005). Predictors of posttraumatic growth following bone marrow transplantation for cancer. *Health Psychology, 24*, 266–273.

Wood, A. M., and Joseph, S. (2010). The absence of positive psychological (eudemonic) well-being as a risk factor for depression: A ten-year cohort study. *Journal of Affective Disorders, 12*, 213–217.

Wood, A. M., Joseph, S., and Linley, P. A. (2007). Coping style as a psychological resource of grateful people. *Journal of Social and Clinical Psychology, 26*, 1076–1093.

Wood, A. M., Linley, P. A., Maltby, J., Baliousis, M., and Joseph, S. (2008). The authentic personality: A theoretical and empirical conceptualization and the development of the authenticity scale. *Journal of Counseling Psychology, 55*, 385–399.

Woodward, C., and Joseph, S. (2003). Positive change processes and post-traumatic growth in people who have experienced childhood abuse: Understanding vehicles of change. *Psychology and Psychotherapy: Theory, Research and Practice, 76*, 267–283.

Worsley, R., and Joseph, S. (Eds.). (2007). *Person-centred practice: Case studies in positive psychology.* Ross-on-Wye, UK: PCCS Books.

Yalom, I. D. (1980). *Existential psychotherapy.* New York: Basic Books.

Yule, W., Hodgkinson, P., Joseph, S., Murray-Parkes, C., and Williams, R. (1990). The *Herald of Free Enterprise*: 30-months follow-up. Paper presented at the Second European Conference on Traumatic Stress, Netherlands, September 23–27.

Zenmore, R., Rinholm, J., Shepel, L. F., and Richards, M. (1989). Some social and emotional consequences of breast cancer and mastectomy: A content analysis of 87 interviews. *Journal of Psychosocial Oncology, 7*, 33–45.

Zoellner, T., and Maercker, A. (2006). Posttraumatic growth in clinical psychology: A critical review and introduction of a two-component model. *Clinical Psychology Review, 26*, 626–653.

INDEX